THE ORIGINS OF EUROPE

Neolithic ground stone axe embellished in the Roman period with a gnostic inscription

Frontispiece

THE ORIGINS
OF EUROPE

Four new studies in Archaeology
and History

Edited by
Desmond Collins

with contributions by
Desmond Collins
Ruth Whitehouse
Martin Henig
David Whitehouse

Thomas Y. Crowell Company
Established 1834
New York

Apollo Edition 1976
Copyright © 1975 by George Allen & Unwin Ltd

Printed in the United States of America

L.C. Card 75-42837
ISBN 0-8152-0396-9

ACKNOWLEDGEMENTS

The authors gratefully acknowledge permission to use in this book the following illustrative material:

PART ONE: The Royal Ontario Museum for the frontispiece. The Clarendon Press and Dr M. Day for Figs 2 and 3. Jonathan Cape and Dr C. Coon for Fig. 9. The late Dr Leakey and Mr R. Beatty for Plate I. Dr H. de Lamley for Plate IIc and Figs 6c, d, e. The late Dr M. Gerassimov for Plate III. The Trustees of the British Museum for Plate V.

PART TWO: Prof. C. C. Lamberg Karlovsky for Plate VIa. Mr G. Sholl for Plates VIIa, b, c. The Society of Antiquaries and Sir Mortimer Wheeler for Plates VIIIa, b. The Trustees of the British Museum for Plates VIb, IXa, b. The Clarendon Press and Prof. A. Thom for Fig. 18. Methuen & Co. and Prof. C. Renfrew for Figs 20, 21. The Edinburgh University Press and Prof. S. Piggott for Fig. 22.

PART THREE: The Cambridge University Press for Map 9 (from *The Cambridge Ancient History* XI). Thames & Hudson and Mr Barry Cunliffe for Fig. 24 (from Fishbourne. *A Roman Palace and its Garden*). Instituto Espanol de Arqueologie and A. Garcia y Bellido for Fig. 25 (from *Colonia Aelia Augusta Italia*). The Historischen Museum, Basel, and Mr R. Laur-Belart for Fig 26 (from *Fuhrer durch Augusta Raurica*). The Society of Antiquaries and Mr Barry Cunliffe for Fig. 27 (from *Roman Bath*). Routledge & Kegan Paul and Mr W. F. Grimes for Fig. 28 (from *The Excavation of Roman and Medieval London*). *Antiquity* and Mr Barry Cunliffe for Fig. 29 (from 'The Temple of Sulis Minerva at Bath', Vol. XL, 1966). Methuen & Co, Mr R. G. Collingwood and Mr I. A. Richmond for Figs 30, 31 (from *The Archaeology of Roman Britain*). Penguin Books and Mr I. A. Richmond for Figs 32, 34 (from *Roman Britain*). *Current Archaeology* for Fig. 33 (Vol. II, 1969, 1).

PART FOUR: Mr G. Sholl for Plates XVI, XXIa. Antiquity Publications and Prof. J. Werner for Plate XVIIa. The Trustees of the British Museum for Plates XVIIb, XVIIIa, b, XXa, and Figs 37, b, c, d. Batchworth Press for Plate XIXa. HMSO for Plates XIXb, XXII. Thames & Hudson and Prof. D. Wilson for Plate XXb. The Phaidon Press for Plate XXIb (from *The Bayeux Tapestry*). Sadea Editore for Plate XXII. J. M. Dent & Sons and Mr R. S. Lopez for Fig. 35 and Map 13 (from

The Birth of Europe). Antiquity Publications and Prof. L. Alcock for Fig. 36. W. Heffer & Sons and Dr N. Aberg for Fig. 37a. Thames & Hudson and Dr J. Beckwith for Fig. 38. Antiquity Publications and Dr M. Biddle for Fig. 39. Thames & Hudson and Prof. C. Thomas for Map 12.

The Cambridge University Press especially for the use of material included in the same authors' *Background to Archaeology*, which covers the ground in a briefer fashion.

CONTENTS

ILLUSTRATIONS

TABLES

INTRODUCTION

The purpose of this book is to discuss some of the forces that shaped the development of Europe from the emergence of man until *c*. AD 1200. It consists of four short studies, each covering a separate period. The scope of the four studies varies, partly because different kinds of evidence survive from different periods and partly because the authors have approached their subjects from similar, but by no means identical, points of view. In Part I and most of Part II we are concerned with prehistory and all the evidence has been recovered from the ground by the archaeologist or anthropologist. In Parts III and IV we deal with historical periods and much of our knowledge comes from written records. Nevertheless, the later sections make full use of archaeological evidence – the authors are archaeologists, not historians – in addition to the evidence of documents, inscriptions, coins and other written sources.

The geographical scope of the studies also varies. In Parts I and II the discussion ranges over much of the Old World, for European developments can be understood only in relation to a wider background: Part I considers developments in Africa and Asia, Part II developments in Western Asia and Egypt. In Parts III and IV the scope narrows to focus on Britain and its European context.

We have not written a textbook for advanced students. We have kept technical terms and concepts to a minimum, and tried to avoid long explanations, in the hope that readers new to archaeological writing will find the text clear and concise. One point does, however, require an explanation – the problem of dating. The dates quoted in Parts III and IV, and some of the dates in Part II, are derived from historical sources and, in most cases, are fairly accurate. However, most of the dates quoted in Parts I and II are *not* historical; they have been calculated using a variety of laboratory techniques, notably the potassium-argon and radiocarbon (C14) methods, which depend on measuring the time taken for particular radioactive isotopes to decay. For many reasons, these techniques cannot provide precise 'historical' dates; they offer instead a *period of time* within which the age of the sample probably lies. Thus, archaeologists quoting C14 dates do so with standard deviations, for example 3200 BC ± 100 years; in this general account, we shall omit the pluses and minuses. Moreover, a new problem has arisen over radiocarbon dating: the calibration of the C14 time scale with the time scale provided by the annual growth rings of the Californian bristle cone pine, *Pinus aristata*, which is enormously long-lived. Comparison of the two time scales has shown that 'radiocarbon years' have differed in length from 'real' calendar years by different amounts at different periods in the past. Archaeologists can now calibrate C14 dates which are younger than about 4500 BC with calendar years, and we find a maximum divergence of 800 to 900 years in the fifth millennium BC. We cannot at present calibrate dates older than 4500 BC. The current convention – which we shall adopt throughout the book – is to indicate that a date is an uncorrected C14 date by using the letters bc in lower case type; corrected dates have BC in small capitals. Thus, a date written as *c.* 4000 BC (*c.* 3200 bc) means that radiocarbon tests gave the date as *c.* 3200 'C14 years' before Christ, which after calibration was corrected to *c.* 4000 calendar years BC.

D.C. R.W. M.H. and D.W.
October 1972

PART I
EARLY MAN

Desmond Collins

Chapter 1

HUMAN ORIGINS

According to normal evolutionary theory man is of great antiquity and his ancestry passes back through geological time. Geologists recognise three successive eras, called Palaeozoic, Mesozoic and Cenozoic, which are thought to span the last 600 million years or so. They and the periods into which they are subdivided have boundaries defined by particular rock strata and their fossil content.

Before the Palaeozoic, rock strata contain few fossils; the planet earth came into existence before 4500 million years ago (hereinafter abbreviated MYA). Rocks nearly 4000 million years old (MYO) are known, and indications of life over 3000 MYO have been found. By the beginning of the Palaeozoic, both protozoan and metazoan (true animal) life had come into existence.

Some of the principal events in the 600 MY record are indicated in Figure 1. From the point of view of human development, the first appearance of the biological groups and sub-groups to which we belong is of most importance. These and their approximate dates are in the right-hand column: the vertebrates (at first like fish); the first land vertebrates (amphibians and later reptiles); the mammals; and finally the primates. This latter group is one of fifteen or so orders of mammals and includes man, monkeys and apes, and lesser known forms like lemurs and lorises.

Biologists think it likely that every species within these groups descends from a common ancestral population. The first appearance of the group in the fossil record is thus often the best indication of when the various ancestral forms came

Era	Period	Epoch	Date in million years ago	Major events	Human emergence	First appearance MYA
C		Pleistocene		Great ice age	Homo	1
E			2			
N		Pliocene		Age ⎫ Deserts expand	Toolmakers	2½
O			10			
Z		Miocene		of ⎬ Alpine mountain	Hominids	15
O			26			
I		Oligocene		mammals ⎭ building	Higher primates	38
C			38			
		Eocene				
			65	Flowering plants	Primates	66
M	Cretaceous			⎫ Dinosaur extinction		
E			136	Age ⎬		
S	Jurassic			of ⎭		
O			190	reptiles First		
Z	Triassic			birds	Mammals	190
O			225			
I						
C						
P	Permian					
A			280	Ice age	Reptiles	280
L	Carboniferous					
A			345			
E	Devonian			Age of fish	Land verte-	370
O			395		brates	
Z					(amphibians)	
O	Silurian					
I			435	First land plants	Vertebrates	450
C	Ordovician					
			500			
	Cambrian			Trilobites		
			570			
	Pre-Cambrian			Rare fossils	True animals	1000+
			4000+		First life	2300+

Figure 1. Geological time and the emergence of man.

into existence. The dates currently favoured, and quoted in this chapter, for the geological time scale are derived from measurement of radioactive potassium (K/Ar dating) or less often other radioactive substances like rubidium. In spite of a number of problems still unresolved, most of the boundaries are probably reliably dated to well within 10 per cent of their total, and usually to within a few million years.

The early primates were small, unspectacular, warm-blooded and probably furry. Biologists call them unspecialised because they were not restricted closely in their diet or habitat or any other aspect of their way of life. Prosimians (lower primates resembling the tree-shrews, lemurs and tarsiers of today) were very successful between 65 and 40 MYA. By 35 MYA their heyday was over. Rodents were now more successful on the ground; and in the trees of the then continent-wide tropical rain forests, higher primates (monkeys and apes) were becoming major colonisers. These latter are man's closest relatives.

There are still sharply divergent opinions on when man's ancestors (the hominids) first became distinct from the ancestors of their closest relatives, the two African apes (the chimp and gorilla belonging to the family Pongidae or pongids). One view, based on biochemical studies of proteins in man and apes, favours a recent common ancestor at 5 MYA or less. Study of fossil remains, on the other hand, suggests a clear separation at least 14 MYA, the divergence occurring perhaps 30 MYA. The contraction of the rain forests 5 to 35 MYA coincides roughly with the emergence of the hominids. This contraction caused the grassland and desert to expand, thus providing an environment ripe for colonisation by primates.

The fossil evidence for hominids before 5 MYA consists of teeth and jaw fragments. Some were found in the Siwalik beds of north-west India in 1910 and again in 1934, but their full significance was not taken seriously till the 1960s; these belong to the species *Ramapithecus punjabicus*. Similar fragments come from Fort Ternan in Kenya. Here they are K/Ar dated to 14

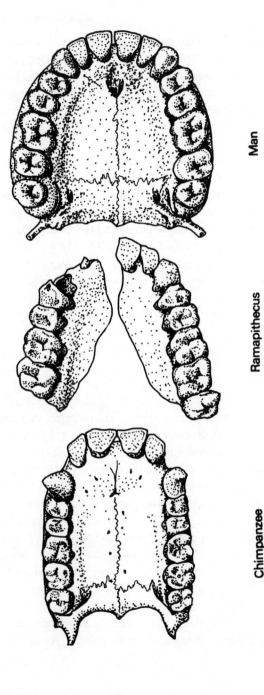

Chimpanzee   **Ramapithecus**   **Man**

Figure 2. The dental arcades of chimpanzee, *Ramapithecus* and man (not to scale).

MYA. The Siwalik fragments probably lie in the bracket 9 to 12 MYA.

The *Ramapithecus* jaws differ from those of the ape in several ways. Perhaps most important is that the canine teeth are short while in apes and monkeys they are long and dagger-like, interlocking with the teeth of the opposite tooth row. Secondly the *Ramapithecus* tooth row is short and parabolic in shape, while the ape form is quite different (Figure 2).

Dagger canines serve important functions for the apes, especially in the realm of self-defence and breaking open plant food. Man does not use his canines in this way. Instead he is a toolmaker, and this is one of the two or three most important things that distinguish him from other animals. In order to use tools one must have hands free from the job of locomotion and preferably developed for gripping to a level better than that found in the apes. If the hands are to be free the legs must suffice for walking and the posture become erect.

An attractive explanation of the reduced canines is that tool using had taken over their function in *Ramapithecus*; genetic mutation had then brought them to their present form, flush with the tooth row. Such tool using would have to be of greater intensity than that found in the modern apes, who are known to use tools to a small extent. Most obviously the tool using might involve sharp stones for cutting open hard-rinded plant food, and secondly some aid to defence such as wielding a club. True toolmaking on the other hand is less likely, and we have no flaked stone tools from the period of *Ramapithecus*.

An alternative theory explains canine reduction as an adaptation to a diet with many grass seeds, such as are likely to have been abundant in the savannahs of eastern Africa. To grind and digest the seeds would necessitate large molars with grinding surfaces, and side-to-side mastication. Only by the reduction of the canines could such mastication be achieved. Apparently similar canine reduction has been documented by Jolly as occurring in the evolution of some large gelada baboons during the last few million years, again for a similar reason.

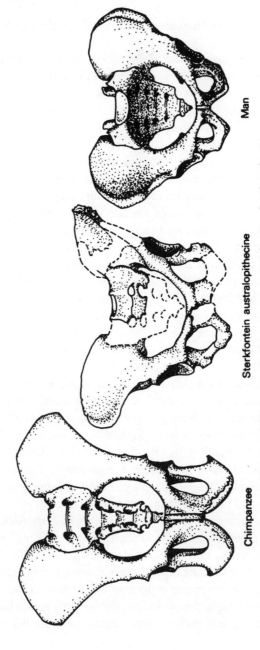

Chimpanzee　　　**Sterkfontein australopithecine**　　　**Man**

Figure 3. Pelvic bones of chimpanzee, a Sterkfontein fossil and man.

Incidentally very precise hand movements would be needed for collecting seeds, and upright posture with free hands would be an advantage.

The theory of *Ramapithecus* as an upright walking hominid has the merit of being testable from the fossil record. For the pelvis and lower limb of an upright walker like man are quite different from that of an ape, even though an ape can walk upright for a time. In fact we have evidence that the early Pleistocene hominid *Australopithecus* was a bipedal walker (Figure 3). Following Darwin most biologists would accept erect posture as the principal criterion of the hominids. When a suitable sample of bones are found we shall be able to decide between a hominid or pongid posture for *Ramapithecus*.

In the meantime a small piece of evidence is consistent with the tool using theory. From Fort Ternan, the east African *Ramapithecus* locality, comes a battered sharp stone; presumably *Ramapithecus* was the batterer. Leakey thinks he may have been battering bones to extract the marrow. Most workers do not think that regular meat eating began so early, but this view needs more investigation.

Late in the 1960s it became normal to talk of a human fossil record going back millions of years into the past. It is easy to forget that as recently as about 1960 an estimate of 300,000 to 500,000 years for man and for the earliest human or hominid fossils would have been considered quite normal. The great extension backwards is only partly due to the new favour in which *Ramapithecus* is held; and he dates back to the late Miocene and Pliocene. It has been particularly noticeable that *Australopithecus* has been given a much greater antiquity than formerly. The early finds at Taungs (1924) and Sterkfontein valley (1936–58) were not, and are still not, easily datable; but the early conservative estimates of half a million years or less are certainly too low. The hominid fossils of Olduvai bed I (especially 1959–63) were quickly dated by K/Ar to at least $1\frac{3}{4}$ MYA. Then in the late 1960s rich new hominid sites were found in the region of Lake Rudolf; Omo valley to the north in Ethiopia has fossil hominids dated to as old as 3½ MYA; and Koobi Fora and Ileret in Kenya, east of lake Rudolf, have fossils dated between 1 and 3 MYA. The highest date at the moment is for a hominid jaw from Lothagam, south of lake Rudolf, being 5 to 6 MYA. Almost all this dating is by the K/Ar method, but some confirmation comes from uranium fission track dating and palaeomagnetic studies.

The gap between existing fossils of *Ramapithecus* and *Australopithecus* may be only 2 to 5 MY, and transitional forms dating from around 6 to 8 MYA may be expected; eastern Africa is a more likely region than Asia or Europe. By 5 to 8 MYA the grasslands were expanding widely in Africa at the expense of the rain forest, and the deserts were already in existence, though for most of the last 6 MY rather smaller.

2. AUSTRALOPITHECUS

Modern studies of fossil man (for example Washburn 1963, Campbell 1966, Pilbeam 1970) recognise besides the genus *Homo* only one (or at most two) other valid genera, and two (or at most three) valid species in each of these (Table 1). A species is a population of animals (or organisms) actually or potentially interbreeding, but reproductively isolated from other species. Even with living species this can leave some doubt. With past species known only from a small sample of fossils, the problem is more difficult, and only a general guide from comparison with the degree of difference in present-day species is available.

The genus should be a group of 2 or more species which are more closely related to each other than to the nearest related genus; a genus contains one species only in exceptional circumstances where the species is found to be equally distant from the several nearest groups of species, and even here a subgenus would normally be preferable. In the past the concepts of genus and species were used less carefully, and often as a way of identifying each new major find of fossil man. In this way at least 16 genera have been created, and 45 or more species – often synonyms; even 4 subfamilies came into use (Table 1). In 1962 a much simplified scheme was tentatively agreed upon by participants of a conference sponsored by the Wenner-Gren Foundation (edited by Washburn 1963). This has received a considerable measure of support. The main exception to the scheme as set out in Table 1 is that of those who recognise the species *robustus* as a separate genus or sub-genus *Paranthropus* of equal status to *Australopithecus*.

The first discovery to which the name *Australopithecus* was given was made in 1924 at Taung, 100 km north of Kimberley in South Africa. It consists of an almost complete skull of a juvenile (Figure 4(a)). Then a selection of adult skeletal remains and several skulls were found at Sterkfontein near Johannesburg in Transvaal between 1936 and 1958, and these

Table 1

Hominid species approved by Wenner-Gren conference on 'Classification and Human Evolution', 1962[1]

genus *Australopithecus* : species *africanus*
genus *Australopithecus* : species *robustus* (ex *Paranthropus robustus*)
genus *Homo*   : species *erectus* (ex *Pithecanthropus erectus*)
genus *Homo*   : species *sapiens*

List of some species, genera and subfamilies of the Hominidae *proposed at various times*

Subfamilies   : Neanthropinae, Palaeoanthropinae, Archanthropinae, Australopithecinae

Species of Homo : *sapiens, neanderthalensis, primigenius, steinheimensis, leakeyi, habilis, heidelbergensis, kanamensis*

Other genera   : *Palaeoanthropus, Protanthropus, Javanthropus soloensis, Cyphanthropus rhodesiensis, Africanthropus njarasensis, Sinanthropus pekinensis* and *lantianensis, Atlanthropus mauritanicus, Pithecanthropus erectus* and *robustus, Telanthropus capensis, Australopithecus africanus* and *prometheus, Plesianthropus transvaalensis, Paranthropus crassidens* and *robustus, Meganthropus palaeojavanicus* and *africanus, Tchadanthropus uxoris, Zinjanthropus boisei, Eoanthropus dawsoni, Paraustralopithecus*

[1] Published by Methuen in 1964, ed. S. Washburn

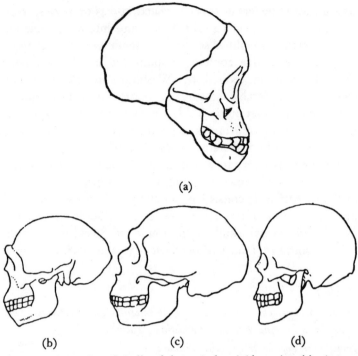

Figure 4. Examples of skulls of the main hominid species: (a) *Australopithecus africanus*; (b) *Homo erectus* from Peking; (c) *Homo sapiens* (Neanderthal type); (d) *H. sapiens* (Modern type). Not to scale.

seem to belong to the same species. Only a few km from Sterkfontein and in the same valley is the site of Swartkrans, which yielded mainly between 1948 and 1952 a second large sample of hominid skeletal parts belonging to a more robust type called *Australopithecus robustus*, in contrast to the slender species *A. africanus*.

One of the most surprising revelations of post-war research on human evolution was that the pelvic bones of both these species are quite clearly human in form and unlike those of the apes (Figure 3). Accordingly few workers would deny an upright posture for *Australopithecus*, and some confirmation of this comes from study of the base of the skulls where the spinal chord meets the skull, and from the foot bones in other early hominids.

Like *Ramapithecus* and man, both species of *Australopithecus* had small canines and a short parabolic tooth row. Like modern man and unlike the apes, both had crowded teeth with no spaces. In contrast with surviving members of the human species who have a brain with capacity averaging over 1,300 c.c., *Australopithecus* had a small brain within the range found in apes, and below 700 c.c. For some six skulls from South Africa whose capacity has been estimated, the values fall between 400 c.c. and 600 c.c., even when higher and lower estimates are taken into account; possible equivalents from Olduvai fall between 500 c.c. and 700 c.c.

Available dating evidence seems to make *A. robustus* contemporary with *A. africanus* and possibly with *Homo erectus* as well. In fact *robustus* is usually regarded as a branch from the line of human evolution, not interfertile with man or leading to him. In stature *robustus* was stocky, perhaps 1 m 30 to 1 m 50 (4½–5 ft) tall and 50 to 55 kg (8–9 stone) in weight. The crucial distinguishing characters are the enormous molar teeth – three times the surface area of contemporary molars – coupled with small front teeth no bigger than those of today. The molars needed an enormous jaw to accommodate them, and to anchor the great chewing muscles the skull had a sagittal crest, thick cheek bones and a generally heavy bone structure.

Australopithecus africanus was a smaller species, perhaps 1 m 05 to 1 m 25 (3½–4 ft) tall and weighing only 20 to 35 kg (3–5 stone). Many of the differences seem again to be related to the teeth. The molars are smaller than in *robustus*, but the front teeth larger, causing the face to protrude like a muzzle. Otherwise the skull is slenderer than in *robustus* or in the apes but is nearer to the juvenile form of apes.

Some explanation of the two types of *Australopithecus* is needed. That they are male and female of the same species does not seem possible. Another theory is that they are successive stages in human evolution: *A. africanus→A. robustus→Homo erectus*. The available dating evidence does not seem to fit this view, but it is worth bearing in mind in case new evidence should support it.

Probably the most explicit theory is that of Robinson, who suggested that the two species were adapted to different diets and ways of life. Large molars would be needed for chewing and grinding a large bulk of low protein vegetable food. The *robustus* teeth are characteristically scratched and chipped, and this may have been caused by the grit adhering to roots and other vegetables not carefully cleaned. Thus *robustus* would be a large-bodied vegetarian adapted to much chewing.

By contrast *Australopithecus africanus* may have derived an important part of his sustenance from animal food, which because of its higher protein content would be eaten in smaller quantities. This factor and the probable intensive use of tools in preparing the food would make smaller molars adequate. But without an efficient knife, the front incisors would remain important and their large size would be maintained or increased.

With new discoveries well over half the localities yielding *Australopithecus* are now in eastern Africa – Tanzania, Kenya, Ethiopia and Chad (Map 1), though the largest samples from single localities are still the Sterkfontein sites. If all the east African material was fully published, and known to belong to *Australopithecus*, our picture would alter somewhat. Olduvai hominid 5 was originally referred to a new genus, *Zinjanthropus boisei*, but along with a robust jaw from Peninj is usually linked with *robustus*.

The gracile Olduvai hominids 7, 8 and 24, together with some smaller and later finds, have been assigned to the surviving genus as *Homo habilis*; indeed some would assign *africanus* to *Homo* as well. The issue is whether *habilis* and *africanus* can be validly separated at the species level, and the poor dating of the Sterkfontein finds complicates the problem. Four characters have been offered as justifying the separation: toolmaking, hand form, dentition and brain size. The first two

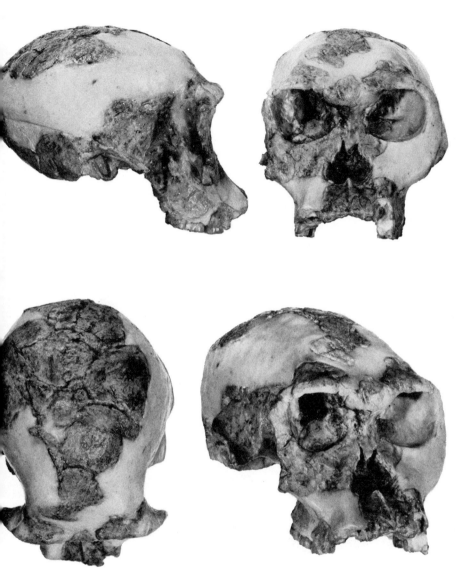

I. Olduvai Gorge. The skull of hominid 24. Four views

II. (a) Hand-axe (right) and Levallois flake

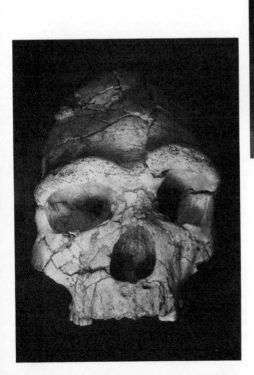

(b) Two Hand-axes

(c) The Arago skull. Facial view

Map 1. Early hominid sites in Africa.

have little relevance since Sterkfontein *africanus'* toolmaking abilities cannot be reliably determined and anyway cultural achievements are not normally accepted as relevant to biological taxonomy; and secondly the hand form of *africanus* is unknown. Experts disagree over the significance of *habilis* dentition, but the rather large front teeth seem to be an *africanus* feature. The brain size of Olduvai hominid 7, once fixed at about 675 c.c., is now placed near 650 c.c.; Olduvai hominid 24 has about 560 c.c. These figures are a little higher than those usually quoted for *africanus*, but still fall within an estimated population range of 375 to 650 c.c. based on six estimates by Tobias. At present there does not seem to be enough evidence to justify regarding '*Homo habilis*' or the new gracile hominid from East Rudolf as a separate species from *africanus*; on the other hand it may prove convenient to place *africanus* in the genus *Homo*.

3. EARLY TOOLMAKING

Toolmaking is probably one of the most fundamental innovations in human development. We shall distinguish it from tool using by insisting that it involves the making of tools with other tools, such as a hammerstone, and that its range should include the flaking of stone and the production of cutting tools. Along with true language, true toolmaking is perhaps the most realistic criterion of man. Man's present-day survival would be inconceivable without tools, and they have played a crucial part in his rise to mastery of the material world.

There is evidence from sites distributed in time over most of the last 2 MY for human meat eating activity associated with stone tools. Sometimes they appear to be kill sites; in other cases broken and cut bones litter surfaces where early man left his tools. The impression that hunting made an important and regular contribution to the diet of early man reinforces the view first offered by nineteenth-century evolutionary anthropologists that man passed through a hunting and gathering stage of development, once called Savagery, and equating with the archaeologist's Palaeolithic or Old Stone Age, followed by the beginnings of food production (Barbarism) in the Neolithic or New Stone Age. Of course it is possible that a hunting people may take only a small proportion of its food by hunting. Modern examples are found in the low latitudes such as Australia and Tanzania, where perhaps only 20 to 30 per cent of the food is meat; but its protein contribution is probably much higher. Hunters of the higher latitudes like the Eskimo or Fuegians usually derive between 80 and 95 per cent of their food from animals.

By contrast with man, monkeys and apes eat little meat, and none live by hunting. Baboons and chimpanzees do consume meat, but in default of exact figures, anything more than a small percentage would be surprising. At some point in our ancestry, therefore, regular meat eating originated, probably just once, and this would have been impossible without regular hunting or culling of animals. Also it is overwhelmingly probable that this would have been impossible without cutting and piercing tools flaked from stone. For our nails and teeth are quite unsuited to killing and dismembering animals; moreover the potentially useful canines with dagger points had disappeared millions of years previously.

Thus it seems reasonable to expect stone toolmaking to coincide with the first regular meat eating, for there was no obvious prior use for the stone tools; notwithstanding the difficulties of testing, this view fits the available evidence well. Such an event has sometimes been called the Human Revolution; and the theory may be summed up in the simplified formula: man = true toolmaking = meat eating adaptation = regular culling/hunting.

Criteria for recognising human workmanship have been developed over many years, and in sealed deposits in which stones have obviously not been subjected to natural battering and crushing, quite simple flaking can be distinguished from nature's handiwork. Such stone tools are known from a number of sites dated between 1 and 2 MYA. The earliest flaked tools of all are from two hominid localities near lake Rudolf, and fortunately they are radiometrically dated. Tools from Omo valley are about 2·1 MYO, and from Koobi Fora about 2·6 MYO. More such sites in the 2 to 3 MY time span can be expected. None are known from the 3 to 5 MY span at the time of writing, and it will be interesting to see if this remains true, and how it relates to the first appearance of the two types of *Australopithecus*.

The best site known at present for following the continuity and development of human culture over the last 2 MY is Olduvai Gorge (see Map 1), lying between the Serengeti game park and the Rift valley. The long sequence of geological strata

Dates	Thick-ness (metres)	Main strata (forma-tions)	Tuffs	Main hominid remains	Cultural type
C 14 8450 BC 15600 BC	10	Naisiusiu		1 burial	Kenya Capsian
29000 BC	18	Ndutu			Middle Stone Age
Erosion of gorge					
Dates in million years ago (K/Ar 0·5 position in strata doubtful)	12	Mesak	Norkilili		Evolved Acheulian
	24	Bed IV		28 (pelvic bones) 12 *Homo* skull	Acheulian
	9	Bed III			
	28	Bed II — Upper II C, Mid II B, Lower Lemuta II A		9 3 *H. erectus* *robustus* 13 late *habilis* 16	Pelorovis kill site Primitive Acheulian and Developed Oldowan
K/Ar 1·57 ? K/Ar 1·75 [Fission track 2·0] K/Ar 1·92 K/Ar 2·0	42	Upper Bed I Basalt Lower Bed I	I F I D I C I B I A	7 5 *habilis* *A. boisei (robustus)* 24	Typical Oldowan ? stone shelter

Figure 5. Strata, hominids and culture sequence at Olduvai Gorge.

is given in diagram form in Figure 5. The dating of the lower part is unusually well fixed, from K/Ar dating, from uranium fission track dating and from cross-checking for reversed and normal magnetisation, which changed several times in this span. Hominid remains and tools are found almost throughout the sequence.

The recognition of cultures or traditions from the study of stone tools is a controversial subject. For those workers who believe it is a worthwhile objective, it is usually attempted by comparison of assemblages for systematic similarities. The 'traits' used in this comparison are mostly types of tools (artefact-types). These are recognised by their shape and the pattern of flaking on them. To be of any use as artefact-types, they must occur again and again in some assemblages, but equally they must be absent in some contrasting groups of assemblages. The types are of lessened value if they grade smoothly into one another; but on present evidence types do intergrade, either over time, or in part of their geographical range.

The artefacts from bed I at Olduvai, some over 1¾ MYO, are quite numerous, and their style or culture has been named Oldowan. Quartzite, basalt and other siliceous rocks were used. In a recent study (1971), M. Leakey lists up to six types from this level – 'choppers, polyhedrons, discoids, subspheroids, scrapers and burins'. Of these perhaps only two can be accepted as standardised types recurring within and between assemblages – the chopper group (of which the most distinctive form is more correctly known as a 'chopping tool', Figure 6) and the discoid, though with the low degree of standardisation this might better be included in the chopper group. The other types listed have low standardisation. There is thus some justification for calling the Oldowan simple compared with later cultures; but it is fashionable at present to stress how complex and varied the earliest cultures are. This is mainly due to confusing lack of standardisation with variety of well defined types.

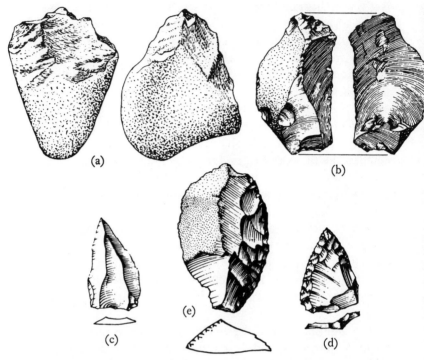

Figure 6. Types of stone tools. (a) Chopping tool. (b) Clactonian flake. (c) Levallois point. (d) Retouched Levallois point. (e) Racloir (side-scraper).

Inevitably the reader will wonder what these and later tools were used for. In particular he will assume that terms like chopper and scraper have come into use because we have some knowledge of their function. But the truth is that the names merely reflect early guesses, and the function of early stone tools (even in the unlikely eventuality of their having a single well defined function) is unknown and possibly unknowable.

It follows as a consequence of the theories about the origin of toolmaking discussed previously that some of the tools were used for cutting and piercing the game eaten by earliest man. The 'chopping tools', and indeed the flakes off them, could easily have served this purpose. But there is no direct evidence of the function of most stone tools; instead the indirect evidence of the context seems to be our best guide and the usual context of Oldowan tools is with animal bones.

One. question that most strongly suggests itself is that of the hunting capabilities of earliest man of the Oldowan culture. Later hunters, still probably over a quarter MYA at sites like Torralba, had begun to hunt even the largest animals such as elephants, and had begun to 'specialise' in hunting particular species presumably selectively, till such a species made up over half the animals killed. The evidence from Olduvai is not altogether clear. There is one case (FLK N/6) near the top of bed I of an elephant carcase, almost complete, with tools of early man scattered round it. Whether the animal was hunted and killed by men, or only found, is not easily decided. Near the base of bed II (FLK II) a skeleton of *Deinotherium* (large relation of the elephant) was found in similar circumstances.

Otherwise the hunted animals associated with the Oldowan of bed I and lower bed II are rarely large and often very small. M. Leakey comments that remains of large mammals such as hippo, *Libytherium* (a large giraffid), giraffe and rhino are more common at sites in middle and upper bed II than in lower levels. At some Oldowan sites, but not all, frogs and toads, lizards and snakes, birds, and small mammals such as insectivores, rodents and bats were very abundant. Detailed figures for this microfauna are unfortunately not available. Excluding the microfauna the commonest component of the fauna consists of tortoises, antelopes, pigs and crocodiles. It is unlikely that the latter were hunted. At fifteen out of sixteen sites African bovids (mostly antelopes) were dominant, usually well over 50 per cent of the fauna, but they include many different species from small gazelles and kudus to the rather larger sable antelope. Sometimes juvenile animals predominated as in the case of level FLK NN2 where pigs were commoner than antelopes. All things considered it is hard to deny that even the tiny hominids of the Oldowan were regular hunters of not only small but of medium-sized game also.

In the earliest Oldowan level of bed I at site DK, excavation revealed a ring of basalt blocks, concentrated round the circumference, less common inside and quite absent outside the circle of some 4 m diameter. Some of the stones are in small piles (15–22 cm high). Six such piles were found at intervals of 60–75 cm. Probably they supported the posts of a simple circular shelter. Such an early date for simple architecture is surprising, but a second east African site of 1 to 2 MYA has revealed traces of a circular construction, a raised circular platform of 2½m diameter with similar piles of stones possibly acting as supports for pole bases. This is Melka Kontoure, near Addis Ababa in Ethiopia.

Melka Kontoure is perhaps the most promising Oldowan site after Olduvai. Here too living floors have been uncovered with abundant remains of animal bones, like those of Olduvai, in sediments which were probably laid down by a lake. Also belonging to the true Oldowan we may probably include some sites in north-west Africa, notably Tardiguet and Douar Doum in Morocco, as well as numerous less well-documented sites.

At the base of bed II at Olduvai we seem to have the transition to a later form of Oldowan, which M. Leakey calls Developed Oldowan A and B. Spheroids, particularly those with multiple facets, become common and sometimes outnumber the chopper group. Such an evolved Oldowan with faceted balls or polyhedrics is also found in north Africa at Ain Hanech in Algeria and at coastal Moroccan sites like Souk el Arba. It almost certainly begins over 1 MYA.

The spheroids are puzzling in that they have no cutting edge. One theory is that they were throwing stones or even bolas attached to two or three thongs. An alternative theory is that they were for tenderising the meat in times before cooking or cutting into small portions was practised.

Closely similar to the assemblages from the upper half of bed II with numerous spheroids and a small number of handaxes are assemblages from the Sterkfontein valley at Swartkrans and West pit. Here they were associated with hominids to be mentioned below. While Sterkfontein is some 2,500 km south of Olduvai, the other main culture sequence comparable to Olduvai and Melka Kontoure is some 4,000 km north, and the only such site outside Africa. It is Ubeidiyah in the Jordan valley of north Israel. The Oldowan levels here are like those of upper bed II, and as at Melka Kontoure are overlain by true hand-axe assemblages. Once again we are probably dealing with a series of buried lakeside occupations. Two possible European localities with evolved Oldowan are Carmona near Seville, and Vallonnet near Menton. The former is a larger assemblage, but the latter though better documented has only some twelve artefacts.

The earliest toolmakers may have lived in a relatively small area of eastern Africa, perhaps under 2 million square kilometres (MSK) compared with 30 MSK for the whole of Africa. After 2 MYA they are found in north Africa as well, and may soon have occupied 15 MSK with a population approaching one-tenth of a million. With the dispersal of man to southern Asia, the area occupied may have increased to about 32 MSK and the population approached half a million.

4. MODELS OF HUMAN EVOLUTION

In the 1960s it became fashionable to use an interpretation of the fossil record in which the main groups of fossil man – Sterkfontein and Olduvai (*africanus*), Java man and Pekin man (*Homo erectus*), and some 'neanderthals' like Steinheim and Saccopastore (early *H. sapiens*) – were seen as stages in human evolution. Three decades earlier, a very different view had been fashionable. Each main fossil group had a species and genus name of its own, and was the result of branching in the early Pleistocene or even Miocene into separate evolving lines genetically isolated, and all doomed (with the possible exception of only one) to extinction. This latter can be called the Branching-Extinction model; while the former can be called the Linear-Continuity model.

Each of the two models has an extreme and a standard version, together with a series of gradations from one to the other, many of which can be grouped as an Intermediate (limited branching) model. Proponents of Linear-Continuity would accept the hominid status of almost all the fossils under discussion, but some proponents of Branching-Extinction have preferred to regard the *Australopithecus* group and even Java man as pongids. Although there are almost as many versions of these models as there are fossil men and experts on them, most versions fall easily into the categories mentioned above.

The extreme linear view is that there was never more than one hominid species at a time. This would allow no branches at the *Ramapithecus*, *Australopithecus* or *Homo* level. It would also deny the extinction of the Neanderthals, even at the level of a local subspecies. A view not unlike this was taken by Brace in the 1960s. Long before most of the fossil hominids were discovered, T. H. Huxley took a similar view, and it may reasonably be regarded as the simplest view. But the standard linear view of the 1960s, which underlies the 1962 terminology discussed previously, involves two branches of *Australopithecus*, rather than the simple stages envisaged by Brace. Quite a few standard linear theorists would also postulate some kind of Neanderthal extinction, but this is not essential to the model.

The extreme form of branching model would exclude all fossils from before the Cromagnon stage (that is pre 35,000 BC) from membership of species ancestral to modern man. Essentially this kind of view was taken by Teilhard de Chardin, the Catholic philosopher. More commonly a few selected fossils are regarded as ancestors of *Homo sapiens*. Such a view was held by Boule, one of the most influential figures in anthropology of the early twentieth century. Boule's model of evolution has been called hominid Catastrophism. At first he selected two fossils, Grimaldi and Piltdown, as the sole representatives of the line leading direct to modern man. He was succeeded as the main proponent of this view by Vallois, whose candidates for the distant ancestry of modern man were skulls from Swanscombe and Fontéchevade. On this view fossils could be accepted as ancestors only if the skull shape closely resembled modern man. Not surprisingly this view denied *Australopithecus* a place in human evolution.

Intermediate views have many adherents. Two English workers illustrate the trend during the last half century from a branching model through an intermediate model to a linear model. Sir Arthur Keith, a distinguished anatomist, was originally a proponent of a view with much early branching but in his latest work he moved towards a linear model. Le Gros Clark held an intermediate view in the 1940s and 1950s. Latterly he preferred a linear model.

One other issue is important in the interpretation of Java and Peking man; it is the question of the antiquity of racial divergence and adaptation. In the 1930s and 1940s Weidenreich, chief investigator of Peking man and one of the most original thinkers in anthropology, proposed that races began to differentiate as early as the time of Java man. This view has been called the polyphyletic theory, of parallel phyla evolving into modern races: Java man into the Australoids; Peking man into the Mongoloids; Mauer and Ehringsdorf into the Caucasoids (Europeans); Broken Hill (Zambia ex N. Rhodesia) man into the Africans (negroids, etc.). In fact Weidenreich's view on examination is very close to the standard linear model, and the phyla are only at the subspecies level, even though Weidenreich's use of the old generic names *Pithecanthropus* (Java man), *Sinanthropus* (Peking man), etc. could have led the unwary into supposing that he had proposed branching at the generic level. Coon has elaborated the polyphyletic model with the aid of new data, and suggests five phyla or lines passing from *Homo erectus* to *H. sapiens*. The most controversial part of Coon's version is that the *erectus/sapiens* boundary is claimed to be much later in some lines than in others, and it is fixed on morphological grounds in each line. The idea of the delayed *erectus/sapiens* boundary is in no way essential to the theory of early racial divergence.

The story of human evolution on the standard linear model is relatively simple. The small-brained gracile hominid of the late Pliocene and earlier Pleistocene (usually attributed to the species *Australopithecus africanus*) evolves into the larger-brained form *Homo erectus* between $1\frac{1}{2}$ and $\frac{3}{4}$ MYA. The best-known fossils of *H. erectus* are from Java (skulls P 1–7), and from near Peking (skulls CKT 1–12); a more complete list is in Table 2. Brain capacity ranges from 775 c.c. in a skull from

Table 2

List of fossils attributed to Homo erectus

Choukoutien (near Peking)	L	China
Lantian	M	China
Trinil	M	Java
Sangiran	E and M	Java
Modjokerto	E and/or T	Java
Ubeidiyah ?	?	Israel
Ternifine	L	Algeria
Sidi Abderrahman ?	?L	Morocco
Olduvai H. 9	M	Tanzania
H. 13–16	E or T	Tanzania
H. 12+28?	?L	Tanzania
Swartkrans SK 15+45	E or T	Transvaal
Sterkfontein SE 255	E or T	Transvaal
Mauer	L	Germany
Vertesszöllös	L	Hungary
Prezletice ?	?M	Czechoslovakia

L signifies late in *H. erectus* range (? 250–500,000 years ago)
M signifies middle of range (? 500–700,000)
E signifies early in range (? 700–1 million plus)
T signifies late Australopithecus or transitional form

Sangiran in eastern Java to 1,225 c.c. from Choukoutien (CKT 10). A figure of over 1,400 c.c. has been claimed for an occipital bone from Vertesszöllös (a possible Hungarian example of *H. erectus*), but the true figure may be much lower. The achievement of the larger body and brain size, as well as the rugged features, thick skull and big brow ridge of *H. erectus*, can most

easily be explained by a process of giantism (or hypermor-
phosis).

The latest fossils that can be regarded as close to *Australo-*
pithecus africanus are from the Sterkfontein extension site
(SE 255 etc., upper jaw and teeth) and from Swartkrans (SK
15, SK 45, etc., lower jaws and skull pieces). These are poorly
dated, being perhaps 1¼ MYO and ¾ to 1 MYO respectively.
The bed II hominids Olduvai H 16 and H 13 may represent
the same evolutionary stage, perhaps transitional to *Homo*
erectus. Early forms of *H. erectus* are skull P 4 from Sangiran
in Java, perhaps three-quarters MYO, and some other archaic
jaw fragments from Java often compared to *Australopithecus*.
The P 4 skull has 900 c.c. cranial capacity, nearly twice that of
A. africanus, but an early *erectus* skull from Lantian in central
China is only 778 c.c. Olduvai hominids 16 and 13 are still
small-brained (640 and 620 c.c.), so that the species boundary
might conveniently be drawn where the mean brain size of the
population rises above 750 c.c. All the late *africanus* fossils
have teeth strongly reminiscent of *Homo erectus*.

5. THE EMERGENCE OF EARLY CULTURE TRADITIONS

In Africa and the immediately adjacent parts of south-west
Asia and south-west Europe, the Oldowan gives way to one
culture or more exactly a group of related culture traditions.
The stone tool assemblages that succeed the Oldowan in the
Moroccan coastal sequence, at Melka Kontoure and Olduvai
in eastern Africa and at Ubeidiyah in the Jordan valley, all
contain one well-known tool type regarded as highly distinctive by archaeologists; it has the somewhat misleading name
hand-axe (Plate II). Actually it consists of a number of closely
similar types, normally intergrading to form the class hand-axe.
Usually associated with hand-axes, we find a second type called
a cleaver. Other more technical distinguishing features have
also been recognised.

The hand-axe was one of the first tools to be recognised in

Europe as the work of Palaeolithic man (early Stone Age man contemporary with the ice ages and extinct animals). For over half a century the term Acheulian was used to denote an epoch of time early in the Palaeolithic, and characterised by assemblages with hand-axes. It is still just about possible to use it in that sense in Africa as the epoch succeeding the Oldowan. But in Europe the epochal system created by de Mortillet in the nineteenth century has been overthrown, and under the influence of workers like Childe, Warren and Breuil the idea of cultures or traditions has become more orthodox since 1930. Warren recognised the existence of a 'Clactonian' tradition evolving contemporary with the Acheulian in Europe, and these two traditions are now rather well documented (see references in Collins 1969).

The hand-axe assemblages of Africa are almost universally accepted as belonging to a tradition related to the true Acheulian of Europe. However there are undoubted differences; and the African assemblages must presumably represent a separate tradition or several separate traditions, belonging to a wider 'Acheulian' group of traditions or super-tradition which includes the true Acheulian. Confusingly the term Acheulian is used in both these senses, as well as others even less justifiable. One solution is to use a term like Pan-acheulian for the wider sense.

It is still difficult to put a precise date on the beginning of the hand-axe tradition in Africa. Not long ago, a date of 300 to 500 thousand years ago (ThYA) would have been thought high. Recent estimates for bed II at Olduvai would put the early hand-axes over 1 MYA. A compromise figure of around three-quarters MYA may be used here pending accurate dates. It is clear that the simplest explanation of the Pan-acheulian traditions is that they evolved, presumably in Africa, from the Oldowan. Individual tool types like the hand-axe may have been invented in one area and spread only slowly to others, but a model of local continuity, which we may call the cultural continuity model, would still be appropriate.

A cultural extinction model has recently been proposed by M. Leakey in which the Oldowan is replaced at Olduvai by an Acheulian originating elsewhere. Apparently two assemblage-types are found in the upper part of bed II, though one of them from site EF-HR is based on a single small assemblage; this assemblage, called simply Acheulian, has more hand-axes proportionately than has the other type, called Developed Oldowan B. I still prefer the continuity model and would regard the Developed Oldowan B, which has both hand-axes and cleavers, as a primitive form of local Acheulian.

There is some circumstantial evidence that the hominid responsible for making the early hand-axes was *Homo erectus*. Both are found in Olduvai upper bed II, and are more directly associated at Ternifine, an early hand-axe site in Algeria. In my opinion the early tools from Java called Patjitanian represent an early local form of the Pan-acheulian and were most likely made by one of the later Java man hominids from the Trinil period (one-half to three-quarters MYA). *H. erectus* is of course usually regarded as a more advanced hominid than *africanus*, nearer to modern man in his larger body and brain, and also in his smaller teeth.

Archaeologists have been singularly unsuccessful in documenting any way in which the later stone tools represent a cultural advance. A well made hand-axe is probably more difficult to make than any Oldowan tool, but this is a rather trivial point. Probably more significant is the indication that big game and large herd animals were regularly hunted. Torralba and Ambrona, two sites in central Spain thought to belong to a rather early Acheulian, some 300 ThYO, and of African style, have provided evidence for the killing of full-grown elephants (species *Elephas antiquus*), apparently on a large scale. The hand-axes and cleavers found amongst the carcases were presumably used for dismembering and flensing the elephants (Figure 7); over forty have been found. Deer and horses were also found, the latter dominant in one upper level.

Olduvai provides an excellent example of this level of hunting

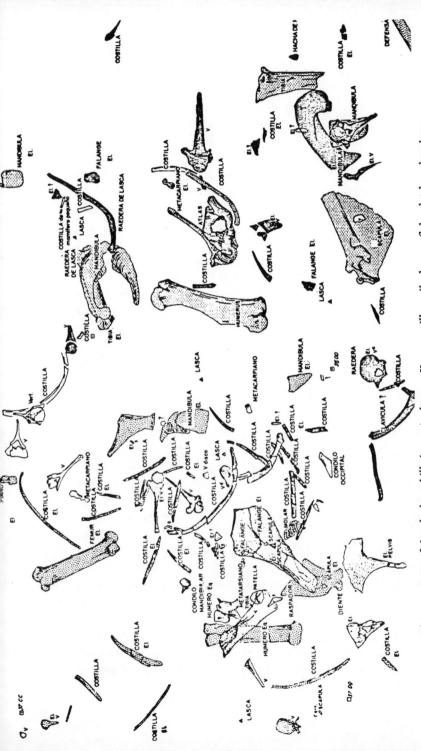

Figure 7. Part of the elephant kill site at Ambrona. Key: costilla = rib; lasca = flake; hacha = handaxe.

from site BK near the top of bed II (one-half MYO or 1 MYO depending on whether a short or long chronology is used). Here a herd of twenty-four animals had been killed; they belonged to the species *Pelorovis oldowayensis*, a large and strange extinct bovid once thought to be related to the sheep. They had apparently been mired in the muds of a backwater, and one remained intact with its legs vertically in the mud as when it had become stuck. Other large animals were probably killed here, including an elephant, a *Deinotherium*, a *Liby-therium* (giant short legged relative of the giraffe) and a rhino. Other examples of a single species featuring in the kill fauna to the near exclusion of others are the large gelada baboons hunted at Olorgesailie in Kenya by hand-axe makers. There thus seems little doubt that big game hunting and specialist hunting go back to half a million or more years ago.

While there is the possibility that big game from Oldowan levels was representative of the contemporary hunting ability, it is more interesting to seek a reason why big game hunting should have become normal in the traditions that succeeded the Oldowan. The large body size (1 m 50 to 1 m 65 or 5–5½ ft tall) is one obvious factor, and the large brain (750–1,300 c.c.) may also have been significant in the improvement of hunting strategy. The Acheulian hand-axe and cleaver may have been more efficient utensils for getting meat morsels from newly killed thick-skinned animals to the mouth of a hungry hunter. But perhaps most useful of all would have been a sharpened wooden spear, a metre or more long. The earliest certain example of this is of rather late date, probably less than 100 ThYO, from Lehringen in north Germany. A much shorter pointed stick from Clacton, not necessarily a hunting spear, is perhaps about 250 ThYO, while the only possible example from the period of *Homo erectus* is from Torralba, and is a doubtful example.

In addition to the emergence of distinct traditions since 1 MYA, we have good evidence that a progressively larger area of the Old World was being occupied by man. Much of this new territory is in the middle latitudes where winter temperatures are much colder than anything the apes are adapted to. Such areas would have been even more cold in glacial periods, but the sea barriers which had to be crossed would have been easier when the glaciers had locked up water and lowered world sea level. Population increase (a normal biological phenomenon until checked) would have made territorial expansion desirable, and large body size with bigger food requirements would have exacerbated this situation. Bigger body and better hunting would perhaps have facilitated the expansion. By about 200 ThYA man was much more widely distributed than in the Oldowan, covering perhaps 50 MSK and numbering perhaps a million people.

Newly occupied areas are found in China, north India, Romania, Hungary, Czechoslovakia, Germany and eventually Britain. In each of these areas, I have argued that traditions related to the Clactonian are to be found, forming a super-tradition across Eurasia with a bias for more continental and interior geographic situations. In Hungary, Romania and China this can be traced back to before 300 ThYA. The characteristics which bind the Clactonian group together are of a rather technical nature and the whole notion has been disputed by some authorities.

Fire came into use in a number of areas contemporary with the species *H. erectus* (that is about 350 ThYA). Traces were found with Peking man at Choukoutien, with the Vertesszöllös human remains, and at Torralba and Ambrona, the Spanish Acheulian sites. Fire of similar age is known from St Estève in south-east France, but the cultural context is not known. The use of fire may well be connected with the problem of survival in Eurasia during the third to last glacial period. Skin cloaks were probably also used as protection from the cold. One should not perhaps too readily conclude that any efficient method of making fire existed so early. There are no clearly defined hearths of this period; the evidence of fire is scattered fragments of burnt wood and bone – only bone from

Vertesszöllös. Later (about 100–150 ThYA) true hearths become a common feature. The first fires may have been taken from natural fire and carefully conserved; some 200 thousand years may have elapsed before they could be rekindled at will. Only then is fire found in the tropical regions.

Chapter 2

EARLY HUNTERS IN EUROPE

DATING THE PALAEOLITHIC

The development of man from 10 ThYA back to over 2 MYA, which archaeologists call the Palaeolithic period, took place in a context of changing climate popularly called the ice ages, and coinciding roughly with the geological epoch called the Pleistocene. By geological standards the oscillations of temperature are quite exceptional, but the total time span is very short.

A century ago almost nothing was known of the duration and subdivisions of the Pleistocene. In fact the main issue was whether there had been one or several ice ages, and the 'monoglacial' theory, being the simpler, was more widely held. Instead the archaeologists were finding a great wealth of stone and bone tools in Pleistocene deposits; most typically these were in front of rock shelters occupied by Palaeolithic man, notably those in the Dordogne in south-west France.

The first great specialist in Palaeolithic tools was de Mortillet, and he recognised many of the characteristic types which form the basis of the study today, such as hand-axes, 'scrapers' and other flake tools, burins and the main sorts of blade tools, and of course the carved bonework. Between 1867 and 1883 he developed the idea of using tools to define a series of quasi-geological periods and epochs; the 1881 version of this epochal scheme is set out in Table 3. For half a century the epochal scheme went without effective criticism, and the epochal names are still in use today with a more or less different meaning.

The reasons why the theory underlying epochalism has subsequently been rejected are easy to understand. It would be inconceivable if the distinctive tool types of the Magdalenian and Solutrian 'epochs' were to be found in every continent; it would be surprising if even in one region, a single tool or set of tools was exclusive. Instead one would expect a situation more analogous with that found in Africa, America and Oceania, where early settlers found tribal groups, often in quite small regions, each with a distinctive culture often sharply contrasting with its neighbours. We now know that this is much closer to the archaeological situation than de Mortillet's model, and the

Table 3

A nineteenth-century table of archaeological classification

Ages	Periods	Epochs	Archaeological characteristics
Iron Age		Hallstattian	
Bronze Age		Larnaudian	
		Morgian	
	Neolithic	Robenhausian	Polished stone tools
Stone Age	Palaeolithic	Magdalenian	Blade + bone tools
		Solutrian	Blade tools only
		Mousterian	Flake tools
		Acheulian	Core tools
		Chellian	
	Eolithic	Ottaian	Chipped stones
		Tortonian	
		Thenaisian	
		Aquitanian	

only reason this was not realised earlier was that in the nine-teenth century the Palaeolithic of other continents was almost entirely unknown.

In the 1920s these objections were forcibly raised, most effectively by Childe for the Neolithic and later periods; Warren, Peyrony and others showed that separate tool types or rather associations of tools (assemblage-types) were contemporary even in quite small areas and these refuted the epochal theory in its classic form. A number of attempts to modify the theory have been tried, notably by invoking retardation so that a particular mode of toolmaking is allowed to survive contemporary with a new mode. But the dominant theory from the 1920s onward has been the assignment of archaeological assemblages to cultures or traditions, with a defined area of distribution. Apart from the Oldowan, they are found to be contemporary with other cultures. It must however be admitted that especially for early times, types like the hand-axe are very widespread, and 'epochalism' can almost be made to work. The French tradition of research still leans heavily on archaeological evidence in dating the Palaeolithic, while an

Table 4

The Alpine Sequence of Glaciations (Penck and Bruckner, 1909)

Name selected	Glacifluvial terrace
Würm	Lower terrace
Riss	Higher terrace
Mindel	Younger plateau gravel
Günz	Older plateau gravel
Donau[1]	Higher plateau gravels

[1] Added by Eberl, 1930.

opposed school rejects all such practice. The important point is that the study of artefacts is no longer regarded by most archaeologists as the primary method of dating.

Related to the abandonment of the concept of archaeological epochs, there has been a greater readiness to use geological evidence to provide a time scale. This has coincided with a great improvement in the geologist's understanding of the Pleistocene over the last twenty-five years, and particularly the development of dating techniques based on radioactive break-down, which give a date in years. At least before the last 50,000 years however, there remains much doubt and disagreement about dating in years.

Standard geological practice is to establish regional strati-graphic sequences, and to be wary of correlating them. This is unfortunate for the archaeologist, who would find a single sequence of periods of general applicability more convenient, even if doubts existed on how some strata and some regional sequences should be fitted in. In fact such is the attraction of a general sequence that one particular terminology, worked out in the Alpenvorland of south Germany around 1909, has come into very wide use by archaeologists, and is used by geologists in most of France and southern Europe. Ironically this Alpine sequence (Table 4) is one of the least secure in Europe, and lacking faunas and floras is virtually impossible to correlate with other areas. Of the numerous archaeologists who use this terminology, almost none imply any particular view about the sequence in the type region. Instead they usually use the names as periods of time with equations like those shown in Table 5 to much more widely correlatable stratigraphic units, or in the case of the main French school of Pleistocene specialists for periods defined by French type sites and archaeological phases.

The position adopted in this study is that while the best local sequences are of great relevance, a general terminology based on the best sequences is desirable if not indispensable. Probably the best sequence is that adopted tentatively by the Subcommission for European Quaternary Stratigraphy in 1967 as a standard for Europe, and based on deposits in the region of the lower Rhine and immediately adjacent areas (Table 5). This sequence is built up largely from the alternation of organic deposits of temperate or interglacial periods (having a highly structured and characteristic vegetational history) with deposits indicating colder climate. Typically the latter are deposits left by continental ice build-up (the 'tills' and outwash), but for the earlier part of the sequence the evidence is more often vegetation indicating boreal forest or tundra, or frost phenomena indicating permanently frozen ground.

The tills left by the ice-sheets extend eastward into Poland and Russia, and northward into Scandinavia, thus linking several sequences. Those of Denmark, north and central Germany are well understood. A second excellent but more

Table 5
Stages of European Pleistocene

T = temperate or warm / K = glacial or cold	Holland–Germany	West E. England	Important events (and stages of fossil man)	Possible Dates	European mammal stages	Common conventional usage of alpine names for glacial age time units
T	Holocene	Flandrian			Postglacial	
K	Weichsel	Weichselian	Last major ice advance (Neanderthals)	8300 BC	Glacial	(Würm)
T	Eem	Ipswichian		0·1 MY	and	
K	Saale	Wolstonian	Second major ice advance		Interglacial	(Riss)
T	Holstein	Hoxnian	(Early H. sapiens, Swanscombe + Steinheim)			
K						
T						

Table 5 continued

	Elster	Anglian	First major continental ice extension		Cromerian / Villafranchian	
K					Cromerian	(Mindel)
T						
K						
T	'Cromer'	Cromerian		0·4 MY		
K		Beestonian		0·7 MY		
T		Pastonian	(H. erectus)			
K	Menap	Baventian	Oldowan + (A. africanus)		(upper) Villafranchian	(Gunz)
T	Waal	Antian				
K	Eburon	Thurnian				
T	Tegelen	Ludhamian				
	Praetegelen	Waltonian				
K						
T	Reuver	Gedgravian		2·0 MY	(lower)	(Donau)
(Pliocene)						

localised sequence is found in East Anglia (Table 5). It is very similar to the north European sequence and is based on a similar alternation of deposits indicating cold and temperate climates. Some of the tills are believed to have been continuous with those on the continent.

Near the margin of the glaciated area and someway south of it, deposits of loess (wind-blown dust) have been used to construct local sequences; there are more than eight of these from north-west France to south Russia, and some as in Belgium and Germany are easily integrated into the north European sequence. Cave and rock shelter deposits have been used to construct sequences, particularly of the later Pleistocene, notably in south-west France, south-east France and several other Mediterranean areas; archaeological data are usually involved. Local names have not usually been used for cave sequences, and often not for loess sequences. Instead, as explained previously, the Alpine names have been used. The alternation of marine and continental strata has also been used to construct sequences, especially in Italy and Morocco, but this has proved abnormally controversial.

We have already mentioned the possibility of a late Oldowan culture in south-west Europe at sites like Carmona and Vallonnet, dating from over three-quarters MYA. It is also likely that early phases of the Acheulian and Clactonian were established in Europe before the Holstein, about 250 ThYA. Possible sites of such an early Acheulian are Torralba and la Janda in Spain, Alpiarça in Portugal, Terra Amata in southeast France, and of the early Clactonian, Vertesszöllös in Hungary, Dirjov and Farcasele in Romania and Achenheim in Alsace, France.

2. THE EARLIEST MEN IN BRITAIN: THE LOWER PALAEOLITHIC

The first reliable evidence of man in Britain comes from the Holstein (Hoxnian) period. Claims of earlier toolmaking are based mainly on specimens of doubtful geological age, or on 'eoliths' whose status as artefacts is not widely accepted at present. Most eoliths are not humanly struck flakes, but stones fractured by thermal action, usually frost. The only evidence for human workmanship is the small-scale flaking or 'retouch' round their edges. By contrast evidence of deliberate flaking is much clearer in the Oldowan, in spite of its higher age and worse raw material. The best criterion is probably assemblages, which are absent in the earlier Pleistocene of Europe, but present in Africa.

On theoretical grounds, the purpose of retouch should be to sharpen or regularise the tool edge for some cutting or scraping purpose. But eoliths have a kind of crushed retouch which is blunter than most naturally broken stones, as well as often being irregular. The theory that they preceded the first competent chipping of stone is no longer attractive in view of the African evidence. A further point is that the 'crag' deposits, which are the only dated early Pleistocene deposits in which they have been found, are mostly marine; and Britain was largely isolated during the time of their formation.

When all claims for man in Britain not supported by assemblages of undoubted artefacts from a dated context are left aside, it is the last but one interglacial (Holstein or Hoxnian) that has yielded the first clear evidence of man's arrival. The temperate or interglacial periods in Britain as in most of northern Europe are mainly distinguished from one another by pollen analysis, and West (1970) has shown that their vegetational history characteristically has four stages, of which the second and third with warmth-loving trees are usually distinctive (Table 6). The British Hoxnian interglacial has yew and silver fir as its distinctive features and the first two sites investigated by pollen analysis both had evidence for early man. They are Hoxne, type site of the Hoxnian, which has Acheulian, and Clacton, which is the type site of the Clactonian.

The strata of Barnfield pit at Swanscombe consist of several Acheulian levels overlying some Clactonian levels. Acheulian also overlies Clactonian at Barnham in Suffolk, but the reverse

Table 6

The last five temperate periods of the British Pleistocene. Characteristics
the four-stage vegetational history according to West (1970) and evidence
early man

FLANDRIAN	III	MOF, *Fagus*	
	II	MOF	
	I	*Betula, Pinus, Corylus*	MESOLITHIC
		WEICHSELIAN (DEVENSIAN)	Occupation sparse
IPSWICHIAN	IV	*Pinus*, NAP higher	
	III	*Carpinus*	Little evidence of man.
	II	MOF, *Pinus, Acer*, high *Corylus*	Cultures poorly underst⸱
	I	*Betula, Pinus*	
		WOLSTONIAN (GIPPINGIAN)	ACHEULIAN + CHARENTIAN
HOXNIAN	IV	*Pinus, Betula*, NAP *higher*	ACHEULIAN
	III	MOF, *Abies, Carpinus*	
	II	MOF, *Taxus, Corylus*	CLACTONIAN
	I	*Betula, Pinus* .	
		ANGLIAN (LOWESTOFTIAN)	
CROMERIAN	IV	*Pinus, Picea, Betula, Alnus,* Ericales	
s.s.	III	MOF, *Abies, Carpinus*	
	II	MOF, high *Ulmus*, low *Corylus*	Man absent?
	I	*Pinus, Betula*	
		BEESTONIAN	
PASTONIAN	IV	*Pinus, Picea, Betula, Alnus,* Ericales	
	III	MOF, *Carpinus, Picea, Tsuga*	
	II	MOF, low *Carpinus, Picea, Corylus*	Man absent?
	I	*Pinus, Betula*	
		BAVENTIAN	

MOF	mixed oak forest	*Abies*	silver fir
NAP	non-arboreal pollen	*Taxus*	yew
Fagus	beech	*Picea*	spruce
Betula	birch	*Alnus*	alder
Pinus	pine	Ericales	heathland shrubs
Corylus	hazel	*Ulmus*	elm
Carpinus	hornbeam	*Tsuga*	hemlock spruce
Acer	maple		

situation has not yet been found in Britain. Apparently the Clactonian is typical of the first half of the Hoxnian (I and part of II), while the Acheulian is typical of the second half (III and IV) and the succeeding glacial period. The Clactonian is thus the first well-defined tradition in Britain.

The Swanscombe sites have yielded a remarkable amount of evidence concerning stratigraphy, river level, erratics, vegetation, molluscs and vertebrate animals (Figure 8). Above all,

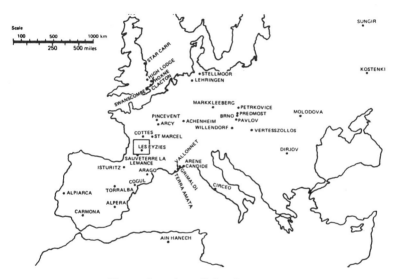

Map 2. Location of sites in Europe.

few Lower Palaeolithic sites have yielded a more abundant series of stone artefacts. These assemblages have formed the basis for several theories of the stages in the earlier Palaeolithic culture sequence. There is some evidence that, as with Olduvai at an earlier date, such sequences have a rather wide validity over large parts of the continent. The evidence for the distinctiveness of the Clactonian and Acheulian is strongest in Britain, but the main axis of distribution of each is very different. On a world scale it seems that the 'Pan-acheulian' is found in Africa, south-west Europe and southern Asia; the 'Pan-clactonian',

Thickness (metres)	Deposit	Culture	Mammalian fauna	Mollusca
1·5	Valley bottom peats	Roman, Neolithic		
1·8	Loessic Uppermost loam	?Acheulian (MAT)		
1·0	Fluviatile Temperate bed	?Acheulian, atypical with denticulates	Red deer and horse commonest. Mammoth and 'woodland' elephant present	*Lymnaea* commonest of 16 freshwater species, 24 land species
2·1	Loessic Middle loam with solifluxion			*Pupilla muscorum* dominant in 3 land species
1·0	Ebbsfleet Lower loam			*Bithynia* only species present
0·6	Ebbsfleet Lower gravel	?Acheulian with Levallois flakes and bipolar cores (Northfleet II stage)	Mammoth, woolly rhino, horse and *Megaceros* giant deer	
3·0	Main Coombe rock Chalk solifluxion	?Acheulian with tortoise cores and Levallois ovates (Northfleet I stage)	Mammoth dominant with horse	

Base of Ebbsfleet channel. Later than Barnfield middle gravels, possibly contemporary with upper gravel

Down cutting through Barnfield pit series to near modern sea level

Thickness (metres)	Deposit	Culture	Mammalian fauna	Mollusca
1·0+	Upper gravel	Acheulian (poor)	Presence of Gipping erratics, absent in lower deposits	
1·2	Upper loam	Acheulian with ovates and limandes, some		

0·15	Solifluxion gravel			
1·0	Top of middle gravel and silt bed	Acheulian (pointed hand-axes in minority) (Cuxton I stage)	*Microtus ratticepoides* present (cold adapted vole)	*Lymnaea* and *Bithynia* commonest in 25 species *Belgrandia* and *Corbicula* present *Valvata antiqua* and *V. naticina* index fossils
3·0+	Upper middle gravel	Acheulian (pointed hand-axes 50%) (Barnfield II stage)	Horse and Ox dominant in 10 species Archaic *H.Sapiens*	
2·4	Lower middle gravel	Archeulian (pointed hand-axes dominant) (Barnfield I stage)	Horse and Ox dominant in 10 species	*Ancylus*, *Lymnaea*, *Valvata* commonest in 43 species
	Soil. B-horizon of brown or red earth	Clactonian (with biological cores) (Jaywick stage)	Land surface	
1·8	Lower loam	Clactonian	Fallow deer and woodland elephant	60 species including *Valvata cristata*
1·8	Lower gravel	Clactonian with 'chopping tools' dominant (Rickson stage)	(*E. antiquus*) dominant in 16 species	*Ancylus*, *Lymnaea* and *Bithynia* commonest of 53 species *Clausilia ventricosa* present

Base of Barnfield pit series. Bench of '100 foot' Swancombe Terrace

Figure 8. Sequences of strata from Barnfield pit in the Swanscombe high terrace, and the Ebbsfleet channel at Northfleet.

found in eastern and central Europe and eastern and central Asia, is above all from the continental interiors of Eurasia, often from sites where environmental evidence of the time indicates greater continentality than today, with little influence from oceanic climates.

The distribution of Acheulian in general is most concentrated in areas where grassland and open woodland prevailed and sometimes where the greatest density of game is found today, like the game parks of east Africa. In view of the rather clear circumstantial evidence for big game hunting at Acheulian sites, one is tempted to label them as big game hunters. But paradoxically it is in the tropical grasslands today that surviving hunters rely most heavily on plant food. Some estimates put this at 80 per cent, while in the middle and high latitudes the game assumed a dominant role of 75 per cent or more.

The Clactonian of western Europe is found in environments where game animals were scarce, for they seem to have lived in the more densely wooded areas, and a more widely spread subsistence base including invertebrates, fish, birds, small mammals and much plant food such as hazel-nuts would perhaps have been the optimum exploitation of such environments.

Archaeologists are not agreed on the cultural succession of the succeeding Riss or Saale glacial period and the last or Eem interglacial. But a continuation of the Acheulian through this time, and a continuation of the Clactonian, particularly in the form sometimes called Charentian, seems very likely. In fact the Riss age Charentian site of High Lodge in Suffolk was long called Clactonian. The Charentian has numerous convex-edged and steeply worked 'racloirs' or 'sidescrapers', which may have been used for preparing skin cloaks, such as would have been a useful adaptation to a glacial period.

The first indication of man living in the tundra zone comes from this glacial period. At sites such as Baker's Hole, Swanscombe and Markkleeberg near Leipzig, assemblages including some Acheulian types are found in association with geological evidence of permafrost (perennially frozen ground typical of the tundra), and with tundra animals like mammoth, woolly rhino and reindeer.

Perhaps the most significant overall development of this time, about 200 to 100 ThYA, is that artefacts are found in caves and rock shelters in sufficient intensity and number of cases to indicate true occupancy as opposed to fleeting rests and picnics. It is also from this time that hearths become common, surviving as major blackened or ashy layers sealed in the cave strata. This seems to be the beginning of an adaptation more characteristic of the last glacial period, when Mousterian (Middle Palaeolithic) and Upper Palaeolithic cave occupation becomes so typical. Fire was not a novelty at this time as it seems to go back to at least 300 ThYA, but the ability to make fire at will (either by a percussion or a friction method) and the sophisticated equipment such as dry tinder and containers which are essential for this, may all date from the Riss.

A number of house plans have been identified from this time. The best is probably from Terra Amata in southern France, but they are also known from Latamne in Syria and Wadi Halfa in Egypt. A construction of birch branches matted with clematis and ferns was found in the Stoke Newington deposits in London. None of these are likely to have been very well built or wind-proof.

There are probably more problems connected with the Lower Palaeolithic in need of further research than for any other period. We have only touched on the question of distribution, economy, adaptation to cold climate and cultural division. There are many more problems too poorly understood to be worth discussing in a general book, such as why the last interglacial has left such a small amount of archaeological evidence compared with the last glacial or even the penultimate interglacial (Holstein) period. Again there is the question of adaptation to cave living and probably semi-sedentism in the Riss, which contrasts with the life-ways of the better known surviving hunters like the Eskimo, Bushman and Australian Aborigines; and the question of whether the adaptation to the

Riss cold climate was totally lost and reinvented in the last glacial period or whether there was some continuity of this adaptation.

Two skull bones found in 1935 and 1936 and a third in 1955 from close together in the upper middle gravel hand-axe level in Barnfield pit at Swanscombe have been pieced together to form the much discussed Swanscombe skull. It is the back part of a cranium. No forehead, facial or jaw parts survive. The cranial capacity of about 1,270 c.c. is in excess of any brain case of *Homo erectus*, and the overall shape of the skull differs from that of Pekin or Java man in that the sides are rounded rather than tapering towards the crown (Figure 9).

Potentially more important is the Steinheim skull from south-west Germany found in 1933 in a crushed condition with frontal, facial and maxillary regions all surviving. Dispute about date and reconstruction of the skull as well as the poorer cultural context have detracted from its importance. These are the two most complete skulls of the period 300–100 ThYA. The new skull from the Arago cave near Tautavel in the east Pyrénées is not fully studied at the time of writing, but has well preserved facial parts (Plate II (c)). The area of Africa and the Far East, so productive of human fossils of earlier date, is disappointing for this period. The few hominid remains known from this period here are not sufficiently complete or well dated to supplement the picture much. Possible examples are Omo I and II and Olduvai H 12. The significance of some other European skull fragments, Lazaret and Fontéchevade in France and Cova Negra in Spain, is also unclear. The Steinheim and Swanscombe skulls have nevertheless been thought sufficiently distinct from *H. erectus* to mark the beginning of *H. sapiens*, but their relationship to the Neanderthals is a complicated problem to be considered in the next section.

3. THE NEANDERTHAL PROBLEM

Because the small number of fossils found from the period

300–100 ThYA have some similarity to the large number dating from 70–40 ThYA (the Mousterian of archaeologists) usually known as Neanderthals, the two groups are often considered together. The earlier fossils (Swanscombe, Steinheim) are sometimes considered early Neanderthals, sometimes as the precursors of modern man or sometimes as forms transitional from *H. erectus* to *H. sapiens* (in the wide sense). According to what interpretation one places on the main Neanderthals, so a particular interpretation of the 'early Neanderthals' is likely to be favoured.

The alternative explanations of the Neanderthals well illustrate the three main models of human evolution mentioned earlier: the Branching-Extinction model; the Linear-Continuity model; and the Intermediate (limited branching) model. The best-known extinctionist interpretation is called the Presapiens theory (formulated by Vallois in the 1940s); it holds that skull fragments from Swanscombe and Fontéchevade are to be considered as Presapiens, that is the true ancestors of the surviving human species, and all the Neanderthals were doomed to extinction. The Vertesszöllös occipital has been added by Thoma to the list of European Presapiens ancestors. A more African-oriented version favoured by Leakey at different times has listed Kanam, Kanjera and Omo I.

It is important to realise that the controversy is not over whether these Presapiens fossils are human ancestors, for this is common ground between all sides. The controversy is rather about the extinctionist claim that all the fossils contemporary with Presapiens (the 'neanderthaloids') belonged to one or more separate species and were doomed to extinction. So many neanderthaloid fossils have been discovered that extinctionists do not usually list those that belong to doomed species according to their model; in any case most of the 100 or so discoveries are either very fragmentary or poorly dated. The extinctionist model was most widely held between 1910 and 1950.

The linear-continuity model is both older and more recent

than extinctionism, since it was common in the nineteenth century among evolutionists like T. H. Huxley at a time when few fossils were known. It has been proposed more recently in the light of new evidence by a new generation of workers like Brace. Others things being equal, it is hard to deny that the general evolution of modern races of man in different parts of the world from their widespread predecessors of neanderthaloid type would be the more economic view.

Nevertheless before either of the two preceding views had been fully considered or fully eliminated, preference for a compromise view grew up around 1950. Le Gros Clark suggested that a group of generalised Neanderthals gave rise to modern man, while extreme or classic Neanderthals became extinct. A similar version by F. Clark Howell distinguished 'early' Neanderthals from classic Neanderthals; extinction was reserved for the latter, whom Howell suggested were isolated in western Europe. Membership of the classic group is not very closely defined. Le Gros Clark specified 'gross exaggeration of the brow ridges, a large brain and the development of specialisations like taurodontism'. The large brain can hardly be regarded as a sign of inferiority; taurodontism turns out to be much commoner and more marked in the generalised group like Krapina, and thus Clark's definition comes down to a subjective definition of how big the brow ridges are, for no one has introduced a satisfactory way of measuring them. Actually when people refer to classic Neanderthals, they usually mean the well-known 'type skeleton' from La Chapelle aux Saints and a few like it. A short list of favourite 'classics' appears in Table 7.

The Presapiens theory has been much discussed in recent years, and (at least by English speaking authorities) usually rejected. In its classic form the theory insisted that Swanscombe and Steinheim stood astride two diverging lines already separate one-quarter MYA; and Fontéchevade and the early Neanderthals (Ehringsdorf, etc.) are supposed to belong later on the same two lines: (1) Presapiens leading to modern man, and (2) the Neanderthal line leading nowhere. Detailed study of the Swanscombe and Steinheim remains using statistical comparison (by Campbell and Weiner) showed that they were more similar to each other than to any other known skulls; similarly Fontéchevade is not unlike skulls from Saccopastore and Le Moustier in its surviving parts. So the evidence for two

Table 7

Fossil finds frequently cited in the Neanderthal and Presapiens controversies

Favourite 'classic' Neanderthals
La Chapelle, La Ferrassie (2 adults), Spy (2 adults), Circeo, La Quina 5. Also often included but morphologically quite different: Gibraltar I and Le Moustier

Favourite generalised Neanderthals
Ehringsdorf, Saccopastore I and II, Krapina (numerous and fragmentary), Mt Carmel (11 individuals), Solo River (11 individuals),

Presapiens candidates: Boule 1913, Piltdown, Grimaldi 'negroids'; Vallois 1954, Swanscombe, Fontéchevade

distinct human types in Europe between 300 and 30 ThYA is poor.

The generalised Neanderthal or Preneanderthal theory is more difficult to test. It relies heavily on the sharp distinction, discussed above, between the classic Neanderthals and a contemporary group of generalised Neanderthals. Actually the generalised Neanderthals are a very motley crew. In Africa they include the Broken Hill skull (Zambia ex N. Rhodesia) and other 'Rhodesioids' (Saldanha, Eyasi, Omo II). In Java there are the Solo skulls, and in China the Mapa skull piece. All these can be seen convincingly as local continuations of *H. erectus* populations like Peking man and Java man and Olduvai H 9. Indeed it has even been suggested by Coon that Solo man and Rhodesian man should be classified as *H. erectus* because the skull shape in rear view is more like Java–Peking than like Swanscombe–Steinheim (Figure 9). However the

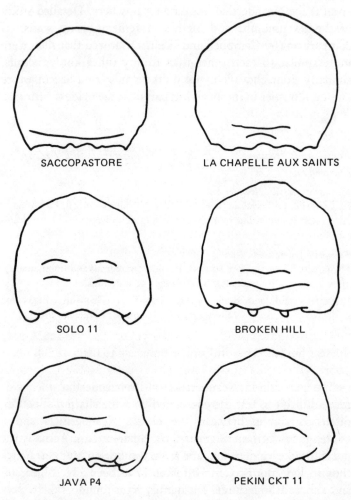

Figure 9. Skull shapes of Neanderthal man and *Homo erectus* in rear view.

boundary between two successive species, as defined by geneticists, is a single time point and cannot be locally delayed, even though average morphology of a widely distributed species may locally be delayed relative to other areas.

Even among the European Neanderthals, there is much

variation, though in rear view the skull is always rounded or even puffy, unlike the shape of Solo, etc. (Figure 9). This character the west European skulls share with skulls from western Asia, a skull from Teshik cave in the west Himalayas, central Asia, and possibly some new skull finds from Jebel Ighoud, Morocco. The brow ridge is very variable in size and shape in Neanderthals and many other species. Contrary to Le Gros Clark's model, relatively small brow ridges are found in western Europe (Gibraltar, Le Moustier, Saccopastore) as well as in western Asia. Prominent brow ridges are also found in many areas. The backward funnelling of the cranium found in La Chapelle, La Ferrassie and other classic skulls is also found in the western Asiatic Neanderthal from Shanidar in Iraq. A non-funnelled, rounded skull back is found in some west European Neanderthals (Gibraltar, Le Moustier), contrary to the theory of two geographically separated groups of Neanderthals.

Finally the taurodontism supposedly indicative of classic Neanderthals is absent in Ferrassie, Quina and Regourdou which should all have it on this theory, but is present in Mauer, Steinheim, Saccopastore and Krapina, all supposedly non-classic Neanderthal fossils. Actually it is beginning to look as though taurodontism is specifically absent from the true 'classic' group (all of which are associated as we shall see with the Charentian culture division).

The group of Neanderthals most different from the classics and most like modern man are from the eastern Mediterranean region. The Mount Carmel fossils have been the subject of much dispute since some ten burials were found in the Skhul cave around 1932. The classic La Chapelle features (elongated low skull, funnelling of the skull back and relatively large brow ridges) are absent in this series. Nevertheless the brow ridges are large by modern standards, the face is large and so are the teeth, which are also more taurodont than in the classics. Faced with this combination of characteristics some workers have suggested that they represent hybridisation between Neanderthal and modern types. Alternatively they can be regarded as transitional from an archaic Neanderthal stage of evolution to a more modern one. This latter view tends to be common ground to the adherents of both the intermediate and the continuity models of evolution. Le Gros Clark saw the Mount Carmel fossils as Preneanderthal in date and ancestral to two divergent branches required by his theory. Howell saw them as contemporary with the classic Neanderthals and an indication that the continuity and transformation took place in western Asia but not in western Europe.

The dating of the Mount Carmel fossils is thus crucial, though not as easy as one would hope, since C14 dating, which has been tried on samples from the site, is known to become more erratic at over 30,000 years. All workers seem to agree that the Skhul burials are later than layer C of Tabun cave, which has a single Neanderthal burial and a C14 date of 38,950 bc ± 1000. This would be consistent with an age for the Skhul fossils anywhere between 30,000 and 38,000 bc. As such it is clearly later than the classic Neanderthals of western Europe, and roughly contemporary with the beginning of the Upper Palaeolithic in Europe at about 35,000 bc. Such a dating would fit a transition from a Neanderthal to a Postneanderthal population around 40,000 to 30,000 bc, in western Asia or indeed all over the Neanderthal world.

Little detailed information is available at the moment on two other hominid sites in Israel, Qafsa near Nazareth and Amud cave near lake Tiberias. The Qafsa burials, found in 1934 (only one skull well preserved) and in 1967, are less Neanderthal than Skhul, even though they are under five Mousterian layers. They have been classified as modern type *H. sapiens* by Vandermeersch, and this means that the usual equation Mousterian = Neanderthal is untenable. The Amud skeleton, found 1961, is provisionally classified as Neanderthal and comes from an early Upper Palaeolithic level, Emiran, which would destroy the equation Upper Palaeolithic = Postneanderthal or 'Cromagnon' man.

The generalised or Preneanderthal theory of human evolution, which involves selective extinction of some Neanderthal populations and continuance of others, is difficult to test partly because of its several versions. This would be an attractive theory from a scientific point of view if the following patterns could be observed in the data: (1) two quite distinct groups of Neanderthals were present in the period 70,000–40,000 bc; (2) two geographical and cultural provinces were inhabited by these two groups; (3) evidence for prolonged genetic isolation of the two groups existed and differential selection factors could be found which caused the differences in the two hominid types. Since nothing approaching evidence for these patterns exists in the present data, I am personally inclined to reject this intermediate Preneanderthal model, leaving only the simple continuity model.

It may be useful to consider why the continuity model, which is unquestionably the simplest and most obvious, should not have been more generally held. A widely expressed argument is based on the archaeological evidence, supposedly indicating an abrupt break between the Mousterian and the Upper Palaeolithic which succeeds it. But currently there is a lot of archaeological evidence which indicates that the earliest Upper Palaeolithic cultures in different regions closely resemble the preceding Mousterian. In any case the equations Mousterian = Neanderthal and Upper Palaeolithic = Postneanderthal are now dubious.

Most of the arguments have been based on fossil evidence. Firstly the presence of fully modern man or Presapiens before the Neanderthals has been repeatedly claimed. In discussing the Presapiens theory we noted that the evidence for this has failed to satisfy most authorities. Secondly the absence of intermediate fossils has been used as evidence of a break. However from most parts of Europe, fossils of the period 45,000–25,000 bc are not definitely known. Furthermore the Mount Carmel and Qafsa fossils of western Asia are excellent intermediates, and early Upper Palaeolithic hominids from central Europe (Brno, Předmost and Zlatý Kun) also show intermediate or mixed features. Thirdly it has been argued that too little time separates Neanderthal man from Cromagnon man to allow an evolution from one to the other. However classic Neanderthals are not definitely known after 50,000 bc, and Cromagnon skeletons not reliably known before 20,000 bc. Furthermore no reliable evidence of the rate of evolution possible under certain circumstances is available. None of the reasons given so far can be seriously regarded as sufficient to reject Neanderthal continuity, but they do demand that any version of the Neanderthal continuity should take these points into account.

The final argument for Neanderthal extinction is perhaps the weakest of all. It states that Neanderthals were too special-ised to evolve into modern man or Cromagnon man. But as to what they were specialised in doing, apart from being Neander-thals, little constructive thinking has been forthcoming. The only serious possibility that has been offered is that they were adapted to cold climate. This however can hardly explain the Neanderthals of the last interglacial, and the short cold part of the Mousterian does not seem long enough for such a major adaptation. Furthermore the generally cold climate from 30,000 to 10,000 bc apparently favoured no comparable adaptation, though people were living in the same part of Europe and rather nearer the ice-sheets, and even colonising Siberia and north European Russia at this time.

Most Neanderthal features bear no known relation to the rules for adaptation to cold climate proposed by biologists. The rule most likely to be applicable is 'Allen's rule', which states that the projecting parts of the body will be shorter and stockier in cold climates. The legs and arms and perhaps the whole bodies of European Neanderthals are relatively short and stocky, consistent with this rule, but such a specialisation would obviously not lead to their extinction. Eskimoes are stockier still but they are not Neanderthals by any means. The very large nasal sinuses of the European Neanderthals may be an adaptation to cold, but the whole issue of adaptation to glacial climates in fossil man is poorly understood, and contributes nothing to the solution of the Neanderthal problem.

Perhaps the only well-published theory of how Neanderthals might have evolved into modern man is the view of Brace that the size of the teeth, especially the front teeth which are large in Neanderthal man, determines a large and heavy face necessary to accommodate and operate them, and that the brow ridges and other Neanderthal features were necessarily retained as concomitants, for attachment of the chewing muscles. The reduction of the whole complex is attributed to an improvement in food preparation at the end of the Mousterian, allowing a reduction in size. Brace attributes this reduction to a peculiarity of genetic mutations, which tends to cause overall size reduction in organs not maintained at full size by natural selection. Whether this theory explains the transformation of a long low brain case into a shorter, higher and more rounded one is questionable.

A second theory which deserves more careful attention than it has hitherto received is that the process of neoteny was the main cause of the transformation to modern type man. Neoteny (used here in a wide sense to include processes sometimes called foetalisation, paedogenesis or paedomorphosis) has occasionally been documented in living species like the axolotl salamander, and de Beer (1950) has made the best-known study of it. Most evolutionists believe it was important at several crucial points in evolution, notably the first appearance of the chordates and the first appearance of the mammals.

Neoteny involves two contrasting schedules. The first is the orderly process of development of the individual, whose growth speed is controlled by hormone secretion from the pituitary gland. This growth can evidently be slowed or speeded quite easily by genetic change or even by damage or pathology; neoteny requires slowing. The second is the schedule of the major thresholds, birth and puberty. Apparently this can be kept stable so that the intervals conception/birth,

birth/puberty and possible puberty/death remain unchanged while the first schedule is much slowed, so that the latter part of it is never attained. In non-mammals this often means sexual maturity in the larval stage. Alternatively the first schedule could be speeded relative to the second, and this would produce such results as giantism and acromegaly, an interesting medical condition which can lead to near-Neanderthals.

The fact that successively appearing primate groups take longer to reach various stages in their physical development is shown in Table 8. Tooth eruption and postnatal growth take

Table 8

Differential growth rates in primates. Some approximate average figures from various sources

	Lower primates	Gorilla, Chimpanzee	Man
Features delayed in successive primate groups			
Milk tooth eruption	birth	3–4 months	8 months
Permanent tooth eruption	1 year	3 years	6 years
Length of postnatal growth	3 years	11 years	20 years
Size of brain at birth, as % of full size	over 75%	about 55%	23%
Relatively stable foetal and pre-pubertal periods			
Foetal duration	5 months	8–9 months	9 months
Female fertility	3 years	9 years	13 years

twice as long in man as in apes, but the foetal period has hardly changed in length. Possibly the clearest example of human neoteny is that the human infant is helpless for several years, while most primates and other mammals are fully able to cope within a few months of birth. Our remote mammalian ancestors were obviously like other mammals in this respect, and since then, natural selection for neoteny has introduced the slow maturation which is so highly characteristic of man. Most likely neoteny has set in on several widely spaced occasions, the emergence of the gracile form, *africanus*, being one.

There are several reasons why the onset of a burst of neoteny at the end of the Neanderthal period would fit the facts well. Juvenile Neanderthals (and to a lesser extent all juvenile early hominids and primates) resemble modern man more closely than their adult forms do. Two Neanderthal infant skulls, Pech de l'Azé and Staroselie, indicate this well; the Modjokerto baby skull of *Homo erectus* from Java and the Taungs child *A. africanus* show the same point for earlier periods. Older Neanderthal children are represented by skulls from different parts of Europe and Asia: Gibraltar, La Quina in France, Subalyuk in Hungary, Teshik cave in the Himalayas, Shanidar in Iraq. The brow ridges are always slight, the chin less receding than in adults, the faces and teeth smaller and the brain cases more bulbous.

Some advantages of neoteny, which would have been useful to most early human populations, would be the longer period of optimum learning ability it provides, and the relatively larger and more rounded frontal lobe of the brain, supposedly the seat of much higher mental activity. A third more debatable point would involve sexual selection of women who were paedomorphic (smooth-browed and child-like) in preference to gerontomorphic women (heavy-browed, coarser-featured, hairier and older-looking). Many human characteristics are neotenous, and vary from race to race. Hairlessness of the body (at least to the degree that the hair is barely visible) is a neotenous feature more pronounced in Bushmen and Mongoloids than in Europeans. Again the light skin of Europeans is neotenous, but this pulsation of neoteny failed to affect many African peoples. Apparently light skin improves the absorbtion of vitamin D from sunlight. Since many Neanderthals north of 40° show signs of rickets, this may have been a crucial adaptation.

One other advantage of neoteny 30–50 ThYA may overshadow all the others in importance. Between 2 MYA and 300 ThYA the human brain size increased by about 150 per cent from about 500 c.c. to 1,200 c.c., while the size of the pelvic aperture in women, through which birth must take place, increased by much less. Natural selection would keep increase of the pelvic size in check, because over-increase would unbalance the whole locomotor system. Presumably the 'slack' in the system which makes for easy childbirth in primates was taken up in this period, and childbirth must have become increasingly difficult.

Between 100 and 50 ThYA human brain size in Europe and western Asia seems to have increased from around 1,300 c.c. (a figure a little under the present mean) to over 1,600 c.c. in some populations (an increase of nearly 25 per cent, to a figure appreciably above the present mean), and there is no indication that pelvic aperture kept pace. This rapid increase must have put formidable difficulties into childbirth, since the brain case is the largest part of the foetus to pass through the pelvic aperture, and even today this brain case must be crushed into a bullet shape to pass through. Neoteny is an outstandingly simple solution to this problem since it leads to a smaller brain size at birth; incidentally it would also account for the otherwise inexplicable smaller adult brain size of today relative to some Neanderthals. Probably only a few genetic changes are required to invoke neoteny, and arguably the potentiality for these new combinations has been in the gene pool throughout most of human evolution.

The theory, then, is that neoteny set in among Neanderthal peoples in Europe and western Asia and perhaps north Africa about 50 ThYA and became increasingly common till about 25 ThYA, producing first a few individuals of modern morphology, and later whole populations of this type. The neotenous peoples rapidly replaced the pre-existing types because of a much lower natal mortality. Archaic or gerontomorphic human types still strongly resembling late *Homo erectus* may well have remained common in parts of southern Africa and south-east Asia, particularly if the mean brain size had remained lower than today's. The archaic type seems to have survived most obviously in Australia, although this continent was probably not peopled much before 30 ThYA, since quite recent skulls like those from Cohuna and Talgai are very archaic.

4. THE CULTURE OF NEANDERTHAL MAN

If it were possible to bring the archaeological evidence to bear on the Neanderthal problem, this would be most advantageous, since stone tools are much more commonly found than fossil men. It must be admitted that one section of opinion does not accept that culture tradition can be used to cast any light on problems of population continuity or extinction, but a larger section takes the more constructive view that continuity of culture must mean continuity of a people in the physical and genetic sense. It is strange that dramatic claims of migrations and extinctions have been widely accepted on the most scanty fossil evidence, and sometimes on archaeological evidence, but that evidence for continuity is regarded with such suspicion.

Under de Mortillet the Mousterian was regarded as an archaeological epoch whose beginning and end were defined by changing tool types and coincided with points of time. When this was shown to be unsupported by the evidence, the term did not decline in popularity, but instead continued to be used, sometimes in its old sense, often as a convenient shorthand term for the time span now known to be about 75,000–35,000 bc on radiocarbon evidence, and sometimes referring to a culture or group of cultures. Some workers thought that the Mousterian culture came in at a well-defined point in time and was re-placed equally suddenly by invasion, and this helped to reconcile the conflicting usages. Closer examination of rich sites in south-west France, such as Le Moustier itself and Combe Grenal, has revealed that there are indeed several different sorts of Mousterian with varying degrees of claim to the name. The only real justification for grouping them is that they were all found at Le Moustier and elsewhere dating from approximately the same period, and that at the end of that period there was a change to blade technology typical of the Upper Palaeolithic recognised by almost all workers in Europe.

Bordes (1968) has distinguished six or so types: two successive types of 'Mousterian of Acheulian Tradition', MATa and MATb; two types, Ferrassie and Quina, sometimes grouped as 'Charentian'; a Denticulate type; and finally the least satisfactorily isolated and defined type, found in two layers at Le Moustier, called 'Typical Mousterian'. In terms of convenience, the names of these assemblage-types leave much to be desired. There is little agreement on the area of distribution of the assemblage-types, partly because other areas are so much less rich than south-west France and have not been investigated from the same point of view; but a multiplication of distinct types is probable in many areas. Type MATb is similar to and probably develops into what is conventionally regarded as the first stage of the Upper Palaeolithic in western Europe, the Chatelperron or early stage of the Perigordian. The denticulate type may also persist into the Upper Palaeolithic.

By contrast the Charentian does not seem to continue locally into the Upper Palaeolithic in south-west France. In fact on some interpretations there is a gap of 10,000 to 15,000 years between the end of the Charentian and the beginning of the Upper Palaeolithic. Accordingly the discovery of Neanderthals with the MAT would have a very different significance from their discovery with the Quina or Ferrassie which became locally extinct. In fact all the better preserved Neanderthals from known culture contexts in western Europe come from the Charentian, and therefore represent less than half the Mousterian peoples. Only a few fragmentary or poorly documented discoveries of skeletal remains accompany the MAT or denticulate. This is mainly because the better discoveries are burials, which are Charentian except in the east Mediterranean,

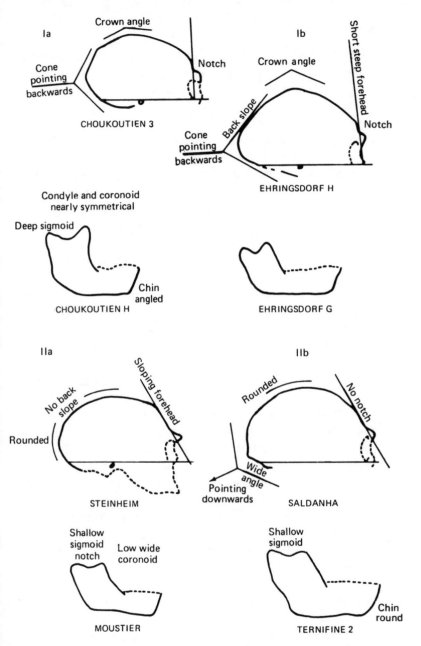

Figure 10. Skull and mandible profiles of human groups I and II.

where the Carmel and Qafsa skeletons from a different culture context are, not surprisingly, physically different. These facts are hardly ever taken into account in discussions of the Neanderthal problem.

It would be a matter of considerable interest to investigate whether different human types were associated with the different cultural traditions. I have suggested a theory in which a human type (I) found at Choukoutien, Ehringsdorf and the main western Neanderthal burial sites is responsible for the Pan-clactonian and derivative cultures, and a type (II) represented by Steinheim, Saccopastore and other skulls is responsible for the Pan-acheulian and derivative cultures (Figure 10). Unfortunately too little attention has been paid to these problems to make it possible to discuss them in a general book.

A widely quoted theory, which concerns the origin of the Upper Palaeolithic and the fate of Neanderthal man, argues for an early appearance of the 'Upper Palaeolithic' or at least its tool types in the east Mediterranean area. This theory, based on archaeological evidence, may be called the Pre-Aurignacian theory, and is analogous to the Presapiens theory of evolution. Under ten Mousterian layers of the shelter of Jabrud I in Syria were two layers claimed to be Upper Palaeolithic, and named Pre-Aurignacian by their discoverer Rust. A similar situation has been claimed by Garrod at the Tabun (Mt Carmel) cave, from a somewhat deeper level than the burials, but the assemblages were not kept separate. Two further examples are Zumoffen shelter in Lebanon, dated by a high sea level, and the Haua cave in Libya, where radiocarbon dates put the layers in question well before 50,000 bc. The complexity of this problem is such that it cannot be adequately treated briefly, and we must go into some detail.

Clearly the Pre-Aurignacian assemblages are not Upper Palaeolithic in the chronological sense of belonging to a later period than the Mousterian, nor in an evolutionary sense of a stage succeeding it. The claim seems to be that the assemblages are Upper Palaeolithic in a typological sense, and hence in an ethnic sense as a human group separate from the Mousterians, but related ancestrally to Upper Palaeolithic peoples. For anyone who believes that the Neanderthals became extinct without issue, that they are uniquely associated with the Mousterian, that the Cromagnons were uniquely associated with the Upper Palaeolithic and that a distinct break separates Mousterian from Upper Palaeolithic, the Pre-Aurignacian theory is attractive; however, as explained in the previous section, none of these points has been established and none is likely.

The typological claim that the Pre-Aurignacian is Upper Palaeolithic is very hard to evaluate, since there is no generally accepted definition of the limits of the Mousterian or Upper Palaeolithic. Perhaps the most striking features of the Upper Palaeolithic of western Europe are the presence of distinctive types of bone tools, representational art and a fast rate of culture change. None of these are found in the Pre-Aurignacian. The usual criterion for distinguishing between the Mousterian and Upper Palaeolithic is the use of blade technology and blade tools, such as burins (Figure 11); the term

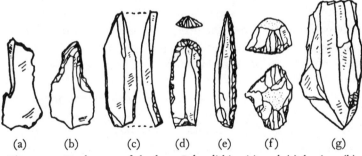

Figure 11. Tool types of the later Palaeolithic. (a) and (c) burins; (b) busked burin; (d) grattoir (endscraper); (e) Gravetto point; (f) Carinate (scraper); (g) blade core.

Leptolithic is sometimes used in this sense, because of the confusions which arise from the use of the older term, but most archaeologists still use the term Upper Palaeolithic and reap the full benefit of the confusions.

In view of the undoubted fact that blades and blade tools occur in the Mousterian, the above definition is useless unless it is made numerically precise. Adherents of the Pre-Aurignacian theory have never applied such a numerical definition to the problem. The nearest to such a definition involves the blade index of Bordes, which ranges up to 40 in the Mousterian, but is usually much higher in the Upper Palaeolithic. The only available figure for the Pre-Aurignacian (Jabrud layer 13) is 37, that is Mousterian. A later layer in the same site, classified as Mousterian, curiously has a blade index of 50. The truth is evidently that an entirely satisfactory typological boundary between two such poorly defined entities as the Mousterian and Upper Palaeolithic cannot at present be made.

There is an even more direct way of testing the Pre-Aurignacian theory than showing that it is not on objective criteria Upper Palaeolithic, namely to see if it appears to be ancestral to one or more European Upper Palaeolithic cultures. The fact is that cultures like the Szeletian, Aurignacian and Chatelperron Perigordian can all be more easily derived from local cultures. Even the Emiran culture found at Mt Carmel seems to develop from a Mousterian source, though there is nothing impossible in the idea of the 'Pre-Aurignacian' continuing into some local culture. The archaeological evidence for a series of invasions of Europe at the beginning of the Upper Palaeolithic is non-existent.

There are further consequences of the theory that only with the arrival of a 'Leptolithic' blade technology does modern-type man arrive. The so-called Middle Stone Age cultures of Africa and southern Asia are not typically Leptolithic, but survive down to around 10,000 bc, which is very late for modern man to appear. In Australia they seem to survive down to about 4000 bc, by which time Australian aboriginal skulls are known; in Tasmania no Leptolithic technology arrived before the white colonists, and few people would claim the Tasmanians were Neanderthal.

Perhaps a more interesting aspect of the Mousterian period

is the evidence it provides that man was no longer simply a functioning animal, but a unique form of life in which the biological necessities of life were joined by specifically human characteristics reaching beyond those essential for physical survival. Artistic and religious activity seems to become common in the Upper Palaeolithic, and these are not in the simple sense practical or functional. In a wider sense, of course, they may perform a function essential for the survival of a community of increasingly sensitive and skilful people. In the Mousterian period we already find evidence of burials, symbols and probably cults, out of which this higher culture presumably emerges.

Burials dating from around 50,000 bc are well enough documented to be beyond doubt. The earliest may be a child burial from the Teshik cave, with a uranium series date of 100,000 years. There are at least four cases of deliberate burial from French Charentian sites. A skull left in a circle of stones in a cave at Mt Circeo is also a kind of burial. Some Neanderthals from Shanidar in Iraq, and most of the Carmel and Qafsa skeletons were buried. There is little standardisation in burial practice. Extended burial is commonest, but contraction is also found, though tight flexing of the knees to the chest is not. Burial on the back is commonest in western Europe, though burial on the right side is also found. Burials on the left side are found only further east in Russia and western Asia.

Several of the burials provide indirect evidence for some kind of closely knit society in which the old and infirm were cared for and fed after they had lost the capacity to hunt and feed themselves. The Shanidar I man had one arm amputated (the earliest known case of an operation), but had survived this to live to an advanced age. He and another old man from La Chapelle were both arthritic to a degree which would have made hunting impossible, and food must have been provided by others. The latter had so little of his tooth row left that his food must have been premasticated for him.

The significance of burial as a spiritual attitude is pointed up by the common occurrence of 'grave goods'. The lower part of a leg of bison with the flesh not removed, a bison horn and a piece of jasper accompanied the La Chapelle burial. Twenty brown bear skulls were found with the Regourdou man. Other examples are deer antlers at Qafsa, a boar jaw 'trophy' at Mt Carmel and flowers at Shanidar. Individually some of these examples could be doubted, but together their significance cannot reasonably be disputed.

The rough triangular gravestone of Ferrassie, over burial VI of a 3-year-old child, has eight pairs of cup marks cut in it. A small pebble from Tata in Hungary had a cross engraved on it. Scratchings with no obvious representational significance are common on bones and stones of this time. Engraved lines spaced out at regular intervals, up to five in number, are known and often interpreted as tallies. Some at least of this evidence suggests the existence of primitive symbolism.

High Alpine caves in Switzerland and Austria have been cited as evidence of cave bear cult activity. Drachenloch, east of Zurich, had a crude stone chamber with bear skulls in it. Long bones had been pushed through the cheek-bone arches of some skulls. At Salzofenhohle in south-east Austria skulls had been set out, each one resting on paw bones and penis bones. There were small cairns of stones with the Regourdou burial as well as the bear skulls. A similar cairn or pyramid of stones was found in a north African site of similar age, El Guettar in Tunisia. Balls of clay had been thrown against the wall of the Mousterian cave of Toirano in Ligurian Italy. Similar balls of loess clay were found at Achenheim, and may be earlier than the last glaciation.

Colouring material of limonite (ferric oxide) and manganese dioxide, the two main colours used in cave art, are found in Mousterian sites such as Pech de l'Azé, La Quina and Le Moustier. Some of the pigment has been shaped into crayons, and the ends are bevelled from use. Such examples are known only from the MAT. Claims of colouring pigment from much earlier periods exist, but may be present accidentally. Altogether there is a lot of evidence for non-material activity by Neanderthal man, certainly by 60,000 BC and perhaps by 100,000 BC. It seems to become commoner as one approaches 35,000 BC.

By the end of the Mousterian, large parts of Eurasia had been occupied. This included the whole of Europe except Scandinavia and north Britain, but during cold periods there was little occupation north of latitude 50°. The major exception to this is that apparently Mousterian occupation had penetrated to 62° and even 65° north in the Pechora valley of north European Russia, in spite of ice-sheets round Archangel to the west, and over Novaya Zemlya and the north Urals to the east. Southern Asia had been occupied extensively by the Mousterian, but north of the Himalayas there was little occupation except a few Siberian sites like Ust Kanskaya, 50° north. Most of southern Siberia was occupied in the succeeding period. Japan and of course China were already occupied. Neither America nor Australasia seems to have been occupied before 35,000 BC, but Australia was occupied shortly after. By this time the inhabited world probably covered between 50 and 60 million sq. km, and the population may have exceeded 2 million.

Chapter 3

LATER HUNTERS IN EUROPE

I. PROBLEMS OF THE EARLIER UPPER PALAEOLITHIC

The main features that distinguish the Upper Palaeolithic (Leptolithic) in the typological sense from what precedes it have been discussed in some length in the previous section. In addition to blade production replacing flake production in providing the main type of blank from which tools were made, the main tool types are the burin, grattoir (endscraper) and backed blade or point (Figure 11). Other types such as pressure-flaked foliates, Emireh points, etc., which are often regarded as Leptolithic types, are included only because of an arbitrary decision. The purpose of the decision was to make the concept of a uniform Leptolithic technology replacing a non-Leptolithic technology workable in Europe and elsewhere over the whole of the later part of the Palaeolithic.

We have already noted that it does not work in most of Africa, southern Asia or Australasia, unless one accepts a retardation in these areas of many thousands of years after the 35–40 ThYA boundary. The example of the Kalambo sequence compared with culture sequences from south-western France and south Russia (Table 9) is given to emphasise this point. Broadly speaking, regions south of latitude 30° north follow the Kalambo pattern in having a 'Middle Stone Age', while those to the north follow the Dordogne pattern with an Upper Palaeolithic; China north of the thirtieth parallel is unfortunately little known in this respect.

The sequence of the Upper Palaeolithic is better known in south-western France than in any other area. It is also far richer in sites and artefacts than any other area except possibly the Mediterranean Levant (Lebanon, Israel, Jordan, Syria). The

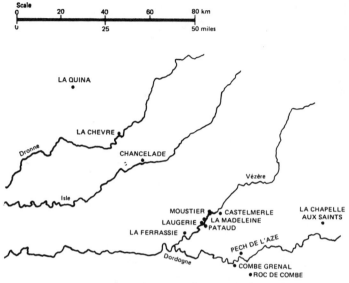

Map 3. Location of sites in the Les Eyzies region.

French sequence has been more effectively radiocarbon dated than any other. A further point which to some extent justifies the high level of concentration on this tiny area is that its archaeology is the key to dating and presumably understanding the world famous mural art of the caves of France and Spain.

More debatable is the effect of trying to date and classify Upper Palaeolithic levels of neighbouring regions like Britain, Germany, Czechoslovakia and even Russia as though it was essentially similar to the classic area. To cite just two examples, the Szeletian of central Europe was long believed to be the same as, and contemporary with, the Solutrian of France, on the basis of the superficial similarity of the foliate leaf points. But it is now clear that this view was mistaken. Sites of the Kostenkian complex of Russia are still often called Gravettian or east Gravettian, although radiocarbon evidence shows they are contemporary with the Magdalenian, and typologically they have no close links with any French culture.

The Dordogne Upper Palaeolithic (summarised in Table 9)

Table 9

Comparison of the culture sequences and C14 dates of Kalambo Falls, Molodova and sites in the Dordogne

Thousands years BC	Kalambo Dates	Kalambo Layer	Kalambo Culture	Kalambo Culture stage	Molodova V Dates	Molodova V Culture layer	Molodova V Culture stage	Dordogne Dates	Dordogne Culture	Dordogne Culture stage
	1790	- -		Late Stone Age			(Mesolithic)	7200	Sauveterrian	Mesolithic
						Ia			Azilian	
	7600	6c	Magosian	Second Intermediate Period	8650	II				Late Upper Palaeolithic (Leptolithic)
					9950	III			Magdalenian	
10					11,430	IV	Late Upper Palaeolithic	15,240		
						V		16,900		
		?			15,150			18,940	Solutrian	
20						VI		21,060	Late Perigordian	Early Upper Palaeolithic
		6b ?			21,750	VII	Early Upper Palaeolithic			
		6a	Lupemban			VIII		26,200		
		5	Lupemban	Middle Stone Age	27,700	IX			II–IV	
30	29,710					X		30,650	Aurignacian I	
								32,300		(Leptolithic)
		4	Lower Lupemban						Perigordian I	
40								37,950		

Table 9 continued

50	over 41,900 44,150	3 Sangoan	First Intermediate	
	over 47,000	2 Acheulian	Early Stone Age	
60	59,750			
70		1 Acheulian		
90+				

XI over 43,650 — Middle Palaeolithic — ?
XII

Late Mousterian 45,550+

Early Mousterian — Middle Palaeolithic

Lower Palaeolithic

has three divisions of long standing: Aurignacian in the wide sense, Solutrian, and Magdalenian. The Solutrian and Magdalenian, forming the later part of the Upper Palaeolithic, are adequately dated and short in duration, lasting perhaps a little under 10,000 years together. Neither is very extensive in distribution; both are absent for example from Italy, the Solutrian does not extend to north-east France, and the true Magdalenian is questionable east of Germany. The complexity of the earlier (Aurignacian) Upper Palaeolithic division has been recognised since 1912, and much work has been done to isolate its components and to date them within its approximately 15,000-year duration.

In 1912 Breuil proposed three stages forming the sequence: lower Aurignacian (Chatelperron stage), middle Aurignacian (Aurignac stage), upper Aurignacian (Gravette and Font Robert stages). In 1938 Garrod proposed that these stages should be regarded as successive cultures replacing one another: Chatelperronian, Aurignacian, lower and upper Gravettian. This terminology, which has achieved very wide currency outside France, is linked to an invasionist model. The cultures originated further east and arrived in the Dordogne as waves of migration. The Chatelperronian came from the undiscovered Asiatic homeland of true man, the Aurignacian from the Iranian plateau, the Gravettian from Russia, the Solutrian from Hungary, and the Magdalenian was of unknown origin.

The main concern in Garrod's theory is with the place of origin of the culture and with its thread of continuity across Europe. It requires that the Dordogne cultures should be continuous across Europe and should appear successively earlier as one moves eastwards. At present neither of these requirements seems to be met, nor does the terminology adequately describe the rather well-established sequence in the Dordogne. One of the ironies of the scheme is that it is favoured by those who would like to see the Dordogne sequence reduced to the status of just one regional sequence, and on the receiving end of a series of migrations from more dynamic regions. But in fact its main effect has been to perpetuate the use of French culture names right across Europe.

In a theory published between 1933 and 1938 and based on the sites of La Ferrassie, La Gravette and Laugerie Haute, Peyrony argued for the existence of two separate traditions, the Aurignacian proper and the Perigordian (Table 10). In

Table 10

Stages of the Aurignacian and Perigordian as illustrated by three sites

	Perigordian V	Aurignacian V
Perigordian IV	Aurignacian IV	
Aurignacian II	Aurignacian III	Perigordian III[1]
Aurignacian I	Aurignaican II	
	Aurignacian I	
	Perigordian II[2]	
	Perigordian I	
La Gravette	La Ferrassie	Laugerie Haute West

1 Now VI.
2 Now Aurignacian.

1946 a second Perigordian tradition was added. Peyrony believed the Aurignacian and Perigordian were different peoples who lived side by side in the Les Eyzies region, but his Perigordian III stage is now known to have been erroneously interpreted. The fact remains that the sites of Ferrassie and Pataud, only some 5 km apart, have a different culture sequence over the same time period, which may imply the coexistence of different peoples. It remains an unresolved question whether in a small area of say 1,000 sq. km it is normal for contrasting cultures to live in proximity. Table 11 indicates the main lines of the sequence near Les Eyzies, and it seems likely that the Perigordian was rare or absent here during Aurignacian stages I and II.

Table 11

Sequence of cultures and stages in the Dordogne, based on Pataud, Laugerie and La Chèvre sites

Layers and C14 dates (all BC) for Pataud and Laugerie (in brackets)

	P	L	C	Stage	Stone tool type	Bone tool type
(18,940)	1	31		Protosolutrian	Protosol. pt	
	–	33		Aurignacian V		Bevel based pt
19,990 (20,030)	2	36		Protomagdalenian	Backed microblade	
21,060	3	38		Perigordian VI	Microgravette	
	3	42				
25,110	4			Perigordian Vc (Noaillan)	de Noailles burin	
26,200	5			Perigordian IV	Gravette pt	
	6			Aurignacian	Busked burin	Lautsch pt
30,950	7			? II–III		
	8			Aurignacian I		
30,650	11				Carinate	
31,310	12		3		Aurignac blade	Aurignac pt
32,300	14					
			2	Perigordian I	Chatelperron pt	
			1			

Column P layers of Abri Pataud
Column L layers of Laugerie Haute East
Column C layers of Trou de La Chèvre, Bourdeilles
Note: The highest C14 date has been quoted in each case, and some may be too high (e.g. Pataud 7).

Nevertheless there is some evidence for continuity between the Chatelperron and Gravette stages of the Perigordian, and for the two traditions being contemporary. At Roc de Combe and Le Piage in the Lot, some 30 km south-east of Les Eyzies, thin levels of an evolved Chatelperron stage are interstratified with an Aurignacian I. Secondly in an area some 200 km north of Les Eyzies, two sites (Cottés and Fontenioux) have assemblages typologically intermediate between Chatelperron and Gravette stages; it had of course long been realised that they were similar. The C14 date for the Cottés (mid-Perigordian) stage at Cottés of 31,350 BC seems to make it contemporary with the Aurignacian I of Pataud at Les Eyzies. It would be possible to incorporate all this evidence in a geographical model in which the two traditions were contemporary but in different regions, the Perigordian surviving in central France, for example.

The role of the Font Robert and truncated element assemblages, Peyrony's PV(i) and PV(ii), is still unclear, and some evidence would support the view that they were part of a separate tradition, perhaps related to the Solutrian, but going back in time to before the Gravette stage. The de Noailles type (PV(iii)) is also under debate. Bordes advocates keeping it within the true Perigordian culture, while Movius and David regard it as a separate culture, as did Peyrony who put it in his second Perigordian tradition. Since the 'Noaillan' is perhaps the commonest element in the Perigordian complex, with more evidence of artistic activity than any other part of the Perigordian, its true affinities are of some importance. It may derive from the Krems-Dufour culture group, which has a wide distribution and close affinity to the Aurignacian.

Of all the cultures before the Solutrian, the Aurignacian phase I is probably the commonest, spanning several thousand years and more than one recognisable stage. Aurignacian II, III and IV are increasingly rare.

The site to which radiocarbon dating has been most systematically applied is the Pataud shelter, within the village of Les Eyzies and at the centre of the richest cluster of Dordogne sites (Table 11). The sequence is continued into the Solutrian at Laugerie Haute, 2 km away, but at the moment the dating of the Magdalenian by radiocarbon is poor. There are unfortunately no dates for the beginning of the Perigordian in the Dordogne, but a date in the bracket 37,000–34,000 BC is probable.

Some of the better known Upper Palaeolithic cultures are listed in Table 12. There are a few rich and well excavated sites like Pavlov and Dolní Věstonice in central Europe, but there are no true sequences outside western Europe except possibly Molodova in the Dniestr valley with a useful series of C_{14}

Table 12

Some Upper Palaeolithic cultures of Europe and adjacent regions

Szeletian complex (including Jerzmanowician and Streletsky-Sungir
    cultures)

Krems-Dufour complex, Willendorfian, Olschevian

Pavlovian complex (possibly including several unrelated cultures)

Kostenkian complex (possibly including several unrelated cultures)

Western Asia Emiran, Halkan, Antelian, Atlitian, Kebaran, Baradostian,
    Nebekian, Natufian

North Africa late Aterian, Dabban, Oranian/Iberomaurusian, Sebilian,
    Sebekian, Silsilian, Qadan

Note: European cultures that do not begin before the Magdalenian are omitted.

dates (Table 9) and the Kostenki sites in the Don valley near
Voronesh. More complete sequences are found in the western
Asiatic caves like Mt Carmel, Jabrud, Ksar Akil and Abu
Halka, and at the Haua cave in Libya. These culture sequences
however have been subject to much less detailed analysis than
those of the Dordogne.

Evidence for Upper Palaeolithic occupation in Britain prior
to the end of the Magdalenian is very slight. Some open sites
in north Kent like Bapchild and St Mary Cray have tools which
may belong to the Chatelperron stage. A busked burin, of the
type found in Aurignacian II, comes from Ffynnon Beuno in
Flintshire along with foliate points. Other such foliates come
from two caves in Creswell Crags, Derbyshire, and some
Mendip sites. Foliates approaching the Font Robert point are
known from Pin Hole, Creswell, from Paviland in south Wales
and Cat Hole nearby. The foliates are similar to those of the
earliest Solutrian, but are closest to those of the Jerzmanowice
culture found in Poland and Germany, and part of the Szeletian group. All this evidence could be incorporated in a single
culture around 30,000–25,000 bc. This is confirmed by two
C14 dates from samples associated with foliates from Kent's
cavern in south Devon – 26,750 and 26,200 bc. That the foliates
are generally earlier than the earliest Solutrian of the Dordogne

(about 19,000 bc) is indicated by the fact that at Pin Hole cave they were from a lower level than the Font Robert points, which would be nearer 25,000 bc in the Dordogne. This British culture, as yet poorly isolated and unnamed, presumably derives from part of the Szeletian, and provides a plausible origin for the French Solutrian. Probably the ice advanced over some of the British foliate sites about 18,000–20,000 bc, and this would have forced the occupants further south.

2. CROMAGNON MAN: BURIALS, ADORNMENTS AND CLOTHES

Prior to the Magdalenian in western Europe, human skeletons are rarely found in reliable archaeological context. The burial from the top of the Pataud sequence is perhaps the only French example. Upper Palaeolithic burials earlier than 20,000 bc are known from Pavlov and Dolní Věstonice, from Kostenki site XV and possibly other Russian sites like Sungir. The Předmost skeletons are probably of similar age. It is clear that man of essentially modern, even European, type was present in Europe by this time.

At the same time several human fossils from Czechoslovakia indicate a strong survival of archaic (Neanderthal) features: Předmost skeleton III, fragments from Zlaty Kůn near Pilsen, and what is possibly the earliest Upper Palaeolithic burial from Brno, skeleton II; the latter two sites are possibly Szeletian. Teeth from the early Perigordian levels at Arcy are taurodontic.

It is often claimed that two French sites, Combe Capelle and Cromagnon, have human skeletons from the beginning of the Upper Palaeolithic. The Combe Capelle skeleton was found under poor excavation conditions at the base of a series of Upper Palaeolithic levels. Presumably it was buried into the early Perigordian level from a higher level, but whether it was from the Aurignacian, the later Perigordian or the Solutrian is unknown. The three Cromagnon skeletons found in 1868 by workmen in a small cave close to Pataud rested on a series of

Aurignacian layers. Whether they were contemporary with the end of the Aurignacian about 27,000 bc, or a little more likely were buried by Magdalenians as most other Cromagnon type skeletons from France were, is also unknown.

The name Cromagnon is often used for the men of the Upper Palaeolithic; as a general term for Postneanderthal man of varied but apparently Caucasoid type, it is convenient for Europe and perhaps western Asia and north Africa. The skulls which most closely resemble Cromagnon man from the type site are in France mostly Magdalenian: Laugerie Basse, Sordes, Bruniquel, Hoteaux, St Germain la Rivière, La Madeleine, Le Placard. The Cromagnons from the Grimaldi caves are poorly dated, either contemporary with the Magdalenian or a little earlier.

Two other races have been claimed as present in the Upper Palaeolithic of Europe. The 'negroids' of Grimaldi, and the 'eskimoids' of Chancelade in the Dordogne. Although another claim for the negroid type has been made for a youthful skeleton from Kostenki XIV – Markina at the other end of Europe, few modern workers accept these as truly negroid. It would be surprising indeed if the negroid physical type, which is adapted to the hot tropics and particularly the vicinity of the humid rain forest, should evolve in or even enter Europe during the last glacial age. The woman and child from Grimaldi do however seem different from most Cromagnons; they are prognathous and big-toothed, and being among the rare examples of skeletons from the earlier Upper Palaeolithic they probably represent a transitional stage from a local Neanderthal population.

The Chancelade man was claimed to be eskimoid or mongoloid. There would be nothing surprising in some glacial or tundra environmental adaptation here, but the racial conclusion has been generally rejected. A child of similar age from Mal'ta in southern Siberia is genuinely mongoloid according to Gerassimov. The Chancelade man and several skeletons from Roc de Sers, 50 km to the north-west, can be most realistically grouped with the Cromagnons, who are probably all cold-adapted without being mongoloid; some minor racial variability within the Cromagnons is only to be expected. The Cromagnons in the wide sense seem to provide an excellent ancestry for the European-Caucasoids, and the following stages may be suggested: late Neanderthals; neoteny→archaic Cromagnons; main Cromagnons; post-glacial European populations.

A total of over sixty burials are known from the European Upper Palaeolithic. Although over 20 of these come from the poorly excavated collective burial of Předmost, burials are clearly not rare. Nevertheless we have no sample of burial from any pre-Magdalenian culture in France, if we discount disputed examples and those with inadequate data like Labattut which was probably a Noaillan child burial. Other than the Magdalenian most burials are from the Szeletian complex (taken here to include Sungir), the Pavlovian complex and the Kostenkian complex.

In a sample of 20 burials where the body position was recorded, 11 are on the back, 4 on the right side and 5 on the left. In 32 cases where the degree of contraction has been recorded, 13 were extended, 8 partly contracted and 11 fully contracted. In the latter case the bodies must have been tightly bound with the knees up to the chin. One burial, Bruniquel, was doubled with the legs straight, feet to head. In the Barma Grande at Grimaldi, a triple burial was found in 1892 (Figure 12).

In contrast to the Mousterian where ochre was not used, most Upper Palaeolithic burials were covered with red ochre made of powdered iron oxide. Twenty-two examples were recorded with ochre and only eight without. The Sungir male burial was accompanied by burnt coals which may have singed the body as in the partial cremation known from classical Greek times; Dolní Věstonice furnishes a second example. True cremation is unknown in Europe, though surprisingly it has been found at Mungo lake in Australia from around 25,000

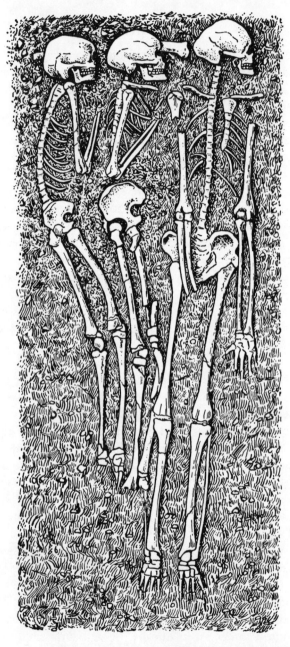

Figure 12. The triple burial at Barma Grande, Grimaldi.

BC. Mammoth scapulae covered burials at Kostenki and on the Czech sites, as grave slabs.

Associated with these burials is much evidence for personal adornment, and occasionally clothes. Usually it consists of shells, teeth, ivory, antler or bone pieces, stone objects and fossils. Many are perforated, but some have only a groove round one end for tying.

Elaborate head-dresses of perforated shells, presumably threaded on a network of cords, are common as at Sungir, Kostenki XV, Brno, four Grimaldi caves, Arene Candide, Combe Capelle, and La Madeleine (Plate IV). The Kostenki XV child's head-dress included 150 perforated fox teeth. Head-dresses are rare in the French adult Magdalenian burials. There seems to have been some standardisation of burial practice here, as all were crouched on their left sides facing right. The child from La Madeleine however, buried extended on its back with head to right, had shell and teeth adornments at ankles and knees, wrists and elbows, neck and head. The Mal'ta Siberian child burial had a diadem of bone pieces on its head.

Evidence for the wearing of strings of beads other than on the head is rarer. Necklaces or collars are found with only seven individuals compared with at least eighteen head-dresses. Apart from La Madeleine and two Czech burials (Brno II and Dolní Věstonice II), the other four necklaces were found at Grimaldi. Waistbands and belts are also rarer, occurring on the two children from Grimaldi, on one other Grimaldi burial, and indicated at Mal'ta by a buckle or stud. Bracelets, armlets, anklets and knee decorations were found on three Grimaldi burials, La Madeleine and Sungir.

Many perforated objects, suitable as pendants or amulets, are known. They are rarely elaborate. A tiny bear statuette from Isturitz is known and little lignite female statuettes from Petersfels in south Germany were perforated. A large number of flat oval pieces of bone have a perforation at one end. Some are probably bull-roarers, designed to make a roaring noise when whirled on a string; some may be pendants or combine both functions. The most elaborate collar, found on the boy in the triple burial of Barma Grande, had two rows of fish vertebrae and one row of *Nassa* shells; after every four vertebrae (and three shells) came a spacer made from a deer canine.

Perforated and grooved adornments begin to occur almost with the start of the Upper Palaeolithic. The early Perigordian level, 10, at Arcy (earlier than the level with C14 date 31,910 bc), had at least six teeth grooved for suspension and one perforated fox canine. There was also a Mesozoic fossil modified for suspension.

Early Aurignacian I adornments from two shelters at Castelmerle including a necklace are only slightly later than the material quoted above, and finds from Fossellone in Italy in a very early Aurignacian context may be contemporary with them. The Fossellone site produced the usual perforated fox and deer teeth. In addition imitation deer teeth had been carved from steatite, and a small pendant of oval shape and plano-convex cross-section was made from a piece of deer antler with double perforation. Subsequent to these finds of 35,000–30,000 BC, adornments occur on hundreds of sites.

The adornments are often simultaneously evidence for clothing. The head-dresses are of course a kind of clothing, and we may begin by noting how common these are. In the Magdalenian cave of Adaouste in Provence it was noted that the chough had been killed and brought to the site. This bird is almost meatless, but has fine feathers for head-dresses.

The Sungir I burial (C14 12,650 bc, but possibly nearer 20,000 BC) contains evidence for extensive clothing. In addition to perforated fox teeth, hundreds of ivory beads were found resting on the skeleton. These seem to have been sewn to skin clothing, and lead to the conclusion that the man wore trousers. He had a shirt of sewn skins without a join at the front, presumably put on over the head like a poncho. Rows of beads were continuous across the chest, indicating this conclusion. Leather shoes sewn to the trousers like moccasins were also claimed.

Several other burials had numerous shells spaced over them, which can be most easily interpreted as evidence of skin clothes. Examples are from Laugerie Basse, four Grimaldi burials, Arene Candide and La Madeleine, but the precision of recording is poor.

Most human figures in Palaeolithic art seem to be naked to judge by the breasts and penises shown. The Laussel male relief however has a belt and perhaps trousers. Two figures engraved on a bone from Isturitz have bands round their wrists, ankles and neck, suggestive of some kind of close fitting suit. However the front figure has breasts indicated, and this presumably makes it more likely that the figures are naked except for necklace, bracelets and anklets. The engraving of a tall cartoon-like man from Montrastruc has apparently seven buttons down the centre of his chest. Perhaps these are the disc buttons so often found in the Magdalenian.

More instructive are the paintings of possibly post-glacial date from Mediterranean Spain, called Spanish Levant art. Most of the numerous human figures are naked but head-dresses, often clearly feathers, are common. A man from Els Secans seems to have trousers to the knees. Knee and waist adornments or fringes, possibly sewn onto clothes, are common. Women from Cogul and Alpera have bell-shaped skirts to just below the knees, but bare breasts.

The best evidence of skin clothing is from two sites in southern Siberia near lake Baikal. A statuette from Buret' seems to be fully clothed from its feet to its hooded head in what resembles a fully tailored eskimo style skin (Figure 13). Three smaller figures from nearby Mal'ta have the same feature, the fur indicated by small incisions. The C14 date for Mal'ta is 12,800 bc, and the likely time range 16,000–12,000 BC. Probably the invention of well-tailored clothing occurred during the middle part of the Upper Palaeolithic, and made the colonisation of Siberia possible. A likely date for its invention is coinciding with the first appearance of finely made eyed needles, in the late Solutrian of France (17,000 bc); they are

Figure 13. The clothed figurine from Buret.

common in the Magdalenian. Examples from Předmost and Kostenki XV may be a little earlier. The colder parts of Europe were presumably the home of these inventions.

3. MUSIC AND REPRESENTATIONAL ART

From an early part of the Upper Palaeolithic we have evidence of musical instruments and presumably therefore of music. A flute was found in a level with mainly Aurignacian tools at Pair-non-Pair near Bordeaux, and no fewer than eight were found in Aurignacian levels at Isturitz. They are all made on bird bones and are of small diameter. Three flutes from central

Europe of comparable age are made on cave-bear bones, and are thus of larger size. The culture has been called Olschevian and has Aurignacian affinities. Another bear bone flute from Pekarna is perhaps Pavlovian, around 25,000 bc. Two lesser-known examples from the Dordogne are in Plate V.

Table 13

Some major finds of flutes in the Upper Palaeolithic

	Western Europe	Central and Eastern Europe
EARLY	Pair-non-Pair[1]	Istallosko (Hungary)
pre 20,000	Isturitz (8)[1]	Lokve (Yugoslavia)
BC	Castelmerle (Roches)[1]	Salzofenhohle (Austria)
		Pekarna (Czechoslovakia)
LATE	Badegoule[1]	Molodova V/4 (USSR)
	Placard[1]	Chernaya Gora (USSR)

Some of the localities in which whistles of Palaeolithic date have been found: D. Věstonice, Pavlov, Istallosko, Pekarna, Solutre, La Madeleine, Kesserloch
[1] South-west France.

As indicated in Table 13, fewer specimens are known from the later Upper Palaeolithic. From Badegoule there is a Solutrian flute made on a reindeer radius; and a four-part pan-pipe has been reported from the early Magdalenian of Le Placard. A later Russian example from Molodova V, level 4, is a pipe of elk horn with six holes. Most of the flutes have only three or four holes. All the later examples are apparently made from cervid bones.

Rather commoner than flutes are whistles made of perforated phalanges (Plate V and Table 13). A specimen from the Mousterian levels of La Quina is dubious, as is a fragment of an alleged flute of even earlier date from Haua cave in Libya. The whistles may have served a practical purpose for signalling during hunts, or for attracting animals. Out of this practice the flute could have developed. An engraving of a man with bison head at Trois Frères cave in the Pyrénées has been variously interpreted as someone playing a flute or twanging a bow held in his mouth.

Quite possibly percussion instruments of stretched skins were made. Some perforated batons have been compared to Lappish drumsticks, and in several caves the stalactites have fine acoustic properties. Another possible acoustic device, already mentioned in connection with amulets, is the bull-roarer. It produces an eerie moaning noise, beloved of participants in religious ceremonies.

Paradoxically cave mural art, the paintings and engravings inside caves in southern France and northern Spain, which is perhaps the best-known relic of early man, is the most difficult of all the surviving traces of the Upper Palaeolithic to date. Instead it is the smaller portable objects that provide an indirect clue to the dating of this art. Over 130 sites with portable art are known and some are very rich, notably La Madeleine, Laugerie, Isturitz and Mas d'Azil. There are ten portable art sites in the USSR, ten in Italy, five in Czechoslovakia, twelve in Germany, ten in Spain and about a hundred in France.

The mural art is found in over 110 sites. One is in the Urals, five are in Italy, over thirty in Spain and the great majority are in southern France, especially from the Pyrénées to the Perigord. Up to one-third of the decoration in caves is close to the entrance. About one-fifth is deep inside, from 50 m up to several km; and nearly half is intermediate between these two situations. Taking into account the many minor sites, engraving is probably the commonest type of art, but painting is also very common and usually easier to see.

Bas-relief sculpting in soft limestone is known only at six or so sites, always near the entrance or in the daylight, but detached blocks with carving are also found. The entrance carving and detached blocks are often sealed by archaeological deposits and are thus datable. A very small number of examples of modelling in clay, smearing of clay and incising of clay are known.

Figures compiled by Leroi-Gourhan (1968) show that horse and bison are the commonest animals represented. Table 14 shows the frequencies of other animals; some are based on the

Table 14

The ten commonest animals in cave art

Horse	610 (228)	Human males	88 (32)
Bison	510 (161)	Human females	19 ?
Red deer	247 (81)	Hands	(14)
Mammoth	205 (50)	Complex signs	(183)
Ibex	176 (75)	Simple signs	? (183)
Aurochs	137 (50)		
Reindeer	84 (25)		
Bear	36 (23)		
Lion/feline	29 (18)		
Rhinoceros	16 (9)		

N.B. The figures in brackets represent the number of compositions in which an animal appears, as opposed to the total number of examples.

number of compositions in which the animals appear and not the number of animals. A puzzling and so far unexplained fact is that the reindeer, which is by far the commonest animal in the food debris, figures only seventh in frequency of representation, while the horse, probably the second commonest hunt animal, is the most represented.

Unquestionably Palaeolithic cave art ('Franco-Cantabrian' art) is animal dominated. The only other major category of art is that of the symbols, some large and rectilinear, some no more than blobs and strokes. Human figures are rare and in no case are they drawn and finished with the care and skill often lavished on the animal representations. Giedion (1963) has said that Upper Palaeolithic man 'considered himself a minor creature, less powerful and less beautiful than his revered fellow creature, the animal'.

Ten Aurignacian sites listed in Table 15 have produced painting or carving from Aurignacian levels. Good examples are two shelters at Castelmerle, Castanet and Blanchard, of early date, perhaps around 32,000 bc, and three levels at La Ferrassie perhaps spanning 29,000–26,000 bc (Peyrony's Aurignacian II–IV). Theoretically any of the dozens of objects from these layers could belong to an earlier period or culture. However the absence of a single example from the Chatel-

Table 15

Sites in western Europe with dated art from the earlier Upper Palaeolithic

Aurignacian: Vezere valley: Castanet, Blanchard, Cellier, Laussel, Gorge d'Enfer, Belcayre, Ferrassie, ?Laugerie. Other localities in south-west France: Bourdeilles/Chevre; Mouthiers/Rois; Pair-non-Pair. Central France: Arcy/Renne. Pyrénées: Gargas and Isturitz. north Spain: Los Hornos. south Germany: Vogelherd.

Noaillan: South-west France: Labattut, Terme Pialat, Laussel, Tursac/Facteur, Pechialet, Rebieres, Planchetorte, Laraux. Other parts of France: Arcy, Isturitz and Gargas

Font Robert and Truncated element culture: Ferrassie, Vachons

Perigordian VI and Protomagdalenian: Laugerie, Pataud

Solutrian: Oullins, Chabot, Solutre, Badegoule, Parpallo (east Spain)

perron Perigordian or Mousterian makes it obvious that it was made by the Aurignacians. Painting on limestone blocks is known, but engraving is commoner. At first (Blanchard and Belcayre) the engraved line is wide and irregular, as though pecked out with a blunt object; later it is much more fine (Ferrassie Aurignacian III and IV) as though done with a burin or special engraving tool. The improvement in engraving seems to be quicker than that in painting.

The commonest motif in Aurignacian art is the vulvar symbol (Figure 14). Early examples are usually pear-shaped; later ones are more triangular. After the Aurignacian they assume the form of a triangle with acute corners, and in the later Magdalenian they are fish-tail shaped. Most vulvas are engraved but one from Ferrassie is in bas-relief. All have a deep groove representing the slit between the labia minora. This emphasis on the sex organs is repeated in a large phallus 18 cm long from Blanchard shelter carved in the round in bison horn, and a second engraved on limestone.

Probably some central European art is contemporary with the Aurignacian. The statuette from Brno of a male figure may be Szeletian and before 27,000 bc. With it were circular vulvar discs. The most famous of all the female statuettes or 'venuses', that from Willendorf in Austria, comes from Willendorfian layers probably contemporary with the latest Aurignacian. Another early venus is from Ostrava-Petrkovice. Animal statuettes from Vogelherd, the best representing the horse, lion and mammoth, are the earliest of this genre, being not much later than 30,000 bc. Possible prototypes of statuettes are known from Ferrassie and Istallosko.

The venuses found in France seem to belong to the Noaillan, about 24,000 BC, but apart from Lespugue and Tursac most are undated. The outstanding bas-relief human figures from Laussel probably date from the same time. Engraved bone and painted or engraved stones are occasionally found in the Noaillan; horse, deer and rhinoceros are among the animals represented. Small dated art finds are absent in Gravette levels, and rare and uncharacteristic in cultures from 22,000 to 15,000 bc. Unfortunately it is not easy to distinguish Noaillan or Solutrian art from the much more abundant art of the Magdalenian.

Probably well over three-quarters of the dated art objects from France belong between 14,000 and 10,000 bc, a heroic age of hunting art. Utilitarian objects were commonly decorated. Strictly speaking the function of many of the carved pieces of antler is poorly established. Spear throwers are fairly easily recognised and the heavy-weighted end is commonly decorated. Half-round rods and other shaft pieces are probably parts of composite spears. Disc buttons and spatulas are also often engraved with animals. Perforated batons ('*bâtons de commandement*') are often decorated, frequently with phallic and vulvar symbols. Some have multiple perforations (Plate V).

Humans figure in Magdalenian engraving. Statuettes of females, less obese than the earlier venuses, are found at Laugerie, Petersfels and Pekarna. Stylised engravings of females in lateral view are common. The head is barely shown, and the feet are often missing. The breasts are often shown but are not large or expanded as was usual in the earlier series. The most

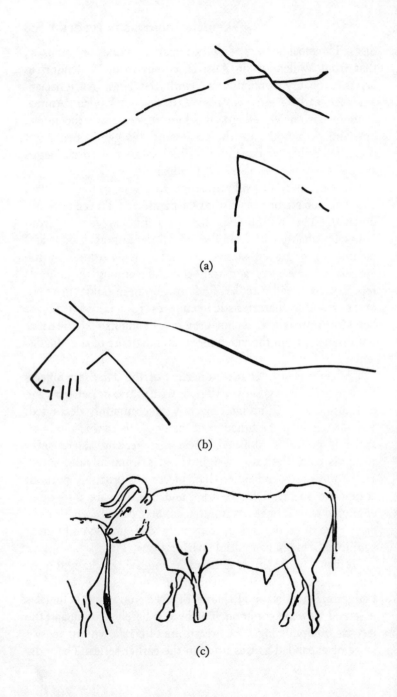

(a)

(b)

(c)

regular feature is that the buttocks are prominent and protruding. The stomach is usually flat or hollow.

Male figures, though dwarfed in size and quality by the animals, also occur. An important group of them have clearly animal attributes such as horns, tails and fur. Many are in animal postures, either crawling or oblique. Often they have cartoon-like heads which may be masks. La Marche in central France has yielded over a hundred such heads. Often the penis is the only clear indication of maleness.

It is impossible even to begin to describe the dozens of mural pictures in detail. All but a tiny minority (Leroi-Gourhan's style I and II) are thought to be late Upper Palaeolithic, though some workers start the main sequence in the Solutrian (style III), and others confine it to the Magdalenian. Some of the most spectacular caves are Lascaux, Niaux, Pech Merle, Altamira, Mt Castillo (four caves), Combarelles and Font de Gaume. Often the pictures are concentrated in particular parts of the cave. But it is at present being debated whether they are in any sense scenes. If they were, then the conventions were quite different from those of later art. The animals are different sizes, on different levels and even at different angles.

There has been much discussion on the purpose of cave art. Art for art's sake, hunting magic, fertility magic, symbolic

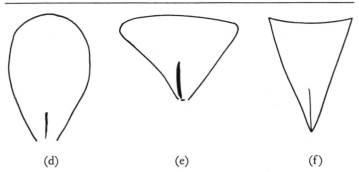

(d)   (e)   (f)

Figure 14. Styles of animals and vulvar symbols. (a) Castanet c. 32,000 bc; (b) Isturitz c. 25,000 bc; (c) Teyjat 11,000 bc; (d) Pear shape, Aurignacian; (e) Triangle, Pavlovian; (f) Fishtail, Magdalenian.

decoration of sanctuaries are some of the theories most often mentioned. It is by now fairly obvious that no one explanation is likely to be the sole answer, and to rule out one explanation in a particular case is not to reject it altogether. There are certain clues about the use of the caves. The hand silhouettes found in several caves are too small to belong to adult males and could be boys'. Footprints of juveniles are common in the caves; at Pech Merle a juvenile and an adult, the latter apparently leaning on a stick, had left prints. In Tuc d'Audoubert, a low chamber had a clay floor marked by heel prints of rows of young people, and at the entrance had been dropped clay 'sausages', possibly representations of penises. At Addaura in Sicily, engravings contemporary with the end of the Magdalenian show figures with penises in a covering or sheath, perhaps following ritual circumcision. Circumcision is a major rite of initiation among many hunting peoples. In Australia it is sometimes accompanied by hand silhouetting. Ideally it is practised in a secret place where uninitiates, especially women, will not blunder in. The painted caves would offer an ideal venue for such ceremonies.

4 THE AGE OF INVENTIONS

The Solutrian spans approximately the period 19,000–16,000 bc, and very few contemporary cultures have been recognised elsewhere in Europe from this time, even though the Solutrian is mainly confined to south-west France and Iberia. The Magdalenian belongs to the period approximately 16,000–10,000 bc. Certainly by the later part of this period, several regional cultures are known: Romanellian in Italy; Hamburgian in northern Germany; Kostenkian in Russia; and other minor cultures. Further research on this regionality would be valuable, as the evidence and dating is for the first time sufficient to allow a detailed study.

During the ten thousand or so years of the later Palaeolithic, a number of key inventions were made, though of course the

III. Reconstructions of Palaeolithic man

(a) Peking (CKT 11)

(b) Neanderthal (La Chapelle)

(c) Mount Carmel (Skhul 5)

(d) Cromagnon

Facing page 112

IV. The Grimaldi burial, Cavillon cave

dates of these can only be fixed approximately. Nevertheless it is clear that more inventions were adopted in this short time than in a million years of the Lower Palaeolithic. The eyed needle, and the tailored skin clothing it made possible, have already been discussed; this invention occurred by 17,000 bc, possibly 20,000–17,000 bc.

A second group of inventions concerns the miniature blade or microblade, removed from a diminutive blade core, and its retouching and hafting. Surprisingly, a certain kind of semi-abrupt retouched microblade (the *lamelle* Dufour) is found widely across Europe about 30,000 bc. The first typical backed microblades in the French sequence date from about 20,000 bc, and the first triangular 'microliths', as geometric forms are called, date from about 15,000 BC. They seem to be present at Pavlov by 23,000 BC. Evidence for the mounting of microliths is rare in the Palaeolithic. An example of micro-blades set in a bone rod has been found at St Marcel in central France and dates from the Magdalenian about 13,000 bc. The triangles probably represent barbs, while the simple backed microblades may in some cases have been set in rows to make a knife or sickle blade. The device of multiple hafting probably first became widespread in the Magdalenian and Romanellian. A tiny waste product of microlith manufacture also came in at this time; it is called the microburin. Microliths are best known as the main constituent in assemblages of the Mesolithic and 'Late Stone Age' across Africa and Eurasia, and there can be no doubt about the importance of this complex of inventions, and of miniaturisation as a progressive principle.

Possibly even more geographically far-reaching was the device of carving a row of barbs on antler, bone and wooden points (Figure 15a). The microliths and barbed points may have been alternatives with a similar function, namely of ensuring that after an animal had been speared, the spear point did not come straight out again. The early barbed heads were almost certainly harpoons with a swelling or loop for attachment of a line, by which the animal once speared could be held and

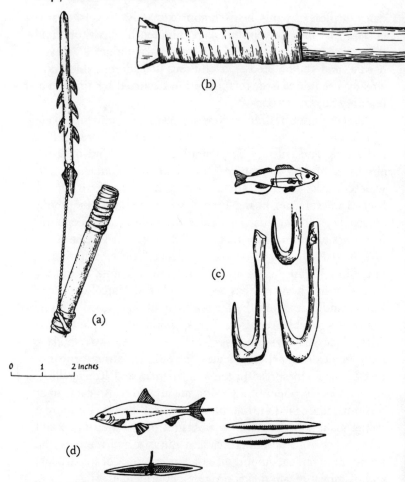

Figure 15. Some late Palaeolithic inventions: (a) Barbed harpoon; (b) Chisel arrowhead; (c) Fish-hooks; (d) Fish-gorge.

played. The development of this device seems to be well documented in the later Magdalenian. Stage IV harpoons (13,000–12,000 bc) have incipient barbs, and by stage V (12,000–11,000 bc) there are uniserial harpoons with fully defined barbs in a single row. The latter are also found in the Hamburgian by about 11,000 bc. Magdalenian VI has biserial

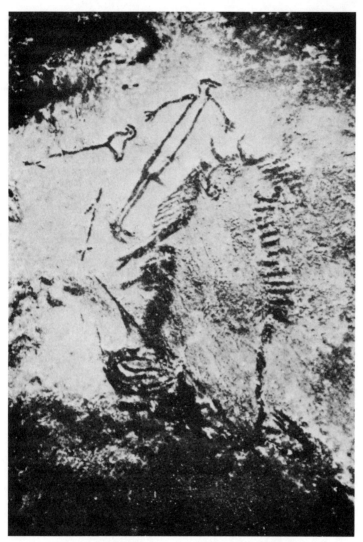

Figure 16. The scene in the Lascaux shaft.

harpoons (Figure 15) and at Pekarna a triserial type was tried.

Later barbed points were often not harpoons. The type became widely spread before, or with, the advent of farming in Asia, Africa, Australasia and the Americas as well as Europe. It was still in use in Tierra del Fuego and the Australian coast in recent times. The continuousness of distribution, short delay in appearance and overall similarity argue for some kind of diffusion rather than independent invention. Diffusion by invasion or 'missionarism' is fairly obviously out of the question. It seems we are dealing with a classic example of the spread of a useful idea by acculturation.

From the later Magdalenian, along with the harpoons, we find the spear thrower, usually a shaft of antler about 30 cm long. A bird-headed spear thrower seems to be represented in the famous Lascaux shaft scene (Figure 16) beside the supine man; it may have been made in wood. Because the painting is probably pre-13,000 bc, it raises the possibility that the spear thrower was in use before the barbed harpoon, but an invention date around 13,000–11,000 bc is also possible. It is a significant invention in that it was the first use of mechanical advantage known, enabling a man to launch his spear faster and further with the same effort. This device also became widely spread, possibly by diffusion with the barbed point.

Similar in purpose is a fourth major invention, the bow and arrow, whose subsequent wide use, even among later literate societies, indicates its importance. Mechanical power is here carried a step further. The bow can also be played, or used to provide rotary motion, as in a bow drill. This invention goes back to late glacial times, but was more used in post-glacial times. The earliest satisfactory evidence is a hoard of more than a hundred arrows from Stellmoor near Hamburg which belongs to pollen zone III (C14 age 9000–8200 bc, corrected varve age 9100–8300 BC according to Tauber 1970), the last period of tundra vegetation in north continental Europe. The earliest bow is from Holmegaard in Denmark at about 6000 bc. The Stellmoor arrows were of pine and were composite. A clear bowstring notch was visible at one end of the shaft and a slot at the other. Into the slot, it seems that the tanged and obliquely blunted Ahrensburg point was inserted. Points of a probably ancestral type are found in northern Europe back to about 12,000 bc and occasionally in the latest Magdalenian. Claims of arrowheads at earlier periods have been made, notably for the fine barbed and tanged tips from the late Solutrian of Parpallo in south-east Spain, but one may doubt if this is correct, because the idea did not catch on at this time.

Some other minor inventions of the later Palaeolithic are pressure flaking, longitudinal grooves on spears (for microliths, for poison or as blood runnels), bird and fish-gorges (15d), disc buttons, and bodkins. Fish-hooks (Figure 15c) were in use before 8000 bc in the east Mediterranean area. The axe was invented by 8000 bc but the flint core axe with 'tranchet' sharpening blow mainly spread to cope with the post-glacial forests.

We now have evidence from almost the whole span of the Palaeolithic which is claimed to indicate traces of dwellings or shelters. These claims have become much commoner with more careful excavation in recent decades, but had been made in Russia as far back as 1927. Although the evidence is always short of conclusive, I imagine most of them are genuine, but with post holes so rarely found, the reconstruction even of the best is difficult.

Only in the later Upper Palaeolithic do they become common, after about 16,000 bc. In the Magdalenian, Hamburgian and Kostenkian complexes twenty-five or more are reasonably documented. Before that only a few Czech sites (notably Tibava, Pavlov and Dolní Věstonice) and some sites near Bergerac in south-west France (Corbiac, Rabier, etc.) can be listed as Upper Palaeolithic open dwellings, though more are to be expected. It has often been said that in cave areas early man had no need to build shelters or tents, and that huts would be found in cave-less areas. This is now seen to be untrue, as huts are found close to caves and several rather convincing post

Figure 17. Reconstruction of Upper Palaeolithic houses at Ostrava-Petrovice.

constructions are known from under rock shelters. The earliest is at Arcy, in the early Perigordian level, and there are Solutrian and Magdalenian shelters that contain structures. A circular dwelling, for example, has been found in the Magdalenian levels of Salpétrière near Pont du Gard; and a central European example is Kniegrotte in central Germany.

In passing we may note the similarity of the structures of Arcy and Dolní Věstonice to two late Mousterian plans from Molodova. They are irregularly rounded in shape, over 40 sq. m in size with multiple hearths. A second small round hut of about 28 sq. m, Dolní Věstonice II, was apparently the workshop of a terracotta figurine modeller who has left us one of the famous venuses. Later, round or oval huts are found commonly in Russia and central Europe, but rarely in western Europe.

Some well characterised house shapes are found in the later Upper Palaeolithic. Remarkable long houses with nine or ten hearths in a row are found at Kostenki; all three are well over 20 m long. Elongated three-hearth or three-cell houses 9 to 13 m long are known from Pushkari in Russia, Borneck near Hamburg and Pincevent near Paris. The long house may be regarded as an invention of the late Palaeolithic. At least two square paved areas, of Magdalenian date (Parrain and Cerisier), and around 18 sq. m in size, probably indicate the existence of square huts at this time. The Hamburgian sites of Poggenwisch and Borneck I have circular houses clearly delimited by a ring of earth or stones.

A claim for seasonal occupation has been made in the case of Pincevent, Dolní Věstonice I, the Hamburgian tents and others. These are usually claims for summer occupancy. The evidence is often far from conclusive and the whole question of seasonal occupation is poorly understood. Once it was claimed that the caves of southern France were only winter occupations, and that the rest of the year was spent moving around. Now there seems good reason to believe that many shelters were occupied through most of the year; claims of seasonality will have to be treated more critically. Semi-sedentism may well have been one of the prime adaptations of the late Riss and Würm in the 'Upper Palaeolithic' province.

Before leaving the subject of the Upper Palaeolithic, we should face the problem that although the beginning of this stage is the most distinct and easily recognised marker in the whole of the Palaeolithic, we know of no major advance in way of life coinciding with it at all comparable to the advent of hunting, fire or farming. The most marked new features were art and music, but the animals hunted and the caves occupied were often the same. Only the regular use of an attached spearhead of bone or stone seems to be new. Instead, I suggest, the real change was in the human type, due to neoteny. It led to a longer learning period and perhaps a more comprehensive language; its first effect was most noticeable in the aesthetic field. The really important long-term effect of neoteny and the 'leptolithic revolution' was a relaxation of the former intense conservatism, leading to a faster rate of culture change, and, after a time lag of between 10,000 and 20,000 years, the age of inventions which we have just discussed, and which saw four or five major inventions, where the previous million years had produced nothing comparable. And the most far-reaching result of the age of inventions was the complex of inventions which led to the 'neolithic revolution' about 12,000–8,000 BC, which is a major subject of Part II of this book. This was nothing to do with close man–animal relationships in the Mousterian as has recently been suggested, but a by-product of the more childlike, dominant and inventive man who evolved in the last 30,000 years.

5. FLANDRIAN HUNTERS

The most important cultural advance of the end of the last ice age was that of animal and plant domestication and associated equipment like sickles and querns. This seems to have happened by 9000 bc in Iraq and probably also in Turkey and the Jordan valley. The hunters of the Flandrian period, that is to say between about 8300 bc when the post-glacial forest history of northern Europe begins and the arrival of farming, are placed by some archaeologists in a Mesolithic period. In western Asia this 'period' is of negligible duration and it is under 2,000 years in parts of south-east Europe. Pockets of surviving hunters may have remained in some areas, reciprocating goods with the early farmers, but they are a minor phenomenon, best dealt with as part of the farming ambit. In the rapidly colonised areas of Europe, like Italy, the Balkans and the Danube, up to 3,000 years of Mesolithic exists, and further west and north some 4,000 years.

The Flandrian hunters were obviously descended mainly from the last glacial peoples we have been discussing. In areas densely populated in the late Palaeolithic like south-west France and parts of Czechoslovakia and Russia, evidence of settlement and presumably population falls off sharply. Seemingly the denser woods and forests dispersed the herds of the treeless mid-latitude 'tundra', and caused reliance on smaller game and individual animals, as well as a host of minor vegetable and other food sources found in woodlands. The long cave sequences of south-west France and western Asia usually cease by around 8000 bc. A rare exception is Sauveterre la Lemance where two cultures succeed the Magdalenian and Azilian; they are called Sauveterrian and Tardenoisian. The latter seems to be one of a group of western Mesolithic cultures which adopted farming.

With the warmer climate of postglacial times, exceeding present-day temperatures by 5500 bc, large parts of Europe were settled, including some like Scandinavia and the Baltic shores not previously occupied. This progressive colonisation added over one million SK (sq. km) to the area of Europe occupied, though much of it is mountainous. The occupation of northern Britain added perhaps 100,000 SK. As much as $2\frac{1}{2}$ MSK may have been colonised in Russia, but this is problematical, for in spite of gaps in the archaeological record some of this area may have been occupied in the late Palaeolithic. The north European plain west of Russia, some 300 ThSK in extent, was more intensively occupied than previously. To this must be added the large tracts of land, perhaps 250 ThSK at 8000 bc, which were dry, but by 5000 bc were submerged under the North Sea and English Channel. In Europe west of Russia, perhaps $1\frac{1}{2}$ MSK were added to the occupied area, but already by 8000 BC territory was being lost in the Mediterranean area by rising sea. I suspect that decreasing density of population in the latitudes 40° to 50° north around 7–8000 BC had more effect on population numbers than the newly occupied territory. Europe's population may well have halved between 11,000 bc and 7000 bc. Only in Scandinavia was the increase important.

As well as being more widely and thinly distributed over Europe, man was probably more regionally diversified. The formation of lakes and peat fens across large areas of Europe previously permanently frozen ensured a high degree of preservation of organic artefacts, and puts a characteristic stamp on the archaeology of the Mesolithic. Probably the low-lying areas of north Europe genuinely were some of the most densely occupied, as the archaeological record implies.

The axe seems to have been the most important new device in the European Mesolithic forest cultures, and was often sharpened with a transverse blow; some were set in antler sleeves. Axes are found at Thatcham, Berkshire, by around 8000 bc. The forests however must have come to more southerly parts of Europe before this, but it is not known if the axe was used. One has been claimed from Kostenki at a date before 12,000 bc. It seems that the axemen of the Mesolithic made little impression on the advancing pine and oak forests, for only the clearance made by the first farmers around 4000 bc is regularly detectable in the pollen record of the vegetational history. The axe was perhaps used for enlarging small clearings, and for felling trees to make platforms as at Star Carr, where one birch tree seems to have formed a sort of landing-stage beside a lake.

The canoe and paddle are found at 6000 and 7500 bc respectively, but it seems inconceivable that primitive water transport had not already been in use during the Würm. Canoes may have been used for fishing and fowling which seem to have become an important part of the economy. The fish-hook, first found in the Natufian of Mt Carmel, came into wide use in Europe. The first evidence of nets made of bark fibres is from Danish peat bog sites of around 6000–7500 bc. The dog was also domesticated at Star Carr by 7500 bc, and may have helped the efficiency of hunting.

Possibly because the more temperate climate did not demand so much protection from the cold, evidence for Mesolithic dwellings is rare. A number of small and rather irregular hollows believed to be semi-subterranean houses are found on British sites like Farnham and Abinger. Rounded huts, indicated by post holes, are known from Retmold in Germany. A spectacular settlement at Lepenski Vir in Jugoslavia close to the Danube Iron Gates Gorge has forty-four huts of curious truncated segment shape. Although the inhabitants of the village seem to have lived by fishing, it is questionable whether they should be regarded as Mesolithic, or as a fishing village in contact with early farming communities around 5000–6000 bc. They carved remarkable stone heads.

Only a small amount of representational art is associated with the Mesolithic cultures, and it is almost all from the Maglemosean of Denmark. Two good examples, both with stylised human figures, are the perforated antler from Jordlose and the ox bone from Ryemarksgaard. The schematised figures on the latter with cross-hatching on their bodies and triangular heads are unlike those of the preceding Palaeolithic. The other designs, such as zigzags, triangles and lozenges, are more reminiscent of the art found later on megalithic tombs in western Europe. Probably the series of rock engravings in Norway and Sweden in which elks are often figured and which have the feel of a hunting art are Mesolithic, or by hunters of Neolithic date. Of the same age would be a number of small animals carved in bone, wood and amber from north Russia and north Scandinavia. A number of stylistic features in this art link it with the later art of the Eskimo and Siberian peoples, and it forms a kind of northern province of hunting art. The famous art of the Spanish Mediterranean region already mentioned is probably also broadly Mesolithic, but its stylistic affinities are not with the northern province or with Palaeolithic art, but more with Africa, forming a southern province of hunting art.

From the point of view of cultural typology, the dozens of local cultures of the Mesolithic can perhaps be grouped into four main traditions in Europe. These are: (1) the tanged point/rhomboid group, with obvious late Würm ancestry in the Ahrensburgian, Masovian, etc. (Kongemose, Carstens-minde, Komsa, Fosna, stretching into the arctic circle); (2) the Maglemosean group with dorsally backed points, deriving from the Azilian and related Tjongerian, etc. (various Maglemosean cultures in northern continental Europe); (3) the geometric microlith group, deriving from the Romanellian or other late Würm Mediterranean cultures (Sauveterrian); (4) the chisel and trapeze blade group, deriving possibly from the Capsian (Tardenoisian, possibly also in eastern Europe). A chisel arrowhead is shown in Figure 15b.

In Britain two of these traditions are easily recognisable, the Maglemosean and Sauveterrian. Star Carr probably belongs to the northerly tradition of Ahrensburgian ancestry. Three other local cultures have also been named: the Horsham culture of south-east England, which is poorly defined and possibly a hybrid of the two main traditions; the Obanian of western Scotland, which is probably of Maglemosean origin; and the Larnian of Ulster, also Maglemosean, which is the first evidence of the colonisation of Ireland. The Maglemosean mainly dates from the Preboreal and Boreal (8300–5500 bc). The Sauveterrian is probably mainly later (6500 onwards). The Horsham culture is also late, from 5500 bc possibly down to the Neolithic. Similarly the Obanian and Larnian are dated late, perhaps not more than a few hundred years before the first farmers came to Britain (C14 about 3400 bc corrected to about 4000 BC).

By 6,000 years ago when farming had replaced food gathering in much of western Europe, man's toolmaking ancestors comprised over 100,000 generations, and were separated from us by only some 240 generations. Even the very earliest farmers were only some 440 generations ago (and Julius Caesar a mere 80 generations). Recent estimates of the total number of people who have ever lived vary somewhat, but correcting for obvious errors like underestimates for the beginning of toolmaking, they can mostly be reconciled to a figure in the region of 80–100 thousand million. Of these $3\frac{1}{2}$ billion are still alive, and 40–50 billion have lived since the inception of farming at the end of the Würm. It still remains probable that approximately half or more of the ancestors of the 3½ billion inhabitants of the world today were hunters, numbering between 30 and 50 billion. Only some 30,000 hunters have survived into recent times, and in a century it is probable that none will have escaped incorporation into the food-producing, literate and industrialised world.

PART II
LATER PREHISTORY

Ruth Whitehouse

V (a) Two flutes from the Dordogne

(b) Two whistles made from perforated phalanges

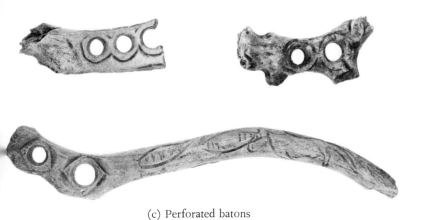

(c) Perforated batons

VI. (a) Clay tablets from Tepe Yahyā inscribed in the Proto-Elamite script. Fourth millennium BC

(b) Clay tablet from Ur inscribed in Sumerian in the cuneiform script. Early third millennium BC

INTRODUCTION

This section documents the story of Europe from the introduction of an economy based on food production to the time when urban civilisation was established over most of the continent under the Roman Empire. The elucidation of this story formed much of the life's work of V. Gordon Childe and the debt owed by the present author to Childe is enormous. It was Childe who drew our attention to the overwhelming importance of two developments in Old World prehistory: firstly the emergence of a subsistence economy based on food production instead of food collection, which he called the 'Neolithic' or 'food producing' revolution, and secondly the growth of urban civilisation, which he called the 'urban revolution'. Moreover it was Childe who demonstrated that the technological developments taken by an earlier generation of prehistorians to define prehistoric periods in fact represented significant stages in economic development. Although new data have made many of Childe's views unacceptable today, his overall assessment of prehistoric economic development still provides the basis of our understanding, and this account preserves essentially the *structure* that Childe gave to the prehistory of Europe.

The prehistory of Europe cannot be understood without an examination of some developments that took place in western Asia. So this section is divided into four chapters: two short ones that deal with events in western Asia crucial to European history and two long ones concerned with the development of Europe itself.

Chapter 4

THE ORIGINS OF FARMING

One of the most important steps ever taken by man was when he changed from a *food collecting* economy, based on hunting and gathering, to a *food producing* economy, based on cultivation of crops and rearing of animals. This change, described as the 'Neolithic revolution' or, more precisely, the 'food producing revolution', freed man from total dependence on the bounty of nature and, by making him at least part master of his food supply, laid down the basis for the subsequent development of mankind. It opened up the way for the emergence of urban civilisation, for it is inconceivable that the density of population associated with urban life could have been supported by the wild food resources of even the most munificent natural environment. Indeed not only was food production an essential prelude to the development of the ancient civilisations, it also provides the basis of modern industrial societies. It is true to say that the population of Europe today subsists largely on the crops and animals that were domesticated between 11,000 and 8,000 years ago in western Asia – wheat, barley, sheep, goat, cattle and swine – although improved strains and breeds have been developed over the millennia. The only significant *staple* crop that has been added to the repertoire is potatoes.

It is currently fashionable to criticise the use of the term 'revolution' to describe this change, as it has become clear that the whole development took a considerable period of time, that it took place in several different areas and that it took various different forms. However, I think it is useful to retain the term, since no other word conveys the momentous and indeed revolutionary effect the total change *once fully accomplished* had on the course of human development.

Farming was invented independently in the New World, in western Asia, in the Far East and possibly in the Indian subcontinent, but for European prehistory only the west Asiatic development is relevant. Within this area, the food producing revolution took place within a wide zone, running east from the Mediterranean coast to the Zagros mountains and northwards from the Red Sea and the Persian Gulf to Anatolia. The development of farming in this area went though three significant phases:

1. Incipient and early food production, beginning before 7000 bc on the Zagros flanks, in the Levant and in southern Anatolia. These communities had some domesticated plants and animals, but still depended to varying degrees on hunting and gathering. The crops included einkorn and emmer wheats, barley and some leguminous plants; the domesticated animals were sheep or goat or both, but not at this stage cattle or swine.

2. Settled village farming, developed in the area of incipient food production, but spread throughout much of western Asia by c. 5000 bc. These communities possessed domesticated plants and animals, but concentrated on cereal production by dry farming. The domesticated animals now included both cattle and swine; both were domesticated in the far northern part of the zone (Anatolia and northern Iraq) or even outside it altogether (the earliest dated domesticated cattle in fact occur in Greece).

3. More efficient farming, based on irrigation agriculture. Irrigation seems to have been used on a modest scale, that is modification of existing stream courses, etc., at Beidha in the Levant before 6000 bc and in south-west Iran before 5000 bc, and subsequently was employed over a wide area. At a later stage, not yet dated with any precision, the harnessing of domesticated oxen to draw ploughs further improved agricultural practice.

Each of these three phases represents a significant improvement in the utilisation of resources and each is associated with evidence of population increase. In the first phase societies practising some degree of plant and animal domestication had economies that were viable alternatives to the traditional hunting and gathering economies, but were not initially noticeably superior: pure hunting and gathering communities flourished contemporaneously with and in the same areas as the early farming societies. As farming practice gradually gained in efficiency and farming became increasingly important in the economy, the inherent superiority of food producing over food gathering became apparent. With village farming – the second phase – not only was there a substantial population expansion, but also the new economy began to spread outside the natural habitat of the wild prototypes of the domesticated plants and animals. It is to this stage that the spread of farming into Europe belongs. The third stage of the west Asiatic development did not immediately affect Europe in any way; it was a specialised adaptation to the environment of parts of the Near and Middle East and was unsuitable for extension into Europe. Its long-term significance, however, was great, since it provided the means of extending the farming economy into the alluvial plains of the great river valleys and thus laid the foundation for the growth of urban civilisation in the Near East. For this reason I shall postpone discussion of the third phase to a later chapter and concentrate here on the first two phases, which provided the basis for the early farming communities of Europe.

THE BEGINNINGS OF FOOD PRODUCTION

The early development of food production took place in a number of different areas and in several different ways. The reasons for the development may also have varied, though there seem to have been some shared preconditions. Firstly, all the areas fall within the zone where the wild ancestors of the cultivated crops – wheat and barley – and of the domesticated animals – goat, sheep, cattle and swine – all occur together. Particularly important was the occurrence together of cereals and sheep and goat, because it was this combination that first provided the basis for a viable farming economy. Leguminous vegetables – lentils, beans, peas, vetch, etc. – and cattle and swine, though valuable additions, were not essential to the original establishment of food production as a way of life. Another shared precondition, it is often suggested, was the changing climate at the end of the Pleistocene, which in this zone took the form of increasing aridity. This may have led to the decline in numbers of the larger game animals, which could have provided an incentive for the development of new methods of acquiring food. Another suggested precondition is the nature of the diet of the later Upper Palaeolithic population of the area, which was of the 'broad spectrum' type, in which almost everything was regarded as potential food; this might have provided a background conducive to experimentation with food production (see paper by K. Flannery in Ucko and Dimbleby 1969). Be that as it may, the domestication of plants and animals took place in several different areas within the general zone in the period c. 10,000–6000 bc. Archaeological evidence available at present allows us to trace the development in three separate areas.

1. The Zagros Mountains and Adjoining Plains

In the northern part of the area domesticated sheep were being kept on the Zagros flanks as early as 9000 bc at Zawi Chemi Shanidar, a settlement that was probably still only semi-permanent, perhaps seasonal. Wild animals were hunted and some crops, probably wild, harvested. In the southern part of the zone in the Deh Luran plain of Khuzistan there were probably permanent settlements before 7000 bc. On these sites in the Bus Mordeh phase (c. 7500–6750 bc) domesticated goats were a major pillar of the economy and there were a few domesticated sheep also; emmer wheat, a little einkorn and two-rowed hulled barley were cultivated and these farming activities were accompanied by the collection of many wild plant foods, hunting and fishing. In the succeeding Ali Kosh phase (c. 6750–

6000 bc), the same domesticated plants and animals occur; hunting and fishing were still of great importance, but there was a decline in the collection of wild plant foods, suggesting that cereal cultivation was proving a more successful way of obtaining plant food. Interestingly enough, the Deh Luran plain, though within the general zone where the wild ancestors of the early domesticates occur, lies outside the belt of oak-pistachio woodland which was their natural habitat. So already before 7000 bc the range of the plants and animals had been extended to include areas where they did not occur naturally. It has been suggested that this was the result of early farmers deliberately seeking lands of high water retention, often near swamp margins, which would have enabled cereals to survive fluctuations in rainfall. More or less contemporary with the Ali Kosh phase in Khuzistan there was a permanent village at Jarmo in Iraqi Kurdistan with an economy based on domesticated goats, cultivated emmer and einkorn wheats, two-rowed barley and also a variety of leguminous crops. Farming was accompanied by hunting and collecting wild plants. The pig bones collected from these levels suggest that pigs were in the course of being domesticated at this time.

The area between Kurdistan and Khuzistan – Luristan – is less well known, but some interesting sites are at present being excavated there. At Ganj Dareh in the late eighth millennium bc goats were in the process of being domesticated and agriculture was almost certainly practised, and at Tepe Guran there was a semi-permanent settlement c. 6500 bc which had grown to a permanent village by c. 5800 bc; domesticated goats and barley are recorded, but other elements of the economy are unknown.

It is clear that throughout this zone in the period before 6000 bc goats were the significant domesticated animals (except for the very early appearance of sheep at Zawi Chemi Shanidar), and that both wheat and barley were successfully cultivated from an early stage. There is no evidence before 6000 bc of large communities, of any social stratification or of any economic specialisation outside the sphere of farming. This contrasts with the other two areas to be discussed.

2. *The Levant*

In Syria, Palestine and Jordan a parallel but rather different development can be traced. *C.* 7500 bc the Natufian culture was characterised by a concentration on gazelle hunting and harvesting wild cereals. This stage was followed at the sites of Jericho and Beidha by the Pre-pottery Neolithic A culture (dated *c.* 6800 bc), with evidence for the cultivation of emmer wheat and hulled two-rowed barley. There is no definite evidence of domesticated animals, except the dog, at this stage, but hunting and collecting of wild plants are well attested. In this phase Jericho was already a site of at least 4 hectares surrounded by massive defences. This suggests a community of some size and probably with an organised leadership.

In the succeeding Pre-pottery B phase (*c.* 6800–6000 bc) a very primitive form of barley is recorded from Beidha and from Tell Ramad in Syria, emmer wheat from all sites, einkorn from Jericho and Ramad, and from the latter site also club wheat. Leguminous crops, especially lentils, were grown at Jericho and Ramad. The evidence for domesticated animals is not definite, but goats may have been kept at Jericho and Beidha; at Tell Ramad the animal diet was certainly based entirely on game. Hunting was important on all the sites and wild plants continued to be collected.

3. *Southern Anatolia*

Information on the earliest phases of food production in this area is lacking; the farming story is archaeologically documented only from *c.* 7000 bc, when a small but permanently occupied village was established at Hacilar. The community there cultivated emmer wheat, naked six-rowed barley, lentils and other pulses. There is no evidence of domesticated animals except for the dog. Hunting and collection of wild food plants were practised. By *c.* 6500 bc there was a large and wealthy – indeed in terms of early farming communities an unprecedentedly large and wealthy – settlement at Çatal Hüyük. The site occupied about 13 ha and the excavated deposits represent approximately a millennium of settlement from *c.* 6500 bc. The subsistence of the community was provided by a well-developed farming economy based on cultivated emmer, einkorn and bread wheats, barley, peas, vetch and bitter vetch and domesticated sheep and goat, still accompanied by hunting and collection of wild plants. To a degree far greater than any contemporary site, Çatal Hüyük has yielded evidence of secondary industries and of trade; indeed trade in the black volcanic glass known as obsidian may partly account for the community's exceptional wealth. There is abundant evidence of elaborate religious practice and the craftsmanship of some of the artefacts, especially of the chipped flint and obsidian objects, is of a truly virtuoso character. It seems likely that there was a considerable number of full-time specialists at Çatal Hüyük and these must have been supported out of the surplus food produced by those engaged in primary production. Indeed this brilliant south Anatolian culture anticipated by three millennia some of the developments that ultimately gave rise to the ancient civilisations. However, some elements were clearly lacking and this precocity came to nothing; by 5000 bc Anatolia was no more advanced than other parts of western Asia and the important later developments all took place in areas further south.

In south-eastern Turkey in an area linking the Anatolian with the Zagros regions, the site of Çayönü Tepesi has provided evidence of domesticated wheat, pigs, sheep and probably goat in the seventh millennium bc; particularly interesting is evidence for the use of copper even before 7000 bc.

One of the most interesting aspects of this whole development is the greater importance of cereal cultivation than animal husbandry in the very early farming practice. Only on the Zagros flanks did the domestication of animals apparently precede that of plants; elsewhere the primacy of agriculture seems certain. Indeed both in the Levant and in Anatolia complex and clearly successful farming societies subsisted without domesticated animals at all. And in all areas the only domesticated animals apart from dog before 7000 bc, and on most sites before 6000 bc, were sheep and goat. Another interesting aspect of these communities is the diversity of food sources exploited, since as well as domesticated crops and animals a great variety of wild plants and creatures were consumed. This 'broad spectrum' diet may represent in this respect a continuation of the preceding Upper Palaeolithic dietary pattern. Its advantages for man are of two sorts: in the first place it is nutritionally sound and therefore healthy, and secondly it is far less vulnerable to climatic unreliability or to outbreaks of disease than any specialised subsistence system. Clearly, if man depends on one or two food sources only, failure of those supplies for any reason can lead to starvation.

By 6000 bc farming communities existed throughout the three zones discussed above and probably elsewhere as well, though this is not yet well documented. In the following millennium domesticated cattle and swine became widespread. With these and other improvements to the farming economy,

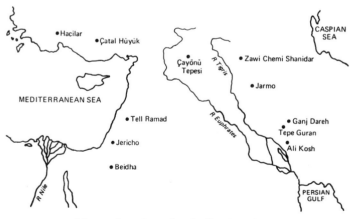

Map 4. Location of early farming sites.

hunting and the collection of wild plant foods declined in importance and these activities were further discouraged by environmental changes produced by early farming practice. During this millennium the farming economy spread to cover

Table 16

Domestic animals and plants present on the early farming sites discussed in the text

	Domesticated animals				Domesticated plants		
	Sheep	Goat	Swine	Cattle	Wheat	Barley	Leguminous crops
Zawi Chemi Shanidar c. 9000 bc	✓						
Ali Kosh 8th–7th millennium bc	✓	✓			✓	✓	
Ganj Dareh 8th millennium bc		✓					
Jarmo 7th millennium bc		✓	✓		✓	✓	✓
Tepe Guran 7th millennium bc		✓			✓		
Jericho 7th millennium bc		?			✓	✓	✓
Beidha 7th millennium bc		?			✓	✓	
Tell Ramad 7th millennium bc					✓	✓	✓
Hacilar early 7th millennium bc					✓	✓	✓
Çatal Hüyük 7th millennium bc	✓	✓			✓	✓	✓
Çayönü Tepesi 7th millennium bc	✓	?	✓		✓		

large areas of western Asia, providing the background for the development of urban civilisation.

There were certainly some connections between the three areas where very early farming communities are known: for instance the plastered floors and the ancestral skull cult which characterise the Levantine Pre-pottery Neolithic B phase are echoed at Hacilar in Anatolia; and, on the other hand, analyses have shown that Anatolian obsidian was traded to the Palestinian sites and even to Ali Kosh. However, it seems likely that the domestication of plants and animals proceeded more or less independently in all three areas.

The sites discussed above are shown on Map 4 and the information about the domesticated plants and animals summarised in Table 16. Interesting papers on these subjects can be found in Ucko and Dimbleby 1969 and Lamberg-Karlovsky 1972, together with further bibliographical references.

THE SIGNIFICANCE OF THE FOOD PRODUCING REVOLUTION

The development of a food producing economy is one of the greatest achievements of mankind. Through direct control of his food supply man acquired a substantially greater control over his natural environment and the increased availability and security of food allowed a considerable population expansion. Only the most tentative attempts have been made to assess prehistoric population densities on the basis of archaeological evidence or of modern analogies, and individual estimates vary considerably. Estimates for late specialised food collecting economies vary from 0·04 to 0·1 people per sq. km, and estimates for primary village farmers from 2 to nearly 10 people per sq. km. These differences in density estimation are partly due to inadequate primary data and partly the result of considering communities in differing environments and at differing levels of food gathering and farming efficiency. In any case we see that the *minimum* population increase estimated is twentyfold, which is very considerable and far greater than any increase documented for any period of comparable length before the food producing revolution (Braidwood and Reed 1957; Hole and Flannery 1967; Deevey 1960). Childe (e.g. 1964: 73) regarded the expansion of population that followed the food producing revolution as proof that the revolution was an evolutionary success for mankind. This view he derived from the biology of Darwin, for in Darwinian terms the multiplication of the species is by definition proof of evolutionary fitness. Such a view takes for granted that all individuals and all species are constantly striving to multiply and that population levels are held down only by a variety of external factors (availability of food, climate, disease, predators, etc.). Undoubtedly the majority of laymen today hold this view.

However, the work of modern biologists, and especially that of Wynne-Edwards (e.g. 1969), has shown that in the animal world most species maintain a population equilibrium, with population levels held down to an acceptable ceiling not by external restrictions, but by *internal social controls*. The survival value of population control in evolutionary terms appears to be the maintenance of an equilibrium between the species and the environment by the avoidance of over-exploitation of the resources on which the species depends. It is probable that in the hunting and gathering stage of his existence man also maintained a population equilibrium, though it is not known whether the mechanisms of population control were genetically organised, as in the animal world, or whether these had been replaced by cultural mechanisms such as abortion, infanticide, etc. This is a question of some importance which deserves further investigation. In any case, with the development of food production the situation changed: although the reasons are not well understood, it is clear that when man altered his subsistence basis, the mechanisms that had previously maintained population size at an acceptable level were abandoned or ceased to function. As a result the population increased dramatically. This probably came about in two complementary ways: on the one hand, the increased quantity and security of the food supply must have led to a fall in death rate, while, on the other, there was probably an increase in birth rate also, since modern analogies indicate that fertility is consistently greater in farming communities than in hunting and gathering ones.

The reasons for this are not well understood. It is sometimes suggested that there is a biological connection between high fertility rates and a diet rich in carbohydrates. An alternative suggestion (made by Lewis Binford during discussion at the Research Seminar on Archaeology and Related Subjects held at Sheffield in 1971) is that the crucial factor was not the diet but the sedentary existence, and that the abandonment of migrations led to a decline in the number of miscarriages and an increase in the number of live births. Yet another alternative is that the increase in control over the food supply allowed people to feel that they could support more children and led therefore to a decline in the practice of abortion and infanticide. Whatever the perhaps complex reasons, a dramatic population increase undoubtedly occurred. Whether this can automatically be considered advantageous is another matter. Certainly the population problem facing the world today is a direct if long-term outcome of the development of farming and the abandonment of adequate controls over population expansion. Indeed we might regard the population increase that followed the food producing revolution not as proof of the biological success of this development, as Childe did, but rather as an example of the problems man has created for himself in his manipulation of nature.

The true measure of the importance of the food producing revolution must be seen not in biological but in cultural terms. For it was followed by a dramatic expansion of the range of cultural activities and it provided the basis for the subsequent development of civilisation. In the millennium or so after the establishment of village farming there were advances in the fields of technology (pottery was invented, new lithic techniques were devised and tentative experiments were conducted with metallurgy), housing (better dwellings accompanying permanence of settlement), trade (increased in quantity, range and scope) and religious life (manifested in a variety of ways). Any of these activities can occur individually or in combination in contexts other than that of settled village farming, but the outburst of new cultural activity that followed the establishment of a viable farming economy and was presumably made possible by it is unmistakable.

The rapid development of cultural activity in this context is often explained as the result of increased leisure accompanying the more efficient subsistence economy, which allowed man to develop his latent cultural potential. This view seems mistaken, since in fact most hunting groups have *more* leisure than farmers, who are tied to the often gruelling agricultural routine. It has been suggested alternatively that the cultural development was related to the increased division of labour that accompanied the food producing economy and to the production of storable surplus food which allowed the support of part-time or even full-time specialists (craftsmen, religious practitioners, etc.). According to this view it was not time man lacked to develop his potential in the earlier period, but rather confidence in the security of the food supply, which alone could free him from preoccupation with his primary need for food.

Chapter 5

EARLY FARMING COMMUNITIES IN EUROPE

A large part of the history of man in the Old World after the establishment of a viable farming economy is the story of the spread of farming almost to the farthest corners of the earth. Indeed so superior has this economy proved to that based on food gathering that, while at the present day large parts of the world are still inhabited by peasant farmers little influenced by the industrial economies of the developed nations, only in isolated areas and extremely hostile environments such as the Kalahari desert or the circumpolar region do tiny groups of hunter–gatherers survive. However, we must remind ourselves that the apparently clear-cut distinction between food gathering and food production is a conceptual one, and that both terms cover a wide range of relationships between man and his natural environment. At the time of the spread of farming into Europe, which concerns us here, the continent was occupied, though sparsely, by small groups of aborigines practising some form of food gathering economy. Each variant economy represented an adaptation to a local environment; in many cases these adaptations had taken place over several millennia and the economies were probably very efficient at exploiting local resources within the limits of the food gathering economy. By contrast, the village farming economy, though potentially more productive than hunting and gathering, was an eastern development adapted to the semi-arid conditions of western Asia and as such initially ill-adapted to the climate, soils and vegetation of Europe, especially temperate Europe. Therefore we cannot assume that in Europe the farming economy was immediately and obviously superior to hunting and gathering and was therefore rapidly adopted by all communities that came into contact with it. Indeed in Europe the early introduced farming economies of western Asiatic type could flourish only in areas with environments similar to those of the Near East. Elsewhere farming would not supersede hunting and gathering until the evolution of a form of farming economy specifically adapted to European conditions. In fact this must have occurred several times over as the major environmental boundaries of Europe were crossed. This situation is reflected in the archaeological evidence in two complementary ways: the rapid spread of farming within a unitary environmental zone (e.g. the northern coasts of the east and central Mediterranean or the loess soils of temperate Europe), and significant time lags in the spread of an efficient farming economy from one environmental zone to another (e.g. from the Mediterranean littoral into continental France or from the Continent into the British Isles).

The expansion of the farming economy into Europe is well documented in the archaeological record and we know that by c. 3500 BC (3000 bc) the practice of farming had reached the northern and western extremities of temperate Europe (only with further technological developments at a later stage did this economy spread beyond the temperate zone). This does not mean that by 3500 BC temperate Europe was occupied wholly by communities of farmers, but that by that date there were *some* groups practising a farming economy in each part of temperate Europe. In some areas pure hunting and gathering groups may have coexisted with the farmers and in many more there were groups with 'hybrid' types of economy – some domesticated animals or plants, but a considerable dependence on wild food products. And in some areas these 'hybrid' economies were the best available methods of exploiting local resources or, in evolutionary terms, the best adaptations to local environments.

It has been suggested that farming was independently invented in Europe. This seems improbable, unless present views about the nature of the wild ancestors of domesticated crops and animals and their original distributions are to be radically revised, for nowhere in Europe, is it thought, did all the important potential domesticates – emmer wheat, barley, sheep, goats, cattle and swine – occur together; yet all the well-documented early farming cultures of Europe have all these crops and animals. Furthermore the many C14 dates available from early farming sites show a chronological progression across Europe from the south-east to the north-west which clearly demonstrates the spread from the original Asiatic sources. This is demonstrated diagrammatically on Map 5.

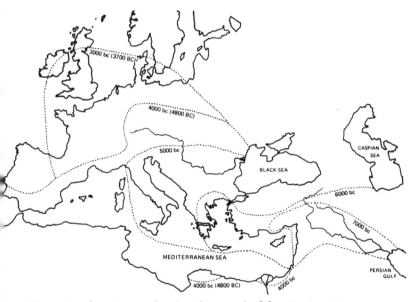

Map 5. Isochronic map showing the spread of farming into Europe.

However, as I have already said, some plants and animals were probably domesticated independently in Europe, including some that had not been domesticated in Asia.

The ways in which the techniques of farming were spread is a matter for discussion. There are two main possibilities.

Firstly, the new economy might have been introduced in its entirety, together with the actual domesticated plants and animals, as part of a total culture by migrating people. Alternatively, farming might have been spread by the process of stimulus diffusion, which means that only the *idea* of food production was spread, being adopted and passed on from one group to another of the indigenous population. Of course both processes might have occurred, with some movements of people introducing the new economy, which was then adopted by the local population. In fact there is considerable evidence that farming was not spread solely through stimulus diffusion. This is indicated, for instance, by the occurrence of plants and animals well outside their presumed natural habitat zone, where they must certainly have been carried by people – at least where formidable natural barriers such as mountain ranges or seas had to be crossed. Moreover the archaeological record indicates a considerable cultural break between the Mesolithic and the Neolithic in most areas of Europe, which suggests that initially a fully developed culture was introduced by a fairly large-scale immigration of people. On the other hand, where the actual farming practice is concerned, there was probably considerable local domestication of native plants and especially animals. In addition it is likely that the introduction of farming to any area was followed by the diffusion of the techniques to local Mesolithic communities. Thus the spread of the farming economy must have been brought about by a combination of migration and diffusion, with the emphasis on migration in the first instance, diffusion subsequently.

The movements of people that spread the farming economy across Europe were presumably not deliberate campaigns to colonise new land, but rather what has been called a 'wave of advance' of population, representing the gradual expansion of an increasing population (Ammerman and Cavalli-Sforza in Renfrew 1973). Such population movements are random in that they are not given a deliberate direction by the moving population; the direction of movement and the area occupied are, however, restricted by environmental factors and it is these limiting factors that give an appearance of conscious colonisation to the settlement of Europe by early farmers. A significant increase in population was, as we have seen, one of the results of the food producing revolution; this increase in fact seems to have been greater than could be comfortably supported by the new economy and this was the reason for the population movements that spread farming across Europe. After all the suitable land had been occupied man was obliged to evolve new mechanisms to contain or absorb the population increase or else fall victim to the cruder natural population controls, such as mass starvation, disease and warfare. The current human situation demonstrates that, overall, this is one of mankind's more spectacular failures to date. At the time we are considering, however, land was abundant and the early farmers spread rapidly to occupy it, diffusing as they went some elements of their economy and culture to the small groups of indigenous hunters and gatherers they encountered.

As I have already mentioned, the farming economy evolved in its spread through Europe and in each environmental zone a new version emerged, particularly adapted to the conditions of that zone. The overall picture is a complex one, but there are some general features that can be noted. In the Near Eastern homeland of farming, cereal crops were the basis of food production; animal rearing was relatively unimportant and wild animals continued to be hunted on a considerable scale. Of the domesticated animals, sheep and goat were the most important in the first two millennia of village farming in western Asia. In parts of Europe with conditions reasonably similar to those of the Near East – south-east Europe and some of the Mediterranean islands and peninsulas – agriculture was also of prime importance, and sheep and goat were the most important domesticated animals. With the spread further into Europe, animal breeding gained in importance and the two creatures native to temperate Europe, cattle and swine, became increasingly important.

The economy was not the only cultural trait to be adapted to European conditions. Many other traits, such as settlement type and tool forms, also evolved, and because of the oriental origin of the farming economy one way in which the European Neolithic can be viewed is in terms of the progressive adaptation of an oriental cycle of cultures to European conditions. Thus, moving west and north, one can see the cultures becoming progressively less 'oriental' and more distinctively European. This adaptation to European conditions also had a chronological dimension, with later cultures being more noticeably European and less oriental in character, though, through new contacts with the east, *some* later cultures also had an oriental aspect.

The farming economy spread into Europe by three main routes: (1) along the northern coasts of the Mediterranean Sea; (2) along the river Danube and its tributaries; and (3) across the north European plain. Along each of these routes a distinct cycle of cultures can be recognised and these form the subject of the next section.

MEDITERRANEAN ROUTE

East Mediterranean
The earliest known farming communities in this area occur in the plain of Thessaly and in Crete and like all but the latest of the Asian cultures discussed so far, they did not use pottery and are therefore described as 'Aceramic' or 'Pre-pottery'. They belong to the seventh millennium bc. This phase was followed in Thessaly by one characterised by plain undecorated pottery, sometimes known by the German name *Frühkeramikum*. Early plain wares have a much wider distribution than is indicated for the Aceramic Neolithic, occurring in southern Greece, in Crete (dated before 6000 bc at Knossos) and in western Greece (dated to *c.* 5700 bc on Corfu). An early phase with plain pottery does not occur west of the Adriatic Sea.

Following the plain ware phase both in Thessaly and north-west Greece was a phase defined by Impressed Ware – coarse pottery decorated while wet with a variety of impressed designs. In Thessaly, but not on Corfu, this ware was often accompanied by simple red-on-white painted ware. In Greek Macedonia, too, painted and impressed wares occur together and at the site of Nea Nikomedeia they occur with C14 dates between 5800 bc and 6200 bc. Impressed Ware does not occur in the Peloponnese or in Crete, where other decorative traditions prevailed (especially painted and incised decoration), but pottery of this type characterises the earliest farming communities in the central and west Mediterranean.

The later phases of the Greek Neolithic are characterised by a variety of more elaborate painted wares, some possibly indicating new contacts with communities in the Near East, which do not concern us here.

Already in the first phase the farming economy differed from that of the early Asiatic villagers. Firstly, the two earliest identified examples of domesticated cattle come from Greek sites – Aceramic Argissa (c. 6500 bc) and Nea Nikomedeia (between 5800 and 6200 bc). On present evidence it is possible that the first domestication of cattle took place in Greece, perhaps contemporaneously with an independent domestication in Anatolia. Domesticated cattle occur in almost every subsequent culture in Europe and can be regarded as a most successful adaptation to European conditions. They occur also in later Neolithic and subsequent cultures in Asia, but not for a millennium or more after the establishment of village farming there. The first Greek farmers may also have initiated the domestication of broomcorn millet (probably cultivated at Aceramic Argissa) and of oats (possibly cultivated at Aceramic Achilleion). Neither of these crops has been identified in domesticated form on early sites in western Asia; both represent successful European adaptations and were in fact cultivated extensively in later prehistoric Europe. Another significant divergence from the Near Eastern economic pattern found in Greece was the relatively small dependence on hunting: the

Greek farmers' meat supplies always came largely from domesticated animals. This is another feature of many European Neolithic cultures making a very early appearance in the east Mediterranean. The significance of wild plant collection in the Greek Neolithic is unknown. The actual farming practice seems to have conformed largely to the west Asiatic pattern. Although domestic cattle and swine occur, they do so only in small numbers and sheep and goat formed the majority of the domesticated stock. The cultivated crops were wheat (einkorn and emmer in the Aceramic phase, bread wheat also in early layers at Knossos), barley (hulled and naked two-row and hulled six-row), and a variety of leguminous crops (peas, lentils and vetch). This coincides with the picture we have of early farming practice in the Near East.

The early farmers of Greece lived in villages and, although it is not proved, these may have been inhabited permanently, as in western Asia. Certainly they are often found at the base of tells (mounds of decomposed mud-brick representing the accumulated remains of successive villages), which are generally assumed to have been permanently occupied settlements. If the settlement type conforms to the Asiatic pattern, the house form diverges from it. Whereas in Asia we find contiguous one-room residential units packed tightly together (though on incipient farming sites separate circular or oval dwellings often occur), in Greece we find separate one- or two-roomed structures, each presumably designed to house a single family. They are rectangular and made of mud-brick or light timber and mud; at a later stage (Middle Neolithic) stone-built examples occur. The 'detached' house is another characteristic European trait.

The artefacts generally have an eastern look – painted pottery, female figurines, etc. – although the pottery styles have a distinctive local flavour.

Thus the culture and economy of the Greek communities were in many respects close in type to those of the Asiatic homeland of farming, but already present were a number of distinctive European traits: domesticated cattle, perhaps domesticated millet and oats, lack of emphasis on hunting, individual detached house form, etc. Thus even at this stage we are witnessing the 'Europeanisation' of the eastern farming culture.

There is little evidence in Greece of any continuity of culture from the Mesolithic to the Neolithic. This may mean that the excavated Neolithic sites were all settlements of immigrant farmers and their descendants, or alternatively this appearance may arise out of our ignorance of the Mesolithic cultures of Greece – an ignorance which is certainly profound. Further work is needed before this point can be discussed profitably.

Central Mediterranean
The Adriatic Sea formed a cultural boundary at this period. Whereas east of it we find the *Frühkeramikum* or early plain ware phase, on the Italian side the earliest farmers were users of Impressed Ware, which in Greece characterises the phase *following* that defined by plain ware. The first farmers in Italy arrived before 5000 bc and were users of Impressed Ware and probably painted wares as well. Settlements occur in eastern peninsular Italy, in south-east Sicily and in Malta. They occur in great density along the Adriatic coastal strip and in the plain of the Tavoliere in northern Apulia. The later phases of the Neolithic in the central Mediterranean are characterised by a series of fine painted and other decorated wares, but there is no evidence of further intrusions from the east.

Very little is known about the economy of these communities, but we do know that emmer wheat and barley (type uncertain) were cultivated and that sheep, goat, cattle and swine were all bred; the relative importance of the different animals varied regionally, probably in relation to environmental differences. The contribution of wild animals to the diet also varied (from *c.* 5 per cent to *c.* 20 per cent of the total fauna), while the contribution of wild plants is unknown. Thus the farming economy was basically of the Greek type, but in some areas at least the 'European' animals – cattle and swine – had become more important.

The settlements were single farmsteads, hamlets and villages, usually surrounded by one or more ditches, which enclosed an area occupied by one or more smaller ditched enclosures described as hut-compounds. It is not known whether they were permanently inhabited. The huts themselves seem to have been circular, built of mud and light timbers, sometimes on a drystone footing, and they were very small (c. 2–3 m in diameter). The contrast to the villages of good-sized rect-angular houses of Greece is strong: the Italian Neolithic villages suggest rather a common African settlement type – the compound containing a number of small huts each de-signed to house not a family, but an individual. Another divergence from the Greek settlement pattern is the occurrence of individual farmsteads as well as villages. If this divergence is a real one and does not arise out of disparities in archaeologi-cal research, it indicates the emergence of another 'European' trait in Italy: the isolated farm is a common phenomenon in most of Europe, while the Asiatic pattern has always been one of farming villages.

The artefacts of the Italian Neolithic seem poor by com-parison with those of Greece: figurines, for example, occur rarely in Sicily and at a rather later stage in Malta; they are not found at all in peninsular Italy. However, these figurines and much of the painted pottery do bear a general resemblance to those found in the east Mediterranean.

Thus, as in the east Mediterranean, we have a culture demon-strating clearly its derivation from an oriental prototype, but demonstrating also several adaptations to local conditions, including some general 'European' traits.

In this area we can distinguish some communities that may represent survivors of the indigenous population. They lived in peripheral locations, often in caves, and practised economies combining elements of farming with varying degrees of dependence on wild food products. Their fate in general was absorption into, or extinction by, the main farming tradition, although some groups may have developed economic adaptations which were distinct and, temporarily at least, viable alternatives to the introduced mixed farming economy.

West Mediterranean

The Apennine mountains formed a second major barrier to the westward spread of early farmers in the Mediterranean, and the early Neolithic groups found to the west of these mountains – in west and north-west Italy, Sardinia, Corsica, southern France and Iberia – though users of Impressed Ware, differed considerably from those found to the east. The characteristics shared by these groups include a high proportion of cave settlements, a considerable dependence on wild food products as well as on farming, the use of many Mesolithic flint types and the absence of painted or other elaborated decorated wares. All these traits suggest a Mesolithic heritage and indeed in most of these areas Mesolithic cultures are well represented. It seems probable that west of the Apennines and the Straits of Messina the numbers of immigrant farmers were small, and that the practice of farming was spread largely by diffusion to the indigenous hunting and gathering population. At the cave of Châteauneuf-les-Martigues in southern France sheep bones are recorded from Aceramic, apparently 'Mesolithic' levels, *underlying* the Impressed Ware deposits. Though it is possible, as Jacqueline Murray has suggested (1971: 24–7), that these animals represent a diminutive form of wild sheep which had managed to survive from Palaeolithic times, it seems more likely that they represent the first stage in the adoption of a farming economy by the Mesolithic population. In the subsequent, Impressed Ware, phase at this site, wild animals were still more important than domesticated ones and of the domestic stock, sheep/goat predominated. A similar situation is recorded in the Impressed Ware levels in the cave of Arene Candide in nearby Liguria, and it seems probable that along the Mediterranean littoral of northern Italy and France the archaeological record documents the gradual taking over of various elements of the Neolithic way of life – domesticated sheep, domesticated cattle, pottery, etc. – by the indigenous population. Agriculture was probably also practised, but we do not know how important it was. The earliest C14 dates for Impressed Ware in the west Mediterranean are *c.* 5500–5300 bc, but most fall between 4800 and 4000 bc and the very early dates (there are only three of them) may be anomalous. In any case the first farmers must have arrived by at least 5500 BC in calendar years (C14 4800–4700 bc).

In Iberia too communities using Impressed Ware lived chiefly in or near coastal caves and used flint types of local Mesolithic origin. Domesticated animals, especially sheep/goat, are recorded, and in Impressed Ware levels at Coveta de l'Or in Valencia, dated by C14 to *c.* 4600–4300 bc (i.e. *c.* 5500–5000 BC in calendar years), remains of cereals were found: bread, club, emmer and einkorn wheats and both naked and hulled barley.

Rather later in date is the Almerian culture of south-east Spain. These communities, in contrast to those using Impressed Ware, lived in open-air settlements in round or oval huts with a wattle and daub superstructure, similar to those found in south-east Italy. The flint industry, like that of the Impressed Ware group, is of local Mesolithic origin, but the pottery is undecorated and bears some resemblance to that of north African cultures. The economy was of mixed farming type, based on both agriculture and animal breeding. The culture was probably of local Impressed Ware origin with some north African influence.

Western Europe

The earliest farming communities of western Europe belong to a group of cultures that are sometimes called 'Western Neolithic'. Important members of this group are Cortaillod in Switzerland, Chassey in France, Lagozza in north Italy and Windmill Hill in England. Some authorities believe that their ultimate origin lies in the Impressed Ware groups, and certainly in southern France Chassey deposits succeed Impressed Ware levels in several caves, and there are similarities with the earlier culture in some flint types and pottery forms as well as a general similarity in economy with a concentration on sheep/goat breeding. In general, however, the Western Neolithic cultures are characterised by a mixed farming economy with an emphasis on cattle breeding. In this way they diverge from the Mediterranean emphasis on sheep and goat and demonstrate a temperate European adaptation of the farming economy. Domestic sheep, goat and pig also occur and emmer, einkorn, bread and spelt wheats and barley were cultivated. The Swiss Cortaillod culture represents a specialised adaptation to a high altitude lakeside habitat and is characterised by a considerable dependence on hunting (wild animals constitute nearly half of the fauna), while wild fruits and nuts were also collected on a considerable scale. In the Chassey and Windmill Hill cultures hunting was relatively unimportant, while very little is known about the role of wild plants.

The Western Neolithic groups used mainly dark-surfaced undecorated pottery of simple rounded forms, though all groups had some decorated wares also, often in later phases.

This group existed in southern France by *c.* 4500 BC (3800 bc) and there are contemporary C14 dates for a possibly related group in Brittany. The earliest dates for Britain are shortly before 4000 BC (3500 bc).

DANUBIAN ROUTE

South-Eastern Europe
The earliest farming culture in this area was the Starčevo-Körös culture, which both geographically and culturally forms a link between the Neolithic cultures of the Mediterranean and those of central Europe. It is found in Yugoslavia, Hungary, Romania and Bulgaria and the majority of the settlements are strung out along the valleys of the river Danube and its major

tributaries. In Bulgaria, as in Greece, the occupied sites built up into characteristic mounds or 'tells' which are usually thought to indicate permanent settlements; elsewhere the sites are not tells but villages which may not have been occupied continuously for long periods of time. As in the Greek Neolithic, the houses were rectilinear, separate and of a size suggesting occupation by a nuclear family unit; they were built of wattle and daub. The economy too was similar to that of the Greek communities: hunting was relatively unimportant and the most important domesticated animals were sheep/goat; emmer, einkorn, barley and probably millet were cultivated as well as some leguminous crops. It is thought that local domestication of wild cattle (aurochs) was practised in Hungary.

The pottery includes barbotine and finger-impressed wares, which link it to the Greek early Neolithic and to the western Impressed Ware groups, as well as undecorated and painted wares. Human figurines and stamp seals are other links with Greece and indeed with the Asian homeland of farming.

The Starčevo culture was in existence by c. 5500 bc.

The Danubian Corridor
West and north of the area occupied by the Starčevo culture, the rich loess soils of the Danube and the other major rivers of Europe opened up to the early farmers a corridor to western and northern Europe. On these soils from Hungary to Holland appeared settlements of the LBK (or linear pottery) culture, formerly called Danubian I, which had reached the limits of its distribution in Germany and Holland by shortly after c. 5000 BC (C14 c. 4200 bc). This was a remarkably uniform culture throughout the vast area it occupied and in many respects it was the earliest farming culture really adapted to temperate European conditions. Most significantly, this is the earliest culture to concentrate on cattle breeding: cattle predominate on almost all sites and overall account for between one-half and three-fifths of the domestic stock; as time progressed this proportion increased to nearly three-quarters. This figure is even

more impressive when one remembers that cattle provide meat weight four to seven times greater per animal on average than sheep or swine, so the vast majority of all meat consumed on LBK sites must have been beef. The LBK farmers were not simply cattle breeders; they were *skilled* cattle breeders. There is evidence that local aurochs domestication was practised in many different areas and that castration was widely practised: in one area studied in detail nearly half of the male animals proved to be oxen. Castration allows control to be exercised over the size of the stock, as well as making the animals more manageable. It is a necessary prelude to the harnessing of cattle for draught, whether for ploughs or carts, though there is no evidence that oxen were used in this way by the LBK population.

Although cattle breeding was the basis of the economy, sheep, goat and pig were also bred and in fact swine became more important than sheep/goat in later phases of the culture. Hunting was also practised and was important in varying degrees. The most important cereal crop was emmer wheat, though einkorn, bread, club and hard wheats have all been recorded. Barley was also cultivated, but seems to have been of little importance. Millet, rye and oats have been recorded also, the last two probably being simply weeds of cultivation. Peas were also grown on some sites and flax is recorded from one site (where it occurred in quantity).

The LBK settlements are distinctive and quite different from those of Starčevo or any other eastern culture. The typical dwelling was a long house built of wooden posts with wattle and daub between the large timbers. This type of construction is an adaptation to temperate European conditions, making use of the best building material available – the fine timbers of the temperate European forests. The long houses are thought to have sheltered extended family units, thus indicating a social system different from that (or those) of south-eastern Europe. In that social systems are ultimately, or directly, related to economy, we can regard the emergence of a different system in

Europe as an adaptation to European conditions, although the way in which such an adaptation takes place is at present, and maybe always will be, beyond the scope of the archaeologist.

The LBK villages, unlike the presumed permanent settlements found in the 'tell' areas of south-east Europe, were occupied for a period, perhaps a decade, after which they were abandoned for half a century or more before being reoccupied. This cyclic system of settlement was probably associated with slash-and-burn agriculture (*Brandtwirtschaft*) with a period of cultivation followed by a long abandonment to allow regeneration of the soil. This system is alien to the eastern cultures and represents another characteristic 'European' trait developed by the early Danubian farmers.

That the LBK farming economy was a successful adaptation to central European conditions is indicated by the rapid spread of this culture across Europe and by the density of settlement within its area of distribution. However, it was adapted specifically to the loess soils and was apparently unable to spread significantly outside this environment. Sites in Holland, on the extreme western edge of the LBK area, seem to have been occupied permanently rather than cyclically, which may indicate a build-up of population in this area: if the continually increasing population was, for environmental reasons, unable to find its usual outlet in continuing outward spread, it may have led to the development of more efficient farming techniques and to the establishment of permanent villages. Be that as it may, it is certainly the case that the LBK culture, having spread almost to the Channel coast early in the fifth millennium BC, never crossed the waters, and it was left to the Western Neolithic cultures of ultimateldiy Meterranean origin to introduce farming to the British Isles almost a millennium later.

The Starčevo-Körös and LBK cultures were followed along the Danubian route by a second wave of cultures, of which the best known are Vinča, Tisza, Herpaly and Lengyel, formerly collectively labelled Danubian II. These cultures are far less uniform than those of the initial spread, though they demonstrate a considerable degree of continuity. This continuity is most marked in the subsistence economy itself, which was very similar in all these groups to that of the LBK settlers, with a concentration on cattle breeding, accompanied by breeding of swine, sheep and goat, some hunting and the cultivation of wheat (mostly emmer), barley and leguminous crops. In some respects these cultures have a more oriental aspect than the LBK culture with traits like painted pottery, stamp seals and animal and human figurines strongly in evidence. These are, however, very generalised traits, and the specific connections often quoted between Vinča and related groups and Anatolian sites such as Troy must now be rejected on chronological grounds: the calibrated C14 chronology indicates that the Anatolian sites are considerably later than the European ones. Therefore, although some connections with the east are indicated, these probably arose through trading relations and the 'Danubian II' cultures can be seen as the direct descendants of the first settlers, perhaps with some absorption of the Mesolithic population.

NORTH EUROPEAN PLAIN ROUTE

This area is less well known than the other two routes and the main settlement seems to have been rather later in date.

Southern Russia and Romania

The first well-known Neolithic communities in this area belong to the Tripolye-Cucuteni culture, which was in existence by *c.* 4750 BC (C14 *c.* 4000 bc). It is very oriental in appearance with sophisticated painted wares, stamp seals, female figurines, etc. and equates both chronologically and culturally with the later Neolithic groups of the Mediterranean and Danubian areas rather than with the first settlers. The settlements are characterised by long rectangular houses which, though differently constructed, recall those of the early Danubian LBK communities and perhaps reflect a similar social system with residential units belonging to extended rather than nuclear families. The economy shows 'European' features: the agriculture may have been of the slash-and-burn kind associated with cyclic settlement and there was considerable emphasis on the breeding of the two domesticated animals native to Europe: cattle and swine. In fact in the earliest phase of the culture two groups of sites have been recognised: one with an emphasis on cattle breeding and the other on pig breeding. The Tripolye culture is the earliest known to concentrate on the rearing of pigs and this can be considered another distinctively European adaptation: pigs are forest animals by nature and even in domesticity often live largely off forest products and thus may well have flourished in the virgin forests of early Neolithic Europe. Local wild boar would almost certainly have been domesticated by the Tripolye farmers. In later phases of the Tripolye culture pig breeding declined in importance, and this may reflect deforestation of the area following clearance for agriculture. In the later phases certainly, and perhaps from the beginning, horses were also domesticated – another local achievement, and one that was to become important in European development at a rather later date. A few domesticated camels are also reported from Tripolye sites and these must indicate Asiatic contacts. Many cereals were cultivated by the Tripolye farmers: emmer, hard, bread and club wheats, barley and millet are recorded. Millet indeed played an important role – yet another European feature. The role of hunting in the economy varied from phase to phase and site to site.

Northern Europe

In northern Europe itself the earliest Neolithic is the TRB (or funnel-neck beaker) culture, sometimes known simply as Northern Neolithic. This appeared in Poland, Germany, Scandinavia and the Low Countries and had reached the northern limits of its distribution by *c.* 3500 BC (C14 *c.* 3000 bc). It is the least oriental early Neolithic group in Europe (which is not surprising since it is both furthest away from the east and latest in date), lacking such oriental traits as stamp seals, figurines and painted pottery. Indeed this culture demonstrates a more obvious debt to local Mesolithic traditions than any other early Neolithic culture in Europe. Traits that suggest a Mesolithic origin include facility in the use of flint (which was mined from early in the Neolithic), exploitation of Baltic amber, pottery based on basketry traditions and the importance of hunting on some sites. In other respects the TRB culture is like the other early Neolithic groups of continental Europe, characterised by long rectangular houses (though different in form from those of either the LBK or the Tripolye group), slash-and-burn agriculture and a concentration on cattle breeding (with evidence of local domestication of aurochs and of the practice of castration). The cereal crops were also similar, with emmer and einkorn the main crops in Germany, Poland and Denmark. In Sweden, however, barley was the chief crop: it is a hardier plant than wheat and its predominance in the extreme north of the TRB area doubtless represents an adaptation to the colder climate of this region.

Either through immigration or through trading contacts, elements of the TRB culture appear to have crossed the North Sea and to have influenced the development of the British Neolithic (which was partly of Western Neolithic type); for instance the practice of flint mining in England may well have been adopted from the TRB people, as may some of the pottery traditions found in East Anglia.

So by 4000–3500 BC (C14 3500–3000 bc) Europe had been opened up by food producers to the extremities of the area that could support primitive farming settlements. Beyond these areas, in the regions where the environment was too hostile to allow exploitation by early farming methods, peripheral groups of hunter–gatherers survived.

In this account I have concentrated on broad outlines of the major cultural groups and have thus drawn a greatly over-simplified picture. I have deliberately chosen this approach, in order to demonstrate one aspect of the spread of farming across Europe – the adaptation of an oriental system to European conditions. It greatly underestimates, however, the extent of human and environmental variability, and detailed studies reveal each community as an individual entity in a distinct ecological niche, with an economy appropriate for its exploitation. I have here travelled rapidly along the main routes – the cultural motorways – of Neolithic Europe, but if we stop for a moment to explore some of the minor roads we find a fascinating variety of cultural and economic arrangements. Among the most unusual of these are communities on the Balearic island of Mallorca who apparently subsisted largely by intensive exploitation of a ruminant called *Myotragus balearicus*, a sort of cross between a deer and a goat, known only from the Balearic islands and now extinct. Another example is provided by a north Italian lakeside community at Molino Casarotto, which bred sheep/goat and cattle, but derived the bulk of its meat from red deer, which may have been in some sense domesticated (or at least manipulated); they cultivated cereals too, but most of their vegetable food came from wild water chestnuts. Such examples could be multiplied many times over, but I have cited these two to indicate the kind of economic variety found in Neolithic Europe, interwoven with the overall pattern which forms the basis of my account.

SUBSEQUENT DEVELOPMENTS

The period that followed the opening up of Europe by farmers was very complicated and here I can only outline a few important trends.

1. One of the consequences of the introduction of farming was the rapid disappearance of pure food collection as a way of life. Indeed only outside the temperate zone in the exacting conditions of the circumpolar region did communities continue to support themselves by hunting and gathering alone. Else-

where the archaeological record shows us communities employing in some degree the practices of farming. This does not mean that the Mesolithic communities were necessarily destroyed or absorbed, but, even where they retained a separate identity, they modified their economies in response to the introduction of farming. Two major factors may have been responsible for this reaction and these would have acted in a complementary manner. In the first place the advantages of food production, or at least of some aspects of it, would have been self-evident and would therefore have attracted the Mesolithic population. Secondly, the arrival of the farmers and their subsequent multiplication would have seriously restricted the territory available for exploitation by the indigenous population. Studies of existing and recent hunting and gathering peoples have shown that very large areas of land are required to support communities on this subsistence basis (the average population density for Australian aborigines was approximately 1 person per 20 sq. km (Yengoyan 1968: 190)). If the available land was relatively suddenly and drastically reduced, it would have become extremely difficult to survive in this manner. The pressure to adapt would have been immense and the solution was to hand in the form of the manifestly successful economy of the intruding farmers. However, hunting and gathering remained important to many of the groups of Neolithic Europe and in some cases the skills and the tools developed by the Mesolithic population made a permanent contribution to the cultural development of Europe. One example of this is the use of the bow. Although bows and arrows were used by some of the early farming communities of western Asia, they were unknown or rare among the first farmers in south-eastern and central Europe. They were, however, very widely used by Mesolithic communities throughout Europe. In the north and west of Europe even early Neolithic cultures used the bow and this weapon again became dominant throughout Europe later in the period. It is probable that this represents the survival and diffusion of a successful Mesolithic (indeed an Upper Palaeolithic) invention.

2. The exploitation of the continent of Europe took on a new dimension. We have already seen how new plant and animal foods were being utilised. In addition mineral resources, such as flint and other stones, were being exploited on a much greater scale than previously and some, notably the rather rare and highly prized black volcanic glass, obsidian, were traded over considerable distances.

Primitive agricultural methods involved wasteful destruction of vegetation and exhaustion of soil. The practice of allowing animals to graze on cultivated land after harvesting, although restoring some fertility to the soil through manure, in the long-run prevented effective regeneration of the vegetation, as grazing animals, especially goats, destroy all growing matter above ground level. The only plants that can successfully withstand this treatment are those which have buds at or below ground level – grasses, herbs, etc. The replacement of forest or woodland vegetation by pasture in this manner would have exposed some areas, especially in the hilly Mediterranean regions, to the eroding forces of wind and water, further discouraging regeneration of vegetation.

Under all these pressures the face of Europe began to change. For the first time in Europe man was materially altering his environment on a considerable scale, thus beginning a long destructive process which has led ultimately to the frightening problems facing us today. In the British Isles man has been seriously manipulating his natural environment for approximately 5,500 years, but has had a Department of the Environment for little more than two years!

3. As in western Asia, the introduction of the farming economy was followed by a population expansion, so that the previously almost empty continent was rather rapidly filled with people. No serious attempts have been made to assess the population of Neolithic Europe and indeed such estimates are beyond the scope of the archaeological evidence available. However, present guesses fall within the range of 1·5–5

individuals per sq. km for the early Neolithic, 5–10 individuals for the later Neolithic. Estimates for the Mesolithic population range from 0·04 to 0·1 individuals per sq. km, so if these estimates are even approximately correct, the order of the increase was between fiftyfold and two-hundred-and-fiftyfold by the late Neolithic. The increase in population led to increasing density of settlement and, combined with the destructive effects of primitive farming, to pressure on the land. The cultural consequence of this was increasing bellicosity, and the later Neolithic cultures of Europe are often characterised by fortified settlements and by increasing numbers of weapons among the artefacts. The economic consequence was change in the subsistence basis: more effective farming methods were developed, including various methods of restoring soil fertility, and there was some separation of groups concentrating on animal rearing; there was also in some cases a reversion to greater exploitation of wild food resources, though in combination with farming, not instead of it.

4. Culturally the period is characterised by the fragmentation of the large culture cycles of the earlier phases into numerous divergent groups. It is possible that these reflect adaptations to smaller regional environments. Some groups indicate a certain resurgence of Mesolithic traditions, with tool types which may be of Mesolithic derivation and with a greater emphasis on wild food resources than early in the Neolithic. It would be a mistake to regard these as retrogade developments: on the contrary they probably indicate a more efficient exploitation of the environment, with fuller use being made of the whole range of available food resources. It is also possible to regard the cultural fragmentation as an indication of a different social organisation, and it has been suggested that it might be correlated with the transition from a band to a tribal structure.

5. We have seen how even the earliest Neolithic cultures in Europe, although derived from oriental prototypes, were distinctively European adaptations. As time progressed, the 'Europeanisation' continued and specifically European traits

appear. Perhaps the best example is the development of mega-lithic monuments in northern and western Europe. These are tombs and temples built of large stones; there are innumerable variations, but they share a general 'family' likeness. The interpretation of these monuments over the last century has reflected in turn the evolutionary and the diffusionist views which have alternately influenced archaeological thinking. Until recently such views reflected little more than the philo-sophical bias of the archaeologist, but with the advent of C14 dating it has become clear that the earliest of the megalithic monuments occur in north-west Europe. Breton examples are dated to the fifth millennium BC (C14 mid-fourth millennium bc), and British and Scandinavian examples not very much later; they are all much earlier than possible prototypes in the east Mediterranean. It is clear that these monuments were devised in north-west Europe and indeed were the inventions of the first farming communities in those areas; we must abandon once and for all the idea current for so many years of missionaries of a 'megalithic religion' hailing from the east Mediterranean and carrying enlightenment to the furthest shores of Europe.

The megalithic tradition was a general west European one, but it developed in many different ways. High points of the development are the decorated passage graves of Brittany, c. 4700–2500 BC (3800–2000 bc) and Ireland, perhaps c. 3200–1800 BC (2500–1500 bc); the cyclopean temples of Malta, c. 3600–2500 BC (c. 3000–2000 bc); the stone alignments of Brittany (of unknown date); and the stone circles of Great Britain, c. 3000–1800 BC (c. 2400–1500 bc), culminating in the magnificent final monument at Stonehenge. These all represent great achievements in terms of social co-operation and organi-sation and in many cases of engineering too. The Breton align-ments and the British circles bear witness also to considerable mathematical and astronomical knowledge. The work of Thom in particular (1967) has shown how the circular, oval, elliptical and egg-shaped enclosures of Britain were laid out according

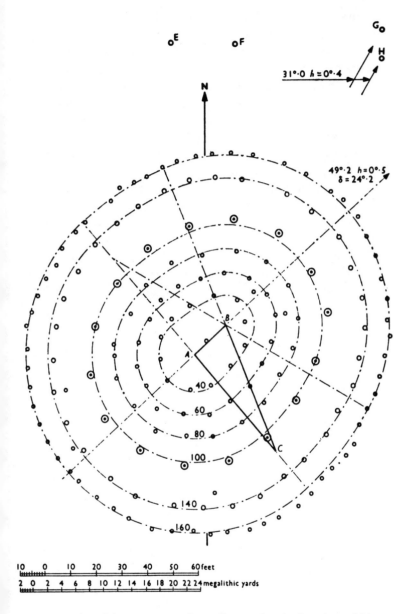

Figure 18. Plan of the monument of Woodhenge, showing how it was laid out.

to rules of geometry and using a standard unit of measurement (Figure 18). Their function is clearly related to astronomy, and even if we hesitate to accept all of Thom's conclusions, we must accept that the people who constructed these monuments made use of an accurate solar calendar and also recorded some of the activities of the moon; they may in fact have been able to predict eclipses of the moon. All these are distinctively European achievements, owing little or nothing to outside inspiration, but all made possible by the liberating influence of the food producing economy.

The development of megalithic monuments overlapped with the invention and spread of metallurgy, which represents a new phase in the technological and economic development of Europe and which I shall therefore treat as a separate topic. First, however, I must return to the Near East to discuss the important developments that were taking place there while Europe was being developed by early farmers.

Chapter 6

THE URBAN REVOLUTION IN WESTERN ASIA

During the fourth millennium BC, while the food producing economy was being adapted to the environmental conditions of temperate Europe, a second economic revolution was taking place in the Middle East and in Egypt. The three great early civilisations of the Old World arose in Mesopotamia, Egypt and the Indus valley, and the earliest of these was Sumer, in southern Mesopotamia. Here before 3000 BC the self-sufficient villages of farmers had been transformed into large cities with an economy based on specialised manufacture and foreign trade. As in the case of the food producing revolution, this was the culmination of a long process and was 'revolutionary' only in its effects. Also like the earlier revolution, it took different forms in different areas.

The growth of an urban economy depended upon the guaranteed production of sufficient food to support not only the population engaged in primary production, but also a large body of non-food-producing specialists: craftsmen, merchants, civil servants, priests, soldiers, etc. Not only did the individual farmers have to produce more food, but the surplus supplies had to be accumulated and redistributed by a central authority. As we have seen, the early farming communities of western Asia were based upon agriculture, especially cereal agriculture, with relatively slight dependence on domesticated animals. The early civilisations in this area were also based to a large degree on cereal agriculture and the necessary increase in food production was achieved by the extension of the practice of farming from the hill and plain zones where it was developed to the alluvial soils of the large river valleys, where flood cultivation, with irrigation, allowed intensive exploitation of the soil and high crop yields. This change has been described recently by Maurizio Tosi (in Renfrew 1973) as a movement from the *areas of agricultural development* to the *areas of productive increase*, and it was clearly crucial to the development of urbanism. The alluvial valleys, as well as permitting intensive cereal cultivation, supported date groves, and there was abundant fish and game, especially in the marshy delta areas. Game continued to be important in the diet of the early civilisations and domesticated animals were naturally kept also. Thus the early civilisations were based on a wide variety of food sources, but the staple foods were undoubtedly the cereal crops.

It was Childe's view that the centralised leadership and stratified society characteristic of civilisation arose as a result of the conditions prevailing in the large alluvial valleys, where the work of draining swamps, cutting and maintenance of irrigation canals, etc., required social co-operation on a considerable scale. Recent work, especially by Adams (e.g. the paper in Lamberg-Karlovsky 1972), has shown that in Mesopotamia massive irrigation works were undertaken only *after* the establishment of civilisation; the early irrigation of the Predynastic period was of a limited sort that could easily be organised by a small kinship group or even a single family. In fact we have seen that this type of irrigation was probably in use in south-west Iran before 5000 bc and even earlier in the Levant, and it seems to have been practised by unstratified egalitarian societies of the type associated with many early farming communities. Modern studies of the rise of the early civilisations (e.g. Adams, op. cit.) favour multi-causal explanations, rather than the earlier simplistic views involving a single cause like the development of irrigation. Some of the factors that may have contributed to the development of urban life are listed in the following paragraph.

The increasing population that resulted from intensive food production would have led to larger population units and to increasing social complexity. The practice of irrigation even on a small scale would have led to inequalities in the value of farming land, which in turn would have encouraged the emergence of social inequalities. The variety of subsistence activities practised (agriculture, herding, hunting, fishing, etc.) would have encouraged economic specialisation and the development of a central authority to co-ordinate the different activities and to distribute the food. Various important technological discoveries and inventions – including metallurgy, the wheel and the harnessing of animal and wind power – led on the one hand to increasing efficiency in primary production and, on the other, to increasing economic specialisation. The role of trade, too, must have been crucial. The alluvial plain of southern Mesopotamia completely lacks mineral resources and even good timber, so all such commodities – including of course the stones and metals needed for every day tools – had to be imported from sources in adjacent or distant areas. One effect of this was to encourage the growth of secondary urban centres in neighbouring areas, but this I shall deal with shortly. Its effect on Mesopotamian society itself was to further encourage economic specialisation and the emergence of a central authority, for trade must have been a full-time occupation for many people and must have been efficiently organised.

All these factors and others as well may have contributed to the development of urban civilisation in Mesopotamia and the positive interaction of different factors – the feedback – meant that the process once under way gathered momentum until the 'revolution' was accomplished. It is impossible to pinpoint a moment at which any society 'became urban', but according to Adams the potential was already in existence in southern Mesopotamia early in the fourth millennium and by 3000 BC Protoliterate – civilised – Sumer can be recognised.

The process of urbanisation in Egypt, which occurred only slightly later than in Mesopotamia, has left us little trace in the archaeological record, though we know much about the end product: the civilisation of the pharaohs. What we do know about the process of urbanisation is, however, of some interest.

About 3000 BC a wave of Mesopotamian features, most con-
spicuously art styles and motifs, appeared in the Nile valley in
the period immediately preceding the political unification of
Upper and Lower Egypt and the emergence of recognisable
Egyptian civilisation. It seems as though in Egypt a largely
independent process of urbanisation was given a fillip by
contact with the already civilised Mesopotamian world.

One of the most interesting discoveries of recent years – the
excavation of the site of Tepe Yahyā in Kerman province of

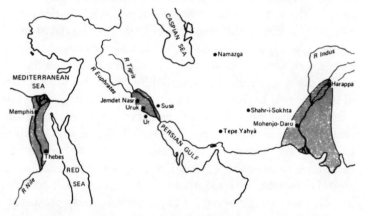

Map 6. The location of important early urban sites.

southern Iran (Map 6) – indicates that urban life was developing elewhere in western Asia *at the same time* as in Mesopotamia.
Tepe Yāhyā in level IVC was an urban literate community: it
has yielded a number of tablets inscribed in the Proto-Elamite
script, certainly produced locally, in association with pottery
and seals of Mesopotamian Jemdet Nasr type and C14 dates in
the late fourth millennium bc (Plate VI (a)); this level is therefore contemporary with the period during which urban life
was developing in Mesopotamia itself. Indeed these Proto-
Elamite tablets are as early as the earliest Sumerian cuneiform
tablets yet found. In the same level at Tepe Yahyā there is
abundant evidence for long-distance trade and for craft

specialisation. Not much later there is evidence also for urban communities in eastern Iran (the enormous site of Shahr-i-Sokhta is thought to have sheltered at least 50,000 people), Afghanistan (Mundigak), Baluchistan (Bampur) and Turkmenia (Namazga, Altin-depe, etc.). Moreover a most interesting possibility is raised by a recent note (*Soviet Weekly*, 14 October 1972, p. 2) that there may also have been communities of urban status at this date in the Ukraine: the very brief note indicates that a site of the Tripolye culture had been found with remains of nearly 1,500 houses, for which a population of 20,000 people is suggested. We await with impatience publication of this most important discovery. In all these areas, with the possible exception of the Ukraine for which we have no evidence, the process of urbanisation was based on local resources (the flood plains of river valleys reproducing on various scales the situation in Mesopotamia), and was initially at least an independent development. The process was further supported by trade between the various zones.

Slightly later, early in the third millennium BC (C14 about the middle of the third millennium bc) another great civilisation arose to the east of Iran, in the valley of the Indus, on a cultural basis closely related to the early urban cultures of eastern Iran, Baluchistan and Afghanistan.

Interestingly enough, although the initial development of urbanism occurred widely in alluvial valleys throughout the Near and Middle East, it was only in the three vast flood plains of the Nile, the Tigris-Euphrates and the Indus that civilisations were maintained. In Turkmenia and eastern Iran after the first flush of urban development there was a decline, resulting apparently from environmental pressures. It seems that the smaller alluvial valleys, especially those vulnerable to changes in river course, were unable to support indefinitely the high population densities necessary for civilised life. Only in the immensely rich large flood plains could agricultural yields be maintained at sufficiently high levels.

None of the developments east of Mesopotamia influenced

events in Europe, whereas the civilisation of Sumer and its successors had a profound influence on European development and there was some influence also from Egypt. So here we are mostly concerned with events in Mesopotamia and Egypt. In these areas the vast surplus produced from the rich soils were concentrated in the hands of central authorities (which arose on a religious basis in Mesopotamia, a military-political one in Egypt). The surplus thus collected was used in part for non-productive purposes, such as the erection of vast temples or, in the case of Egypt, monumental pyramids to house dead pharaohs (though, of course, these activities must have served a social purpose). However, some of it was made available for productive community projects, such as maintenance and improvement of irrigation systems, for foreign trade and for the support of specialist craftsmen. The technological advances on the one hand contributed to greater efficiency in the exploitation of the environment and thus to greater wealth, and on the other hand to the growth of a class of specialist artisans and merchants, all of whom had to be supported out of the surplus produced by the primary producers. The increasing complexity of community life, concentrated in the temples of Sumer and the royal courts of Egypt, gave rise to the invention of writing and developments in fields of knowledge such as mathematics, astronomy and medicine. So new classes of specialists – scribes and civil servants of various sorts – arose to join the craftsmen and merchants. Moreover the incursions of envious neighbours on the peripheries of the civilised areas and the necessity of protecting merchants fetching raw materials from distant regions led to the rise of professional armies, which also had to be supported out of communal funds. The cultures of Early Dynastic Sumer and Egypt were true urban civilisations, literate and with a class society.

THE SIGNIFICANCE OF THE URBAN REVOLUTION

The change from a fundamentally self-sufficient, food producing economy to one based on specialised manufacture and external trade counts as a revolutionary step in human progress. A considerable expansion of population is indicated by the size of both cities and cemeteries. Braidwood and Reed (1957) have suggested, admittedly on a very hypothetical basis, that the population of Sumer about the middle of the third millennium BC might have been around half a million. This represents a population concentration of about 20 per sq. km, which is double the concentration estimated by the same authors for the primary village farming communities of neighbouring areas (and this latter estimate is too high to be acceptable to many authorities). A most interesting speculation is suggested by the evidence of modern urban geography, which has shown that with very few exceptions (all recent), town populations do not increase or even remain stable by themselves; the death rate in towns is always higher than the birth rate. Increase in urban population is therefore always dependent on immigration from the countryside. If this was true also of the earliest towns of all, the Mesopotamian towns would have been absorbing excess population from the countryside. Thus the urban revolution might have provided a solution (though not of course the only possible solution) to the problem of uncontrolled population expansion associated with simple farming communities.

I have attempted to illustrate the differences in population structure between hunting and gathering, village farming and urban communities, though on a purely speculative basis, by the use of population pyramids of modern societies (Figure 19). Figure 19 (a) is a schematic population pyramid of generalised hunting and gathering groups: it has a low wide triangular profile; the broad base indicates that a high proportion of the entire population is young, but this arises more from a short life expectancy (indicated by the low height of the pyramid) than from a high birth rate. Figure 19 (b) is a population pyramid for modern Mexico, which I have taken to illustrate a primarily agricultural society: the triangular profile is absolutely

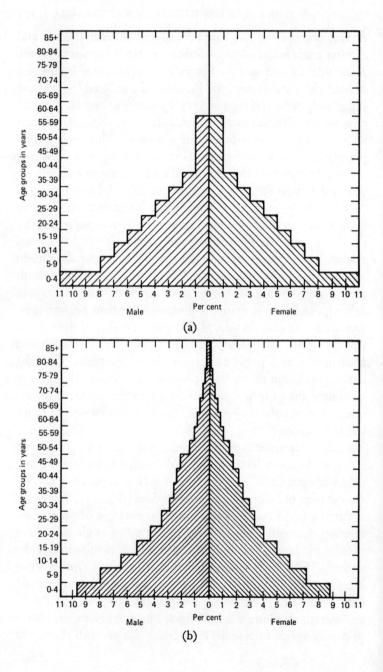

(a)

(b)

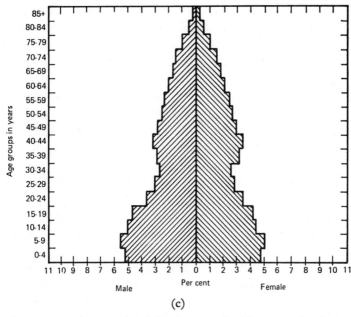

(c)

Figure 19. Population pyramids for: (a) generalised hunting and gathering groups (b) mainly agricultural communities, as exemplified by modern Mexico (c) urban societies as exemplified by modern USA.

typical, indicating a high birth rate (to account for the broad base of the triangle) and a life expectancy considerably higher than in hunting and gathering groups (accounting for the greater height of the triangle). Actually life expectancy in early agricultural communities would have been lower than in modern Mexico, because of the absence of modern medicine, but it would still have been higher than in hunting and gathering groups. Finally Figure 19 (c) is a population pyramid for the modern United States, taken to illustrate urban communities: it is characterised by a much squatter profile, indicating both a reduced birth rate and an increased life expectancy. Both these features may have characterised early urban communities, though not in so marked a degree as in modern north America. This diagram is included to show the kind of changes in population structure (as well as simply numbers) that may have followed the two economic 'revolutions' I have discussed.

The success of the urban revolution, as of the food producing revolution, must be measured in cultural terms; as on the earlier occasion it was followed by a huge growth in the range of cultural activities: there were developments of enormous importance in the areas of technology, architecture, art, religion and in many fields of theoretical knowledge which the invention of writing now allowed to be developed and recorded (mathematics, astronomy, medicine, etc.).

Once the new economy was established in the primary centres it naturally exerted a considerable influence on other areas. However, unlike the village farming economy which was the end product of the earlier revolution, it was not suitable for extension at that stage to large areas of the inhabited world. Before the era of large-scale trade in staple foods (which probably did not precede the vast empires of the first millennium BC), the population of any area was limited directly by the amount of food that could be produced locally. At the time of the emergence of city life in Mesopotamia few areas of the world were fertile enough to support a very large population when exploited with the available technical means. However almost all farming communities, and indeed some hunting and gathering ones, can produce *some* surplus food and thus support a population larger than the maximum engaged in primary production; what is necessary is some incentive for individual farmers to produce more food than is required by their own families. Such incentive appears to have been largely lacking in the era of primary village farming, both in western Asia and in Europe, although there were exceptions, such as the community at Çatal Hüyük, which already in the seventh millennium bc was supporting specialist craftsmen. Incentives appeared with the development of civilisation in Mesopotamia and Egypt, when a whole new range of consumer goods became available: on the one hand, the new efficient tools and weapons of metal, wheeled vehicles, ploughs, etc., and on the other, luxury goods such as fine stone vases, jewellery of precious metals, semi-precious stones, etc. These are directly comparable to the washing machines, televisions, cars, clothes and ornaments which provide the incentives for hard work in our own society.

The availability of these goods in the cities must have inspired envy in communities in contact with them. Some of these were able to acquire the coveted goods because in their own areas lay the raw materials – metal ores, stones, timber, etc. – which were absent in the alluvial valleys, but necessary for the support of civilised life. If the communities were able to support specialists to extract or collect and work these materials, they could exchange them for the manufactured products of the cities; this opportunity provided the incentive for the extra food production necessary for the support of the specialists. In the more fortunate areas, which were well placed in respect to both natural environment and availability of raw materials, secondary centres of the urban economy arose.

It was in this way that Childe explained the early appearance of urbanism thoughout western Asia and Europe (e.g. Childe 1964, chap. 7). Today diffusionist views are unfashionable and for early European urbanism in particular, Renfrew, in a very recent and thorough examination, has suggested an independent evolution (Renfrew 1972). There is a real sense in which the process of urbanisation (outside the context of direct colonisation by imperial powers) is *always* a local phenomenon, since, as we have seen, the population must be fed out of local resources and there must therefore be both the means and the desire to produce surplus food locally. The difference between the two interpretations lies in the field of the *incentives* for increased food production: in the Childe (diffusionist) view, the incentives are external, emanating from already urban societies; in the Renfrew (evolutionist) view, as propounded for the Aegean, the incentives are thought to have arisen locally following the invention of metallurgy. On the basis of the archaeological evidence, it seems probable that Aegean urbanism did arise independently, but the Childe model as outlined above still seems the most plausible explanation of the rise of towns in the Near East and Anatolia.

Even if, as Renfrew argues, the influence of the early civilisations of the East on prehistoric Europe was minimal, it remains true that western culture owes a great deal to these civilisations, especially that of Sumer. For many of the practices and beliefs of Sumeria, as well as much of its applied science, were inherited and further developed by the Babylonians and from them reached, often through conscious borrowing, the Assyrians, the Hittites, the Phoenicians and finally the Greeks and with them our own cultural ancestry. Another, more recent, agent of diffusion was Christianity, which brought to Europe religious beliefs and practices rooted in the ancient East. Specific elements of our own culture that we can trace back to early Mesopotamia include positional numeration and the sexagesimal system by which we divide the clock and the circle, and the story of the Universal Flood.

Chapter 7

ECONOMIC AND SOCIAL DEVELOPMENT IN EUROPE

Until recently it has been orthodox to assume that the important developments of later prehistoric Europe – and especially the practice first of copper and subsequently bronze metallurgy – were, like the practice of farming at an earlier stage, introduced or inspired from western Asia. This view was developed by Gordon Childe over a long period and is still widely held today; indeed there is not a general work on European prehistory in the English language which is not based on this diffusionist assumption. It is nevertheless a view that is losing credence among prehistorians today, for two main reasons. Firstly C14 dating, especially after the tree-ring calibration, now gives us a 'long' chronology for European prehistory, with the result that many developments, including copper metallurgy, appear to be *earlier* in Europe than in the areas from which they are supposed to be derived. Secondly, and partly as a result of the new chronology, diffusionism in general is less popular than it used to be; prehistorians today do not feel, as many did ten years ago, that it is *a priori* unlikely that Europeans invented metallurgy or anything else of importance for themselves. At present, although many authorities still believe that the civilisations of western Asia and the Aegean *did* influence continental Europe, other scholars now feel that it is possible to regard European development as totally or largely independent of such influence.

Whatever the degree or nature of the influence from the East, the development of Europe was certainly very different in kind from that of the East. For environmental reasons there was not in Europe the same kind of population pressure in restricted areas that characterised the Near and Middle East and Egypt. Nor was there the same premium on co-operative effort in Europe as in the alluvial valleys, where an individual had to join forces with his fellows or starve: under European conditions it was almost as easy for a family to farm on its own as in a larger community. In addition Europe lacked the potential for the kind of intensive food production that supported the urban population of the eastern civilisations: although the land could certainly produce more grain than was reaped by the Neolithic farmers, it was not fertile enough to produce the extremely high crop yields achieved by the farmers of Mesopotamia and Egypt. However, the pressures that affected western Asia so profoundly did not leave Europe untouched: for instance increasing population and technological innovations affected both areas and in both were incentives for social and economic change. Population increase in Europe was doubtless less acute than in Asia, but it certainly occurred and probably contributed to the development of new social forms. For instance, Renfrew has recently suggested (in Renfrew 1973) that in the Wessex area of southern England a social system evolved in the later Neolithic of the type described by some anthropologists as a 'chiefdom'; this, though not a form associated with urban peoples, represents a ranked society with a system for the redistribution of wealth through chiefly power. Whether this particular model fits the case or not, the unstratified egalitarian society of the earliest farming cultures in Europe was replaced by other forms – and these were characterised by some degree of social stratification and equipped with some mechanism for the redistribution of wealth.

It is probable that one factor contributing to this development was population increase and the consequent growth in community size. Another and perhaps more important factor favouring social development was technological innovation. The beginning of metal working, whether independently invented or introduced from outside, promoted economic specialisation and led to some division of society on an economic basis. As in the East, the new metal goods were incentives to increased food production and the accumulation of surpluses which could be used to support the metal smiths and other specialists. However, European societies were far less dependent on imported goods for the functioning of their economy than the eastern civilisations, and for a while in Europe the metal smiths may have been almost the only specialists and they may, initially at least, have been shared by a number of communities. So Europe did not at an early stage develop a complex urban organisation as did the East; indeed for a time the Neolithic village structure may have survived, with the extra-local need for metal tools supplied by itinerant smiths, in the same way that stone axes and obsidian tools had been distributed throughout the Neolithic period. However, once the metal tools came to be regarded as essentials rather than luxuries, self-sufficiency was abandoned and the way laid open for the development of larger and more complex economic systems. It was Childe's view that the difference in social and economic organisation between Europe and the eastern civilisations in the Bronze Age laid the foundation for Europe's later development. Whereas the eastern societies which achieved civilisation in the first place eventually reached the point where progress was against the interests of the entrenched ruling classes and therefore ceased to occur, European society, with its less rigid class stratification and higher status for craftsmen such as metal smiths, continued to develop and from the classical period onwards took over the cultural and political leadership of much of the known world.

THE BEGINNINGS OF METALLURGY

The 'orthodox' view about the first appearance of metal working in Europe is that it was developed in the Near or Middle East and introduced into Europe from the south-east. Recently, however, it has been suggested, especially by Renfrew, that it may have been developed independently also in Europe. Its development in the east is well documented: true smelted copper was in use as early as the seventh millennium bc in Anatolia, and by the fifth millennium copper metallurgy was also practised in northern Mesopotamia, Palestine and Iran; in the fourth millennium it was found throughout the Near and Middle East and in Egypt.

When we turn to Europe we find no metal objects nearly as early as the Anatolian finds from Çayönü Tepesi and Çatal Hüyük (indeed most of Europe had not even been settled by farmers at this date). The earliest metallurgy in Europe belongs to the early fifth millennium BC and is found in the Balkans. It must be emphasised that even with the new chronology, the earliest Old World metallurgy was Near Eastern (specifically Anatolian), and it is therefore *possible* to retain the diffusionist view of the spread of metallurgy into Europe from the east. However, the fifth millennium metallurgy

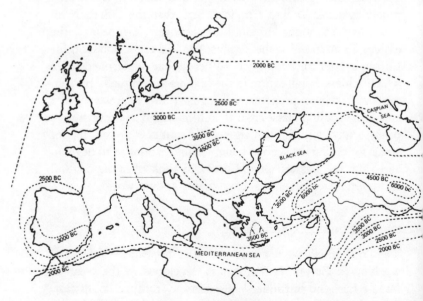

Map 7. Isochronic map showing the development and spread of early metallurgy.

of the Balkans was more developed than contemporary metallurgy *anywhere*: the practice of casting in bivalve moulds and the production of shaft-hole tools by core casting had been mastered by the Balkan smiths, and indeed the tree-ring chronology suggests that these are the earliest shaft-hole tools in the world. It is for this reason that Renfrew (1969) has suggested an independent development of metallurgy in south-east Europe. The isochronic map prepared by Renfrew to demonstrate the development of metallurgy and reproduced here with some modifications supports this interpretation (Map 7) (Renfrew 1970, fig. 10). It is informative to compare this map with that showing the spread of farming in Europe at an earlier stage (Map 5). There is little doubt that the development of farming in Europe was brought about by diffusion or immigration from the east and the isochrons on this map demonstrate a steady spread from south-eastern to north-western Europe, as one would expect. The isochronic map for the development of metallurgy contrasts with this, suggesting instead a spread from several different centres in southern Europe. This seems to be the most convincing interpretation of the evidence at present.

The practice of metallurgy was always dependent on the availability of raw materials, so in the first place its development in Europe was limited to areas where ores occurred; outside these areas it was dependent at all times on imported materials. There were two main stages of development in Europe, which can be taken as approximately equivalent to (a) a phase of copper metallurgy beginning in the fifth millennium; and (b) a phase of bronze metallurgy (true tin bronze with 10 per cent tin) beginning in the late third millennium.

FIRST PHASE

There were four early centres of metallurgy in Europe: the earliest centre of all in eastern Europe, and three in the Mediterranean, in the Aegean, Italy and Iberia.

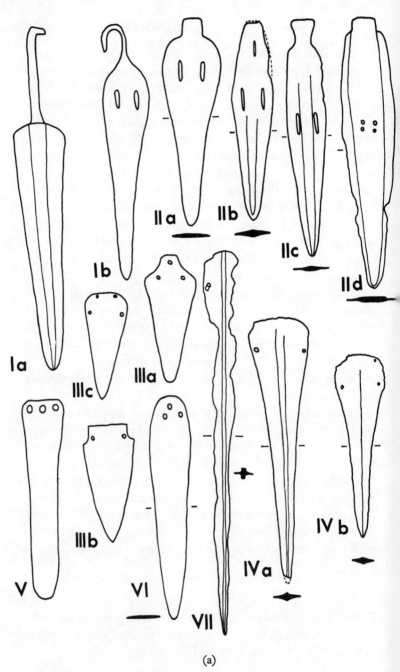

(a)

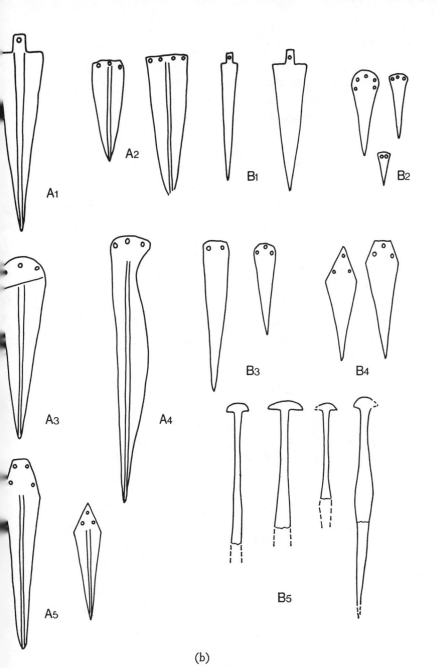

(b)

Figure 20. Early metal tools from: (a) the Aegean, (b) Italy.

1. *Eastern Europe.* The calibrated C14 chronology indicates that there was already a developed copper industry in the Balkans early in the fifth millennium BC (C14 fourth millennium bc). It was based on the ores of Transylvania. As well as ornaments the Balkan smiths were producing shaft-hole axes and axe-adzes. They had mastered the practice of casting in closed moulds and indeed the production of shaft-holes by core casting, so the industry was by no means a primitive one. Indeed, as I have already said, it is probable that these axes and axe-adzes were the world's earliest shaft-hole tools of metal.

2. *The Aegean.* By 3500 BC (C14 2800 bc) metallurgy was practised along the north Aegean coast; this region was an extension of the Balkan province, with many cultural as well as metallurgical connections. By this stage also copper objects, including some smelted ones, occur elsewhere in the Aegean – in Thessaly, Crete and the Cyclades. Copper metallurgy did not, however, become common in the Aegean till the first half of the third millennium BC (C14 second half), when it is found on mainland Greece, the Cyclades, Crete, Cyprus and northwest Anatolia. The tools, made of copper alloyed with arsenic, include daggers (flat and with midribs), spearheads and axes; there was also a variety of ornaments, made of silver, lead and gold as well as of copper (Figure 20 (a)). This industry is often thought to be of Near Eastern origin, but there is no very great similarity in the repertoire of tool forms; whether or not the technological know-how was introduced from outside, the industry must have been largely a local development. It was based on ores occurring in the Aegean: good copper sources are known in eastern Crete and in Cyprus, and silver and lead could have been obtained from more than one of the Cycladic islands.

3. *Italy.* The use of smelted copper was known in Italy, as in the Aegean, in the fourth millennium BC (C14 third millennium bc), and in fact the earliest copper slag, from the island of Lipari, comes from a deposit which is probably earlier than 3500 BC. However, it was not until the first half of the third millennium BC (C14 second half) that metallurgy was widely

practised. At this stage objects made of arsenical copper occur throughout the Italian mainland and in Sicily and Sardinia as well. On the mainland there were two main groups practising metallurgy: the Remedello group of the Po valley exploiting Alpine ores and the Rinaldone group in central Italy exploiting the ores of Tuscany. The island groups were probably using local ores also. The Italian smiths produced flat axes, triangular and tanged daggers (flat and with midribs), halberds, awls and a few simple ornaments. A few ornaments of silver and antimony were probably also made from local metals. An East Mediterranean origin is often suggested for Italian metallurgy, but it is more probable that it was a local development, possibly with a few East Mediterranean metal types being copied by Italian smiths. It has been suggested recently that the halberd was an Italian invention, proceeding from an attempt to mount an ordinary dagger at right-angles to its shaft, like the stone battle-axes that were widely used in central Italy (Figure 20 (b)).

4. *Iberia*. We have very few C14 dates from Iberia and as a result it is very difficult to date the beginnings of metallurgy. However, it is possible that some metallurgy was practised before 3500 BC (C14 2800 bc), and certainly by the first half of the third millennium (C14 second half) the use of smelted copper was flourishing in both southern Spain and Portugal. The industry, which was based on local ores, includes flat axes, flat daggers, daggers with midribs and a number of ornaments. The industry is generally thought to be of Aegean inspiration, and indeed one school of thought holds that it was established by actual colonists from the Aegean. This latter view now seems unconvincing: the Aegean parallels quoted for Iberian cultural traits do not belong to one chronological horizon nor come from one area in the Aegean; moreover the few C14 dates we do have suggest that the 'colonial' traits may appear earlier in Iberia than in the Aegean. It is probable that either there was no connection with the Aegean metal industry at all or that indirect commercial contacts (perhaps via Italy) were responsible for some similarities in the metal forms of the two areas.

All four of these early metal industries probably arose within the context of existing cultures (although this is not universally accepted for any of the Mediterranean areas). The development of metallurgy did more than improve technology: it brought with it at least incipient economic specialisation, since metal smiths are necessarily specialists and usually full-time ones, though initially this may have meant only a few itinerant smiths supported out of the accumulated surplus of several different communities. Moreover the new metal goods, which were relatively rare and therefore expensive, were also extremely desirable; they thus provided compelling incentives for improved primary production and the consequent accumulation of surplus food which could be used to buy the metal tools and weapons (and thus, of course, support the metal smiths). It provided scope also for the creation of 'wealth' and for the development of economic inequalities – concepts which can have had little application during the Neolithic, when technology was simple and when equality of opportunity was the natural result of practising a subsistence farming economy in an environment not yet over-exploited.

The development of metallurgy also encouraged trade, for the distribution of metal ores in nature is uneven and communities in areas without them would have had to buy either the goods themselves or the raw materials from other societies more fortunately situated. In exchange for the metal they would have supplied other raw materials or manufactured goods; we know of a few commodities that were traded – obsidian and amber, for example – but the majority were doubtless perishable objects such as furs or woollen cloth, highly prized foods like honey or minerals like salt. Trade had of course been practised in the Neolithic period, but with the invention of metallurgy it took on a new dimension: not only did its geographical scope increase, but its significance to the communities practising it grew rapidly greater. Thus significant economic and social changes were triggered by the development of metallurgy and the societies that emerged were distinctly different from those that preceded them. It is for this reason that they are so often thought to have been introduced by settlers from elsewhere, although this view is now regarded as misguided in most cases. Of course many factors other than metallurgy can lead to the development of more complex societies, but it does seem that in Europe metallurgy played a crucial role in the evolution of society.

THE DEVELOPMENT OF CIVILISATION IN THE AEGEAN

Although copper metallurgy was practised at an early date in these four areas, only in one of them – the Aegean – did economic and social development continue without interruptions until in the second millennium BC the Minoan–Mycenaean civilisation emerged. This, although having all the diagnostic features of civilisation – urban conglomerations of population, monumental architecture, writing, etc. – bears no comparison with the great civilisations of Mesopotamia, Egypt and the Indus. The Aegean palace-towns were tiny by comparison with the huge cities of the east (Figure 21) and their leaders, though unprecedentedly wealthy by European standards, did not have access to the vast resources of the eastern alluvial valleys. The Minoan civilisation of Crete emerged first and is recognisable by c. 2000 BC, while the mainland Mycenaean civilisation did not emerge for another 400 or 500 years. Both were characterised by towns, each with a palace which was the seat of a prince, serving as a redistributive centre and supporting abundant specialist craftsmen and civil servants. The civilisations were literate, recording first in a non-Indo-European language native to Crete (written in the Linear A script) and later in the Indo-European Greek that was then current on the mainland (written in Linear B). They were also artistic, and craftsmanship reached high levels of technical and aesthetic achievement. They were wealthy and, particularly in the later stages, involved in far-ranging trade.

Childe explained the appearance of civilisation in the Aegean

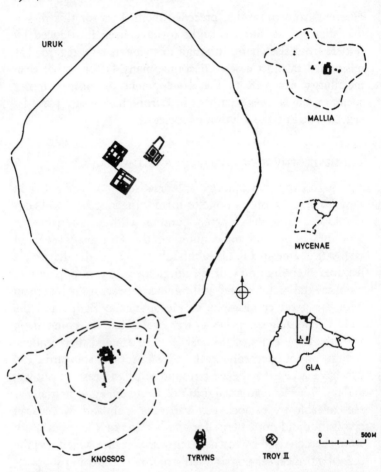

Figure 21. Early Aegean town plans compared with early dynastic Uruk.

in terms of the radiating influence of the eastern civilisations, as described above. However, as we have already seen, Renfrew's recent analysis discounts eastern influence as a significant factor in the rise of Aegean towns (Renfrew 1972). Instead he convincingly explains this development in terms of the inter- action between different factors, operating locally. Particularly important factors were the invention of metallurgy (with all the economic and social implications already discussed) and, in the field of subsistence, the development of Mediterranean polyculture, with the cultivation of the olive and the vine accompanying the cereal crops – a system which allowed a considerable increase in production and a consequent increase in the population that could be supported.

For reasons that are still hotly disputed the Mycenaean civilisation collapsed in the course of the twelfth century BC. Whether it was at the hands of barbarian invaders from the north or for environmental reasons (e.g. a catastrophic eruption of the Santorini volcano), or the result of internal social break-down, the effects were far-reaching. Although there were some elements of cultural continuity, urban life and literacy disappeared from Greece for several centuries and knowledge of the Mycenaeans survived only as half memories recorded in the Homeric poems.

The degree of influence wielded by the Minoan–Mycenaean civilisation over other areas of Europe is another area of controversy. The diffusionist views of Childe and others tended naturally to see many European developments, even in far-off regions like Wessex and Brittany, as related to Mycenaean trading activities. Nowadays these views are rejected by many authorities, and indeed it is hard to see direct Mycenaean influence outside the Mediterranean basin, where evidence indicates flourishing Mycenaean trade westwards to Sicily and southern Italy and east and south to the Levant and to Egypt – but only on a large scale from the fourteenth century onwards. An up-to-date assessment of the Minoan–Mycenaean civilisation, which was without a doubt the earliest civilisation on European soil, would present it as a great achievement, a local product, a specifically Aegean brand of civilisation, but would not claim for it a sphere of influence beyond the east and central Mediterranean regions or, it must be admitted, any lasting contribution to European development, beyond what is incorporated in the Homeric poems.

MIGRATION AND TRADE IN CONTINENTAL EUROPE

The period following the invention of metallurgy in Europe appears in the archaeological record as an era of social and economic change. As well as changes brought about by environmental pressures and those that resulted from the introduction of metallurgy, there seem to have been population movements at this time, which must also have stimulated change. In the past prehistorians have been all too ready to explain any change in the archaeological record in terms of invasion or migration, and by way of reaction present studies, as we have already seen, look instead to local factors for explanation. However, when all is said and done, migration *is* a human activity and we must expect it to have played some role in man's prehistoric past, as it has in history and does at the present day. When the superfluous invasions created by an earlier generation of archaeologists have been expunged from the record, there remain some data that are still best explained in these terms. The millennium *c.* 3500–2500 BC (C14 *c.* 2800–2100 bc) appears as a prehistoric 'Migration Period' in Europe, characterised, like the later period described by that name, by a series of population movements from the east, which resulted in some displacement of existing populations, leading to further westward migrations. Even if the numbers of people involved were very small, their effect could have been considerable. These migrations were different in kind from those that much earlier spread farming communities over the face of Europe: instead of the gradual spread outwards of an expanding population into virtually uninhabited lands, at this period there were probably eruptions of small mobile groups (in some cases horsemen) into areas already settled quite densely by villages of farmers. These intrusions may have been to a great extent peaceable and there must have been much intermingling with earlier populations. The period was very complicated in detail, but in a simplified account one can see two main groups:

1. *Eastern Group*. This group comprises the cultures variously described as Globular Amphora, Corded Ware, Battle-axe and Single Grave cultures. It is found all over eastern and northern Europe and may have originated in the Kurgan (Pit Grave) culture of the south Russian steppes. Important traits of this group are single graves often under barrows, wheeled vehicles, probably domesticated horses, battle-axes and copper metallurgy; in most of these characteristics they contrast with the earlier Neolithic societies of northern and eastern Europe. This group, which had reached Holland by 3000 BC (C14 c. 2500 bc) has been identified by some authorities with the Indo-Europeans; the arguments in favour of this identification are complex, but they include the possession of the wheel and the domesticated horse – which should be characteristic of the 'original' Indo-Europeans – and their possible origin in south Russia, which is a plausible 'original' homeland for them. However, linguists and archaeologists are studying different things: if there was an original Indo-European language – and this is not a universally accepted *linguistic* concept – there is no reason why we should expect it to correlate with a recognisable archaeological culture. Anthropological studies have made it quite clear that there is no necessary correlation between language and other culture traits. Without written records we cannot in fact say what language or languages were spoken by any archaeologically recognised group. In this case all we can say is that the people of the Single Grave/Battle Axe, etc., group *could have* spoken an Indo-European tongue.

2. *Western Group*. This is the Bell Beaker group, which has a fairly dense but discontinuous distribution over an area covering eastern and central Europe, the Low Countries, the British Isles, Brittany, southern France and coastal Iberia, with sporadic occurrences also in the central Mediterranean (northern and central Italy, Sardinia and Sicily). Over this vast area there is a considerable similarity of material. In addition to the typical pottery vessels which have given the group its name,

it is characterised by single graves under barrows (although this may not be an original trait), archers' equipment (flint arrowheads and stone wristguards), and copper metallurgy. Two schools of thought exist about the origin of this group. Many authorities favour an Iberian homeland (with an ultimate derivation out of the Impressed Ware of the Early Neolithic), but the alternative hypothesis of an east European, specifically a Hungarian, derivation seems more probable. The westward movement of Bell Beaker people from eastern Europe may have resulted from pressures on those areas from people still further east, including the Kurgan (Pit Grave) people mentioned above. The Bell Beaker group was certainly in existence shortly after 3000 BC (C14 c. 2500 bc). In the Low Countries it met and mixed with the Corded Ware branch of the eastern group c. 2600–2500 BC (2200–2100 bc) and most of the beakers found in the British Isles indicate mixed Bell Beaker and Corded Ware traditions.

Although these mobile groups retained their separate identities in all areas, they seem often to have mixed freely with earlier groups and with each other. Bell beakers, for instance, are found in megalithic chamber tombs in Iberia, France and Great Britain, and in rock-cut tombs in central Italy and Sardinia, in association with material of local late Neolithic or Copper Age cultures. Corded Ware too occurs in the megalithic tombs of northern Europe, which were constructed by the people of the Neolithic TRB culture.

These mobile groups can claim responsibility for some of the innovations of this period: the eastern group introduced wheeled vehicles and possibly also domesticated horses to northern Europe, while both groups were responsible for extending the knowledge of copper metallurgy from the areas where it was practised initially to the rest of Europe. In fact by c. 2000 BC (1700 bc) the knowledge of metallurgy had been spread almost to the extremities of inhabited Europe, to the British Isles and southern Scandinavia. However, metal was not

Figure 22. Models of wheeled vehicles from Hungary.

very important to any communities at this period, except possibly in the areas of origin discussed above. Other changes occurring at this time cannot simply be laid at the door of the migrating groups and must be explained rather in terms of local environmental and social factors. These include a shift in emphasis in the subsistence economy towards stock breeding, increasing bellicosity in social relations and the growing importance of trade. No serious attempt has been made to explain these changes in detail, but the kind of factors we may expect to furnish such an explanation include the pressures created by over-exploitation of arable land during the previous Neolithic period, improvements in farming techniques, increasing population densities and the social and economic changes, discussed briefly above, which were set in motion by the invention of metallurgy. Indeed the population movements just described may have been as much a symptom of the changing times as a prime causal factor. Whatever the explanation, the archaeological record is emphatic about the degree and significance of these changes: in contrast to the long and peaceful continuity of the Neolithic period, the millennium 3500–2500 BC appears as an era of rapid development. As well as the documented changes in economy, there were certainly social changes and hints also of changes in religious belief, with the earlier dominance of the mother goddess giving way to a sun cult, possibly reflecting, as do the warrior graves, a male-dominated society. There are, however, no indications of any division of society into classes on an economic basis.

SECOND PHASE OF DEVELOPMENT OF METALLURGY

Possibly as early as 2400 BC (2000 bc), certainly by 2200 BC (1850 bc), a more developed metal industry was established in Europe. This industry was technologically more advanced than the industries of the Copper Age: true tin bronze was now in use in place of the pure copper or arsenic-copper alloy of the earlier period, and the employment of closed moulds for casting had become commonplace. The appearance of this industry is traditionally taken to mark the beginning of the Early Bronze Age in Europe. The origin of the bronze industry itself is in some doubt. It has been customary to look for an origin in the Near East and specifically in Syria, where indeed a whole range of tools and ornaments finds very close parallels: these include daggers, neck-rings (known as ingot torques) and a variety of bracelets, anklets and pins. However, the tree-ring calibration of C14 dates gives a date earlier by several centuries for the European examples than for the supposed prototypes in the Near East. It seems probable that we must look for a local origin for the European Bronze Age, as for the Copper Age. There is nothing in the metal technology to argue against this interpretation: all the developments of the Bronze Age could have arisen as simple improvements to Copper Age practice. However, there was a geographical shift of emphasis at the beginning of the Bronze Age: whereas the early industries of the Copper Age developed in southerly locations, in the Balkans and the Mediterranean, the centre of the metal industry in the Early Bronze Age was in south central Europe, and it is usually named after the Czechoslovakian site of Aunjetitz or Unětice. This geographical shift probably indicates the opening up on a large scale of Czechoslovakian and other central European ore sources, which had been worked only slightly or not at all in the earlier period.

The Unětice bronze industry consists of a rather wide variety of tools, weapons and ornaments, of which the most important are low-flanged axes, triangular knife-dagger blades and solidhilted daggers, halberds, ingot torques, spiral-ended bracelets and racket-shaped and knot-headed pins. These goods are found in considerable numbers and they occur both in tombs and in hoards. It is clear that metal was much more abundant than in the Copper Age and that it was distributed on a 'commercial' scale (the hoards are thought to represent the stock-in-trade of travelling metal smiths, buried in times of trouble and for some reason not retrieved as planned). Some features of the Unětice culture certainly appear to demonstrate continuity from the previous period, for example the use of single graves (sometimes under barrows) and some of the pottery forms; there seems to have been basic continuity of culture, and certainly of population, from the Copper Age into the Bronze Age in central Europe. It still remains necessary to explain the close similarities between the Syrian and European bronzes, for these seem too numerous and too precise to be regarded as coincidental or the results of parallel development, as can be argued for the different Copper Age industries. If we are to believe the evidence of the tree-ring calibrated $C14$ chronology, it was the European industry that influenced the Levantine one, rather than the other way about. In any case, the explanation should probably be sought in terms of trading relationships, rather than migrating populations or even simply immigrant bronze smiths.

Although Czechoslovakia was the focal point of Early Bronze Age metallurgy, early bronze industries closely related to Unětice are known also from Hungary, Yugoslavia, southern Germany and Switzerland. These were all based on local ores, and in spite of their close similarity to the Unětice industry clearly represent separate local industries. At a slightly later date more industries of the same general type were established in areas peripheral to the central zone, but where ores were available: northern Italy, Brittany, the British Isles, etc. All these areas had previously had Copper Age metallurgy and there must have been some degree of continuity; in many cases the Bronze Age metal smiths may have been literally the lineal descendants of the Copper Age ones. The metal tools themselves, however, do not demonstrate continuity, but form part of a 'family' of Early Bronze Age industries, all related to each other but different from the industries of the Copper Age. This relationship is not reflected in other aspects of culture and we must think in terms of a pattern of industrial commerce and practice transcending regional cultural differences. This is perhaps easier to understand if we see it as a primitive precursor of the situation at the present day, when industrial technology is a world-wide phenomenon. To take a single example, a bulldozer is not an artefact that can be considered typical of any culture today: one might find one almost anywhere in the world in a huge variety of different cultural contexts; not only are they very widely used, but they are made in many different countries and traded to many others. This aspect of the situation also finds a parallel in the European Early Bronze Age, since from an early stage imported metal goods were reaching areas without ores of their own, for example southern Italy, the Low Countries, Scandinavia, etc. A little later, in what is usually called the Middle Bronze Age in central Europe, although it represents an uninterrupted development from the Early Bronze Age, *c.* 1700–1300 BC (*c.* 1500–1200 bc), local bronze industries were established even in these areas, based on imported materials.

This period – the Early and Middle Bronze Age – was a flourishing one for Europe, or at least for the better provided and more conveniently situated areas, characterised by technological progress and social prosperity. It was Childe's theory, expounded in great detail and adopted in principle by very many other scholars, that the European Bronze Age owed its origin, development and prosperity to the radiating influence of the urban civilisations of the Aegean, and indirectly of Egypt and Mesopotamia also. According to this view it was the demands of these civilised societies for raw materials available in Europe that gave rise to the European Bronze Age. The most important of these materials were the raw metals and ores (gold, silver, copper and tin) of central and western Europe and amber from the Baltic. However, recent work has shown that most of the materials used by the Aegean civilisation in the early phases at least were of local origin; it is only after *c.* 1400 BC that the Mycenaean cities were supported by a large-scale wide-ranging, truly commercial trading system. This is about 800–1,000 years later than the initial establishment of a bronze industry in Europe. There is, it is true, some evidence of trading contacts between the east Mediterranean and central and western Europe before 1400 BC, but when this evidence is examined critically, it boils down to very little; it is hard to imagine that this commerce was of crucial importance either to the Aegean civilisations or to the barbarians of Europe. It is possible, perhaps probable, that after *c.* 1400 B.C. trade with the Aegean did allow European communities to draw on the accumulated capital of the civilised societies and hence increase their own wealth, as in the model propounded by Childe for the earlier period, but if so, this must have been an *additional* factor contributing to European prosperity and not its chief cause. The European Bronze Age must now be regarded as a largely independent and distinctly European achievement. We need look no further for a reason for this development than the invention of metallurgy itself with all its implications (see p. 190).

What now appears to be a pertinent question is why, outside the Aegean, there was no development of civilisation during this period. The answer to this question is beyond the scope of our knowledge at the moment, but one might guess that one important factor was that the economic and social changes latent in the invention of metallurgy were unable to develop fully because there was no complementary improvement in the subsistence economy (as there was in the Aegean) to allow the necessary population increase. In Europe the archaeological record for this period documents increasing wealth and the emergence of recognisable chieftains, but very little increase in economic specialisation. The metal smiths were certainly specialists, but no others are clearly indicated. Instead in some cases at least surplus wealth and energy were put into economically non-productive projects such as the erection of huge religious monuments like Stonehenge (Plate VII) and the Carnac alignments (which probably required specialist priests to maintain them and the cult and knowledge associated with them). To call these projects economically non-productive is not, of course, to say that they were useless. On the contrary, they doubtless served a variety of social purposes: religion is normally a cohesive force, allowing individuals to identify with a symbol of society itself; it frequently provides a rationale for the phenomena that surround man both in nature and society and a code of practice for dealing with these phenomena; the astronomical activities associated with the megalithic enclosures and alignments may also have provided calendrical information of practical use to farmers and others. However, in contrast to the eastern civilisations (which of course had their own extravagant religious monuments), in Europe little if any of the surplus wealth was ploughed back into the community for productive purposes and although technological progress continued, this period in Europe was not characterised by the dramatic economic and social advance that led to the emergence of civilisation in the East and later in the Aegean.

THE LATE BRONZE AGE AND THE FIRST 'INDUSTRIALISATION' OF EUROPE

The period following 1200 BC was a time of disruption in the Mediterranean and the Near East. The half-century 1200–1150 BC saw, *inter alia*, the collapse of the Hittite empire in Turkey and the fall of the Mycenaean empire in the Aegean. Indeed within the boundaries of Europe civilised life was eclipsed for a while: the art of writing was lost, monumental art disappeared, the elaborate bureaucratic machinery of state that characterised Mycenaean civilisation vanished together with the far-ranging commercial network that supported it; only the deeds of the heroes survived as memories incorporated into the epic poems of Homer. While Greece entered a 'Dark Age' and there was much unrest and disturbance elsewhere in the east Mediterranean, in central Europe the period after 1200 BC represents a time of real economic and social progress, archaeologically identifiable with the Urnfield cultures of the Late Bronze Age. The relationship between events in Europe and those in the east Mediterranean is unclear and there is considerable dispute as to what was cause and what was effect. Did refugee craftsmen from Mycenae establish a more developed bronze industry in central Europe? Or was Mycenaean civilisation brought to an end by invading barbarians from central Europe? Or were the developments entirely unconnected? In fact, whatever the reason for the fall of Mycenae, there seems no reason to look for an external cause for the rise of the Urnfield culture of central Europe. There is evidence of continuity of settlement from the local Middle Bronze Age Tumulus Culture and there are no changes, technological, economic or cultural, documented in the archaeological record that could not have developed locally. Indeed, whatever connections there may have been between central Europe and other areas, it is only by looking at it as a process operating locally that we can make sense of the developments of the Late Bronze Age in Europe.

The Urnfield cultures are a group of related cultures, or alternatively, subgroups of a single culture, of which early centres occurred in Hungary, Czechoslovakia, Austria and the north Alpine area. The adoption of the characteristic burial rite – cremation in urnfields – and some of the metal types, such as swords, began as early as the thirteenth century BC (indeed cremation was practised much earlier in some areas, e.g. Hungary), but the main development of the cultures belongs to the five centuries following 1200 BC. The size and number of the cemeteries suggest a greater population density than in earlier periods and there is considerable evidence for a more developed economy. For the first time in Europe the metal industry was organised on a truly 'industrial' scale:

proper copper mines were now being used to exploit the Alpine ores and these are the earliest known in Europe. In the earlier periods ores were probably collected from the surface or extracted by shallow open-cast mining. These copper mines must have employed a considerable labour force, carrying out the actual mining, felling and transporting the large quantities of timber required for shoring and for the smelting fires, and engaged in the various processes of producing metal from ores. If one adds to this list those engaged in transporting the metal in ingot form from the mines to the settlements and the smiths who actually manufactured the tools, weapons and ornaments (no longer itinerant, but attached to individual communities), one realises that there was a considerable number of specialists employed full-time in the metal industry. And of course they would all have to be supported out of the surplus produced by those engaged in primary production.

It seems reasonable to regard this development in the metal industry as a minor 'Industrial Revolution'. Like the later and much greater economic upheaval that we know by that name, the 'Industrial Revolution' of the Late Bronze Age was preceded and made possible by a minor agricultural revolution, which established a more efficient subsistence economy. This allowed the expansion of population needed to support the new 'industrial' economy. It is probable that this was based, again as in the later period, on technological improvements, in this case the introduction on a wide scale of the plough (although this probably began to be used earlier in the Bronze Age), which allowed more efficient exploitation of the land, since the surface could now be turned over instead of simply being scratched. This not only allowed better use to be made of land already cultivated, but also made possible the extension of agriculture to heavy soils such as clays which were not previously cultivable, and new land was probably taken over for cultivation during the Urnfield period.

The settlements, though less well explored than the cemeteries, indicate clearly the social and economic developments that characterise this period. They are often relatively large, they are frequently defended and tend to be densely settled within the defences. They certainly supported specialist bronze smiths, and there are hints that other crafts may have been organised on a specialist basis as well, at least on some sites – perhaps carpentry and the production of woollen cloth. We know that the distribution of metal was organised on a commercial scale and this commerce doubtless brought in its wake trade in numerous other desirable if less vital commodities. Merchants were probably full-time specialists at this period. So the settlements were no longer simply farming villages: though they cannot yet be described as towns, they were already proto-urban in their economic structure.

The cemeteries give us further information about the economic and social structure of the communities. Their size (the urnfields often contain thousands of urns) indicates that the communities were larger than in earlier periods; they often yield evidence of use over several centuries, indicating that the settlements were permanent and stable. The inclusion of abundant grave goods, many of metal, demonstrates the existence of 'wealth', and the uneven distribution of grave goods within the cemeteries suggests an equivalent inequality in the distribution of wealth within the community. They suggest in fact that there was a gradation from rich to poor rather than a rigid division into two or more economic classes.

As well as the economic and social developments just discussed, technological advances are conspicuous at this period. Though probably occurring in many crafts, they are most noticeable archaeologically in the metal industry, where the techniques of core casting by the *cire perdue* method and beating sheet bronze were now practised with great skill. Indeed the Urnfield bronze smiths were masters of their craft. A wide variety of tools was now regularly made of metal for the first time – chisels, gouges, saws, sickles, etc. – and these must have increased efficiency in agricultural production, in many crafts and indeed in household activities also. Sheet bronze was used for containers (buckets, bowls and dishes), for military purposes (armour, shields, etc.), and for ornamentation. In the military sphere the slashing sword replaced the short thrusting sword or rapier – an increase in efficiency of a different sort. Engraved and embossed decoration was employed, some of it executed with great skill. And, as I have already said, the industry has every appearance of having developed locally: there is no reason to look for influence from outside, whether from Mycenaean Greece or anywhere else.

Urnfield Expansion

The increased efficiency of the subsistence economy seems to have led to another population increase in Europe at this time. This led to expansion outside the area of origin and, as Europe was by now quite densely occupied, this was followed by displacement of populations previously existing in the regions into which the Urnfield peoples expanded. Thus population movements of one kind or another affected large parts of Europe. True Urnfields occur in Romania, Bulgaria, Hungary, Yugoslavia, Czechoslovakia, Poland, Austria, Germany, Switzerland, Italy, eastern and southern France and northern Spain. In addition Urnfield ideas and practices spread through the medium of trade. So, through a combination of migration and diffusion the Urnfield economy, or a version of it, was spread over most of Europe. By c. 800 BC, even in peripheral areas such as the British Isles, Scandinavia, Atlantic France and Iberia, there was a consolidated system of settled farming, based on plough agriculture combined with stock breeding and an economic organisation with, in all probability, specialist smiths in each community replacing the travelling tinkers of earlier periods. The increased density of population led to pressure on the land and to hostility between different communities. The earliest hill forts – hilltop settlements defended by earthen or stone ramparts – belong to the Late Bronze Age, and must reflect the need for defence against raids by neighbours. This form of settlement became characteristic of many areas during the succeeding Iron Age, when the ramparts were sometimes multiple and often attained massive proportions (Plate VIII (a)).

THE INTRODUCTION OF IRON

Iron technology was initially a jealously guarded secret of the Hittite kings, who were producing iron daggers (considered as valuable as gold and suitable for diplomatic gifts for foreign kings) as early as the fifteenth century BC. It was not until the fall of the Hittite empire early in the twelfth century that iron-working began to spread. It spread initially to Palestine, had reached Greece by the eleventh or tenth centuries, Italy and eastern Europe by the ninth, central Europe by the eighth or seventh, western Europe a century or so later. The production of iron is more difficult than that of bronze, since to make it usable, it is necessary to toughen the forged metal; this is done by repeated hammering at red-hot temperatures in contact with charcoal, which introduces carbon and effects the carburisation process. However iron ores are widely available, whereas the distribution of copper ores is restricted and those of tin still more so; therefore once the technology had been mastered, iron became a very cheap metal and thus was used from the beginning, unlike bronze, not only for weapons such as daggers and swords and for basic tools such as axes, but also for agricultural implements such as sickles, ploughs and hoes. This must have increased the efficiency of agricultural practice and thus contributed to the support of larger communities practising greater economic specialisation. The spread of iron technology seems to have occurred largely by diffusion, through the medium of trade, though in central Europe it may have been introduced by small groups of immigrants from the east, and in some parts of the western and central Mediterranean it was introduced by Phoenician or Greek colonists.

THE SPREAD OF CIVILISATION

After the collapse of Mycenae shortly after 1200 BC Greece entered a 'Dark Age'. However, civilised life was gradually re-created during the course of the succeeding centuries and by the eighth century a fully developed urban civilisation had emerged. There were some elements of continuity from the Mycenaean period: a few settlements, including Athens, were continuously occupied, though many more were abandoned; there was a considerable degree of continuity in craft practice, most noticeable archaeologically in the pottery industry; and there was almost certainly much continuity also in religious beliefs and practices (although we depend here on the words of Homer as much as on archaeological evidence for the earlier period). Nevertheless, although these elements of continuity can be recognised, the civilisation of archaic Greece owed remarkably little to the earlier civilisation that arose on Greek soil: the varying political and social organisations of the emerging city states contrast strongly with the uniformity of organisation documented for the Mycenaean centres; the alphabetic script of archaic Greece is quite unconnected with the Linear B syllabary, though the language that both recorded was Greek; the new art and architectural styles were likewise alien to earlier tradition; and burial practices were different. In many of these characteristics 'oriental' influences are apparent: the script was certainly acquired from the Phoenicians, the archaic style of sculpture shows Egyptian traits, and in the technological sphere too these influences occur, since iron was certainly introduced from an eastern source. It seems as though a local development towards civilisation was given a fillip through contact with existing civilisations to the east. During the eighth and seventh centuries, partly for commercial motives and partly as a result of population pressure in the homeland, the Greeks established colonies in Turkey, north Africa, the central and west Mediterranean and on the Black Sea.

Another east Mediterranean civilisation was also developing

VII. (a) Stonehenge, View of the Hele stone from inside the monument through part of the sarsen circle

Stonehenge. Carvings of daggers on one of the sarsen stones

(c) View of the inside of the chamber of the megalithic tomb at West Kennet, looking inwards

Facing page 208

VIII. (a) Maiden Castle, Dorset. An aerial view, taken during the excavations of 1934-7

(b) Maiden Castle. A Late Iron Age hut. The post holes are clearly visible

a 'colonial' interest in the west Mediterranean at this time – the Phoenic.ans of the Levantine coast, who became a considerable maritime power after the fall of Mycenae. According to tradition they established colonies in the west at very early dates, but these are not archaeologically documented before the ninth, or perhaps the eighth, century. In the eighth and seventh centuries, however, they established colonies along the north African coast, in Malta, Sicily, Sardinia and Spain, and these were inherited and expanded by the most important of the African Phoenicians, the Carthaginians. The Phoenicians and the Greeks were responsible for the introduction of iron and of writing (in the alphabetic script invented by the Phoenicians, which forms the basis of both the Latin and the Arabic scripts in use today (Figure 23)) to the central and west Mediterranean.

Meanwhile the rich Urnfield-based Villanovan culture of central Italy was developing towards a true urban civilisation of its own. This development, like that of the Greeks, was given a boost by oriental influences, derived in this instance from extensive trading contacts with Greeks and Phoenicians in the central Mediterranean itself. By the end of the eighth century the historical Etruscans (still considered by some authorities as intruders from the east Mediterranean) are recognisable in the archaeological record. In the succeeding two centuries they expanded to gain control over much of north and central Italy and became a significant power in the central Mediterranean. The establishment of Phoenician, Greek and Etruscan cities throughout the Mediterranean was followed by the growth of towns in surrounding areas, and by c. 500 BC the entire Mediterranean zone had an urban organisation with large and prosperous cities, whose wealth was derived mainly from extensive and flourishing commerce. This is in contrast to earlier periods when urban life was found only in the east Mediterranean. Although the Mediterranean area in general was prosperous at this period, political discord was rife and the fortunes of individual towns rose and fell as a result of military and political activities. It was this land of prosperous but disunited cities

Phoenician	Punic	Etruscan	Early Greek	Equivalent letter
⊀	⊀	A	A	a
٩	⊃	𐌁	∂ 6	b
٦	٦	٦	7 Γ	g
△	◢	◖	△	d
⋺	⋺	⋺	⋺ F	e
Y	५	⋺	⋿ F	v
I	I	I	I	z
�H	⊟	目	⊟	h
⊗	⊜	⊗	⊗	th
⟁	∿	I	�५ ⋜	i
⋎	⋎	⋏	⋏ K	k
∟	↳	⌐	٦ ⋏	l
⋎	⋎	⋎	⋎ ⋏	m
�५	�५	⋎	٦ ⋏	n
⨎	⋋	田	田 ⨎	s
○	○	○	○	o
٦	٦	٦	٦ ⋂	p
⋔	⋎	M	M ⋏	s
φ	⋎	Q	φ	q
⋪	⋪	⋪	٩ P	r
⋎	⋎	⟨	⟩ ⟨	s
X	⊢	T	T	t
		Y	Y Γ	u
		X	X	kh
		φ	φ	ph
		Y	Ψ	ps
		8		f

Figure 23. The development of the Greek and Etruscan alphabets from the Phoenician.

that the Romans ultimately inherited and that formed the basis of their imperial power.

Both Greek and Etruscan civilisations were characterised by a city-dwelling, highly organised class society, literate and artistic, organised politically in self-governing cities. In the long run this political system made both civilisations vulnerable to pressures from outside and was responsible for their defeat at the hands of Rome. However, as a result of the intense admiration felt by the Romans for Greece and all things Greek, much of Greek civilisation was taken over by Rome and eventually passed into our own culture. This was not the case with Etruscan civilisation, which was considered alien by the Romans and was largely eclipsed when the Etruscans were defeated in battle. Thus, while Greek was a language used widely by educated Romans, Etruscan was forgotten and is now one of the outstanding undeciphered languages of the world. However, although the Romans felt no affinity with the Etruscans, they shared a common prehistoric background and in fact held many cultural traits in common as well as a similar economic and social structure. Because the Romans themselves acknowledged no debt to the Etruscans, we need not feel that none was owed.

THE IRON AGE IN CENTRAL EUROPE

The Mediterranean civilisations of Greece and Etruria had a considerable influence on the Iron Age cultures of Europe, of which the best known is that named after the Austrian site of Hallstatt (dated *c.* 700–500/450 BC), which developed directly out of the local Urnfield culture. The impact of the by now largely urban Mediterranean on continental Europe was far greater than that of the earlier civilisations, which were restricted to the eastern end of the Mediterranean and impinged on Europe only slightly. The new cities all along the coasts of the Mediterranean provided access for the communities of Europe to the commercial systems of the civilised zone. Europe could provide metal ores, amber, salt and other products, both raw materials and manufactured goods, which were in demand in the Mediterranean, and in return imported the luxury products of the civilisations. Imported goods, local imitations and their derivatives are common on Hallstatt settlement sites, especially in the cemeteries. Greek and Etruscan fashions in the trappings of warfare, the practice of wine drinking and personal ornament were adopted by the courts of the wealthy Hallstatt chieftains and developed to produce distinctively European forms. In the earlier phase most of the trade passed from the head of the Adriatic up the old amber routes into central Europe, but after the foundation of the Greek colony of Massilia (Marseille) *c.* 600 BC and especially from *c.* 550 BC, the emphasis shifted westwards and most of the Mediterranean goods and influences spread up the Rhône and Saône and across to the Danube and the Rhine.

The subsistence economy of the Hallstatt population was basically the efficient mixed farming practised by the Urnfield people, made still more efficient by the use of iron agricultural equipment. On this basis and with the exploitation on an industrial scale of the metal industry, helped by trade, both with the Mediterranean world and within Europe, the Iron Age communities prospered. Population increased, communities grew larger and there was more economic specialisation. Economic and social disparities are noticeable at this period: rich burials occur, presumably those of members of chiefly families, and stand out in contrast to the ordinary burials of the time. The chieftains were often buried together with four-wheeled wagons, which were probably military parade vehicles rather than everyday carts, and with very rich grave goods, often including imported Greek and Etruscan vessels. Fortified hilltop settlements – hill forts – which were first constructed in the Late Bronze Age were now characteristic of many parts of Europe. They suggest a situation in which hostilities between communities were endemic – probably mostly cattle raids with occasional confrontations of a more serious nature. It is probable in fact that the social and political organisation of the Celts recorded by the Romans a few centuries later was already in existence at this stage.

After *c.* 500 BC the centre of Celtic culture (and by this stage we can feel confident that the population of western Europe was largely Celtic-speaking) shifted westwards, and the successors of the Hallstatt chieftains are found in western Germany and France. Their culture, named after the Swiss site of La Tène, developed out of the Hallstatt culture, but owed much to the influence of the Mediterranean civilisations. The chieftains of this period were buried not with four-wheeled wagons, but with two-wheeled chariots, a type of military vehicle they probably acquired from the Etruscans. The potter's wheel was now in use, another feature which was probably acquired from the Mediterranean world; it suggests that the manufacture of pottery was now organised on the basis of factory production. The practice of wine drinking, which undoubtedly came from a Mediterranean source, brought with it a whole range of vessels of bronze and pottery, used in the preparation and consumption of wine (buckets, jugs and cups). De Navarro once wrote (1928: 435), 'La Tène art may largely have owed its existence to Celtic thirst', and indeed some of the finest examples of Celtic art do occur on vessels connected with wine drinking (Plate IX (a)). The other class of objects commonly decorated is weapons (Plate IX (b)), and it is probably not unfair to suggest that drinking and warfare were indeed two of the main preoccupations of the Celtic chieftains. The art style itself, though demonstrating Mediterranean influences, is a distinctively local and very fine achievement, very stylised and depending largely on pattern for its effect, quite unlike the naturalistic art styles of the classical world and the Etruscans. The ornaments of the La Tène people also demonstrate the adoption of many Mediterranean forms such as types of brooches (fibulae) and bracelets; the twisted neck-rings known as torques, however, are of Celtic origin and not derived from the Mediterranean.

Social and economic life continued to gain in complexity. By the third and second centuries BC the La Tène *oppida* (defended settlements) of France and Germany, of which the most famous example is Manching, had a truly urban economy with a high population density and a class society with wealthy chieftains and their courts, many specialist craftsmen – workers in metal, pottery, glass, etc. – the basic peasant population and, it seems, a stratum of slaves, acquired through inter-tribal warfare. The adoption in the second century BC of a true coin currency (a feature the Mediterranean civilisations did not develop till the sixth century BC) on a tribal basis marks a significant development in both economic and political organisation, since it indicates the establishment of a true market economy and the emergence of tribes as economic units. In the less prosperous peripheral areas of Europe there were varying degrees of development towards an urban economy of this kind. Large parts of Europe indeed had to wait for the arrival of the imperial forces of Rome for the forcible establishment of a viable urban economy. Indeed it was only through an imperial power that had access to the resources of a large empire that towns could readily be established in areas where they had not already developed locally. Once established, however, they could normally be supported out of local resources and by approximately the end of the first century AD an urban economy was established everywhere within the limits of the Roman Empire in Europe.

The importance of the Roman Empire to the development of Europe is well understood. The establishment of urban civilisation brought with it material prosperity (based on more efficient farming techniques, empire-wide trade and the new secondary industries), political security (upheld by the imperial armies) and new technological skills. All the achievements of civilisation – from aqueducts and sewers to monumental architecture, art and literature and all the complex institutions, political, economic and social, of city life – previously restricted in Europe to the Mediterranean zone were now made available to most of the continent. In cultural terms this period is often regarded as the beginning of the modern era. With the fall of the Empire, many facets of civilised life were eclipsed in western Europe; in what had been the outermost provinces urban life itself virtually disappeared. However, the survival of the Empire in the east and the revival of classical skills and institutions in the west from the Carolingian Renaissance onwards meant that our own culture owes a considerable debt to the classical civilisations of Greece and Rome.

PART III

ARCHAEOLOGY AND THE CLASSICAL MIND

Martin Henig

INTRODUCTION

The period of time covered by this section is not a long one. From the repulse of the Persians from Greece (479 BC) to the deposition of the last western emperor of Rome (AD 476) is less than a millennium. Classical civilisation was always centred on the Mediterranean, although under Alexander the Great and his successors its influence was felt as far east as Afghanistan and India, while from the first century BC onwards much of western Europe (Spain, Gaul and even Britain) came firmly within its ambit (Map 8). Apart from such limitations of time and space, there is one of degree. The classical archaeologist has in the past concerned himself mainly with the lives of the middle and upper classes. There is good reason for this, in that the men and women who created and developed Graeco-Roman civilisation were relatively wealthy. Even the vaunted poverty of the early Christians was only a comparative state, and some of them (e.g. St Paul himself) were very well educated and came from good families. In more backward parts of the Roman Empire such as Britain, life continued in upland peasant communities as it had done in the Iron Age. G. J. Wainwright (1971) has recently excavated a settlement site in Pembrokeshire whose 'Roman' phase differed little from its Iron Age antecedents. Even in modern North America, we should recall, a few Red Indians practise their traditional 'primitive' ways of life.

The wealth of material both archaeological and literary is such that it is impertinent to attempt an exhaustive survey in a few thousand words. Thus I have felt it necessary to adopt a somewhat different approach to my period. The following essay is divided into four parts concerned with the extent of

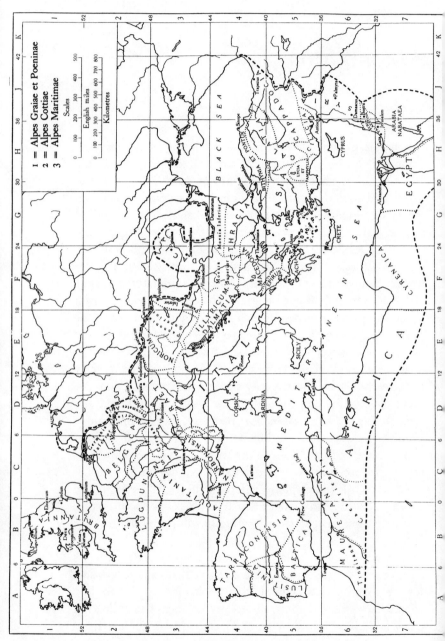

Map 8. The Roman Empire in the reign of Hadrian.

ancient civilisation, the ideals that define it, the material evidence for life in Antiquity, and the history and archaeology of the Roman province of Britain. The last of these topics needs a brief word of explanation: not only have British sites received more detailed attention than those in many other parts of the Roman Empire, not only will the average reader's first experiences of Rome have been at some insular monument – Chedworth, Fishbourne, Richborough, Dover or Housesteads, for example – but Britain is an ideal province in which to observe the impact of civilisation upon barbarians and to observe how the native ultimately became a citizen of the *oikoumene*.

Chapter 8

THE GROWTH OF THE ANCIENT WORLD

Three most potent factors making for continuity in the ancient world are politics, religion and aesthetics. Others such as language and economic organisation are also important, but in my opinion less so than the former group. After all, Byzantium in the east and the 'Latin' states in the west built up very different civilisations in the early middle ages and yet retained much of their linguistic inheritance. Moreover, the social and economic forms of late Antiquity (such as serfdom, clientship, coinage, etc.) also survived until long after the ancient world had passed away. The classical world seems almost as resistant to the passage of time as the Egyptian and Chinese empires; which is only to say that Herodotus would have been more or less at home in a Greek city of the third century AD whereas Plotinus would surely have been bewildered by life in any medieval town.

The essential unit of political organisation in the ancient world was the City. *Civilisation* was everywhere coterminous with it so that to this day most of the language of government has its roots in Greek or Latin. The conduct of public affairs in any *polis* is politics; the word 'municipality' brings to mind the Roman *municipium*. Constitutions varied but few cities were without a system of electing officials from the ranks of their inhabitants, and in many cities (especially in the fifth and fourth centuries BC) direct rule by the citizen body (i.e. democracy) was the normal form of government.

The idea of a community small enough for everyone to know his neighbour and where the interests of the individual and the state coincided was an admirable one. Thucydides sums it up in a speech which he puts into the mouth of the Athenian statesman Pericles.

Our constitution is named a democracy, because it is in the hands not of the few but of the many. But our laws secure equal justice for all in their private disputes, and our public opinion welcomes and honours talent in every branch of achievement .... Ours is no work-a-day city. No other provides so many recreations for the spirit – contests and sacrifices all the year round, and beauty in our public buildings to cheer the heart and delight the eye day by day. (Zimmern 1924, 201, adapted)

The converse of this rosy picture of democracy in action is that Pericles' speech was delivered after the first year of a long, bloody and unnecessary war waged by Athens against Sparta. Greek cities were always quarrelling with one another and treaties between them were notoriously unstable. Defeat in war could be total: in 416 BC, thirteen years after Pericles delivered his noble oration, Athens declared war on Melos without provocation, captured the island and had all the men of military age butchered, all the women and children enslaved. Even states allied to Athens were treated as vassals and given no real say in the conduct of the confederacy. Democracy was criticised by some of the greatest minds in Athens, such as Plato, who perceived in the common will an enemy to true excellence.

However, the alternatives to democracy do not appear to have been any more appealing. In the classical age most Greeks looked on 'tyranny' and on monarchy with equal horror. The former conjured up a vision of overbearing pride (*hubris*) and even of injustice. In literature we only have to think of Creon in Sophocles' *Antigone* and of Oedipus; in history we find Polycrates who learnt the hard lesson that no man can escape his fate (Herodotos III: 40–2), and in Athens Hipparchos, whose assassination in 514 BC by the youthful lovers Harmodios and Aristogeiton was long regarded as a corner-stone of Athenian liberty. Incidentally the tradition fostered by the Athenian democracy that tyrannicide was noble and glorious had repercussions in Rome when Brutus and his associates decided to kill Caesar (44 BC). Monarchy was, by definition, barbarian, although kings in Sparta had a limited importance and the monarchs of Macedon, on the borders of the Greek world, were honorary Greeks. The monarchy *par excellence* was that of the Persian Great King, but the Greeks knew that their tiny city states had challenged the Persian Empire – and won.

Him (i.e. Xerxes) who, transforming the paths of land and ocean, sailed over the dry land and marched on the sea, three hundred valiant Spartan spears resisted. Shame on you, mountains and seas. (*Palatine Anthology*, trans. W. R. Paton, IX: 304.)

Sparta itself, with its narrow oligarchy and contempt for culture, oppressed the Greek helots of Messenia with the sophisticated unpleasantness of a modern police state. It is hard to see it in an ideal light and the enthusiasm of certain non-Spartans for the peculiar system of government appertaining there seems perverse. Other oligarchies, such as Corinth, had a much freer social system and patronised the arts, but lacked the higher ideals of citizenship which made Athens the leader of Greece even after her defeat by Sparta in the early fourth century.

A major failing of all Greek cities was their exclusiveness. Large numbers of non-citizens, foreigners and enfranchised slaves lacked any real opportunity for gaining full civic rights. The foundation of new colonies was a possibility for men free to leave their homes, but the expansion of the Greek world, especially in Italy (*Magna Graecia*) and Sicily, had lost most of its impetus by the time of the Persian Wars.

The ideals of pan-Hellenism were fostered to some extent by such institutions as the Olympic Games and the great shrine of Apollo at Delphi, with its famous oracle. The fourth century sees this attitude gaining ground, both theoretically in the writings of Aristotle and (perhaps) in practice in the brief and glorious interlude between the age of Sparta and Athens and that of Macedon, when Epaminondas (*c.* 362) turned Thebes into the greatest power in Greece and liberated the helots. His epitaph reads, 'By our counsels Sparta was shorn of her glory, sacred Messene received her children at last, Megalopolis was crowned with walls by Theban prowess, and all Greece was free and independent'. But the,independent city state had almost had its day and when Philip II, King of Macedon, destroyed the flower of the Theban army, the famous 'Sacred Band' (a regiment made up entirely of lovers) and also inflicted defeat on the Athenians at the Battle of Chaeronea (338 BC), Greece enters the Hellenistic age of cities that were nominally independent but nevertheless sought the favour of a monarchic suzerain.

Alexander III, Philip's son, enlarged the Greek world to many times its former size by conquering the Persian Empire in the space of a very few years (336–323 BC). He did not attempt to administer his new realms through Macedonian or Greek governors alone, but employed able men regardless of race. Culture was becoming more important than blood as a test of one's Hellenism. Although the years after Alexander's death saw the fragmentation of the Empire, it was not into small cities but into sizable monarchies that it was divided. Sir Mortimer Wheeler is surely right to see Alexander as a precursor of the Roman emperors, the founder of an *oikoumene* which survived both him and his descendants.

One of the most moving inscriptions to have survived from Antiquity is the stone found by French archaeologists in a Greek city on the left bank of the Oxus at Aï Khanum, Afghanistan (i.e. in ancient Bactria). Nothing demonstrates more strikingly how Greek civic ideals might travel than this, for here is a Delphic maxim whose sentiments take us back to the Athens of Pericles (or to the Spartans who fell at Thermopylae): 'In childhood, propriety; in youth, master of oneself; in middle age, justice; in old age, good council; at death, contentment.' (Robert 1968.)

Bactria never became part of the Roman Empire, although it did contribute something to the development of Buddhist art which flourished in Asoka's empire (264–227 BC). Further west, the Hellenistic monarchies lasted much longer. New cities such as Alexandria and Antioch on the Orontes were homes of Hellenism, and developed institutions modelled on those of the city state. It is to places such as Pergamum or Alexandria that we must go to study new developments in Greek art and science.

In the western Mediterranean conditions were very different. There were a few Greek colonies in Gaul and Spain, notably Massilia (Marseille) and Ampurias, and the Carthaginians of north Africa and southern Spain were clearly influenced by the Greeks in some of their arts (e.g. coinage), though in other respects their culture was alien, even repellent. It is well known that the Phoenicians practised human sacrifice and many of the urns in the precinct of Tanit at Carthage contain the remains of infants offered to the goddess.

Elsewhere there were uncivilised tribesmen: Berbers in the north Sahara, Celts in Britain, Gaul, part of Spain and north Italy, Iberians in Spain. As late as the fourth century the barbarians were in the ascendant in western Europe and the few areas of higher culture may be regarded as outliers of a predominantly oriental world. While Greece experienced its golden age, most of the Continent was without the use of writing and can only be known to us through the researches of the prehistorian. It is true that something may be learned from Greek writers such as Apollonius of Rhodes, but archaeological excavation is usually more useful.

In Italy there lived a number of peoples who spoke 'barbarous' languages yet, unlike their neighbours to the north, the Celts, were absorbing and developing a social organisation and artistic sense which were Hellenic. Etruria (and Rome may be regarded as culturally more or less an Etruscan city even though the Tarquins were expelled no later than 475 BC) was to be the pivot of Europe, the centre from which the civilisation of the east was brought to the west.

From Antiquity onwards, the origins of Rome have been debated. The legend of Aeneas seems to have been current in

Etruria at least as early as the sixth century BC and the Romans adopted him as one of the founders of their state. He could not be made the actual founder of Rome – that was Romulus – but was instead connected with Lavinium near the mouth of the Tiber. Romulus and Remus were indeed descendants of Aeneas, being great nephews of Amulius, the last king of Aeneas' house.

So much for myth. The truth may be more prosaic, for even if the Etruscans were subject to cultural influences from the Orient, the indigenous prehistoric culture of Italy gave much to Rome and to the wider Etruscan world. In the classical period the importance of Greek forms in politics as in art cannot be emphasised too strongly, and the foundation myths are useful as evidence for this Hellenisation.

The Roman political system of limited oligarchy (with certain concessions to democracy) lasted for more or less 400 years, despite certain changes during this period. The executive, two annually elected consuls and a senate of elders, was balanced by a popular assembly (*Comitia*) which passed the laws. Such a division in function should have worked admirably, but as the city state became ruler of a larger and larger empire, great strain was placed on this form of government. Power could become concentrated in the hands of ambitious generals while the Senate, by passing *consulta* which had the force of law, could threaten the rights of the assembly. Nevertheless, although in course of time civil strife (what the Greeks call *stasis*) undermined the basis of Roman government, a pattern for civic administration had been set for the cities under her charge. As the election graffiti from Pompeii make clear, politics were by no means a spent force even under the Empire. The Roman assembly might have become a cypher, the Senate might have been reduced to impotence as a mere advisory council to the warlord, who liked to be known as 'Chief Citizen' (*Princeps*), though we call him after his military title, Emperor (*Imperator*); but the ideal of freedom never lacked expression, as long as the ancient world lasted.

Roman expansion began in the fourth century BC with the conquest of southern Etruria and Latium. Near neighbours as they were, this would have availed them little had Rome been a Greek city such as Athens. However, Rome was already developing that genius for rule which Virgil (himself perhaps a descendant of some Cisalpine Gaul) praised her for possessing: 'to spare the conquered and to subdue the proud'. Grants of citizenship might not always be given as freely as they were in the 330s BC but the principle was established.

In the following century Roman interests expanded into Campania. The city thus became the leading power of Italy, and it was natural that she should take an interest in the affairs of the island of Sicily which was partially in the hands of Greek cities and partially in those of Carthage. By helping the former, Rome became involved in the first Punic War (264–241 BC), the immediate result of which was to replace Carthaginian interests in the island with Roman ones. A second (and more ominous) result was to fill the minds of the merchant oligarchy of Carthage with a burning hatred of Rome. In the second Punic War (218–201 BC) the brilliant general Hannibal invaded Italy itself via Spain and the Alps. Several times (e.g. Lake Trasimene 217 BC; Cannae 216 BC) he defeated Roman armies sent against him, but, in the end, he met his match first in Fabius Cunctator and then, decisively, in Scipio Africanus. Scipio destroyed Carthage as an effective power for ever (battle of Zama 202 BC). The end result was the absorption of Carthaginian possessions into the Roman Empire and the emergence of Rome as a major Mediterranean power.

At this point in time, the politics of the Hellenistic world begin to fall within the Roman ambit. The once poor state had become rich and it is a sad fact of human history that wealth always breeds avarice. When in 201 BC Philip V of Macedon's expansionist schemes began to alarm his neighbours, Rome was called in and Macedon ultimately became a Roman province. Although T. Quinctius Flamininus proclaimed the 'freedom of Greece' at the Isthmian games (196 BC), this was mere romanticism. Greece, like other parts of Alexander's former empire, had merely exchanged one master for another. Sometimes the master might be a humane man and philhellene like Flamininus himself, sometimes an insensitive soldier like L. Mummius who is best known as the destroyer of Corinth (146 BC).

The story of Rome's later conquests is confusing, but she continued to acquire territory and wealth in the east at the expense of the Greek kingdoms. Seleucid Syria was annexed by Pompey (c. 63 BC) and Egypt by Octavian (31 BC). Both had been Roman protectorates for some time, although (as is well known) the last years of Ptolemaic Egypt saw a spectacular reversal of the normal processes when Cleopatra VII charmed M. Antonius into serving her purposes. This was the stuff of high drama (and Shakespeare did not miss his opportunity!). The most serious threats to Roman ambitions came from the barbarians, if Pontus, under Mithradates VI, and the revived empire of the Persians (under its 'Parthian' kings) may be described in this way.

In the west the significant conquest of the late Republic was Gaul. The south of this great area had been incorporated into the Empire in the second century BC and is still remembered as the old Roman *provincia* (Provence), but Gallia Comata ('Hairy Gaul'), comprising northern and central France, Belgium, Switzerland and the Rhineland, was not subdued until Julius Caesar was Proconsul between 58 and 51 BC, and its administration was only organised under Augustus.

The Republican system, which had shown signs of strain from the mid-second century, finally broke down in the Civil Wars between Caesar and Pompey (49–45 BC). Attempts to 'restore the Republic' by assassination in 44 BC were doomed to failure (Syme 1939). The end result was that Octavian, or Augustus as he was called after 27 BC, became to all intents and purposes, if not in constitutional theory, a Hellenistic monarch, and in the course of time his successors adopted even the divine honours attributed to these eastern rulers.

Chapter 9

THE CHARACTER OF ANCIENT IDEALS

It is hard to arrive at any accurate estimate of the total population of the Roman world but we are probably dealing with no fewer than 50 million people of whom one and a half million lived in Rome. Two and a half million people lived in Gaul, and Britain may have supported a million. The average population of a market town would have been in the region of 17,000, although there must have been wide variation. Autun is estimated to have supported 50,000 people in the fourth century, and Tacitus (*Annals* XIV: xxxiii) records that 70,000 lost their lives in Boudicca's attacks on Camulodunum (Colchester), Verulamium (St Albans) and Londinium (London).

As in Greek times, every Roman city would have owed especial veneration to its gods. This local religious patriotism is well known by reason of a famous passage in the *Acts of the Apostles* which tells of Paul's sojourn in Ephesus. A silversmith called Demetrius who made silver images of Diana roused his compatriots against the apostle who was guilty of impiety towards 'the great goddess . . . whom all Asia and the world worshippeth', and the cry 'Great is Diana of the Ephesians' was taken up by the populace in the subsequent riot (*Acts* 19: 24 ff.). Diana of the Ephesians with her many breasts was in origin, an oriental deity. Ancient religion was not an exclusive system of belief but rather a synthesis of diverse elements. Its adherents were of necessity tolerant and anxious to reconcile their own ideas with those of their neighbours. Modern scholars use terms like '*Interpretatio Graeca*' or '*Interpretatio Romana*' to explain the fact that the punic Baal of Baalbeck (Heliopolis) was known in the Roman Empire as Zeus (or Jupiter) Heliopolitanus, or that the Celtic goddess of the hot springs of Bath, Sulis, was venerated as Minerva Medica.

Truth for the Ancients took many forms: 'Not by one path alone can man achieve so great a mystery', proclaimed Q. Aurelius Symmachus (*Relatio* III: 10) in his eloquent defence of the ancestral religion against the Christian bigotry of Gratian (AD 384). An earlier pagan, Apuleius (second century AD) makes the goddess Isis address the hero of his celebrated *Golden Ass* to tell him that she is variously known as Minerva, Venus and Diana. 'My divinity,' she continues, 'is adored throughout the world in diverse manners, in variable customs, and by many names [but] the Egyptians, which are excellent in all kind of ancient doctrine, and by their proper ceremonies accustom to worship me, do call me by my true name, Queen Isis.' (*Metamorphoses*, trans. W. Adlington, XI: v.)

The Greek gods and their Roman equivalents were envisaged as human beings living on a more exalted plain; infinitely stronger, wiser and more beautiful of course, but nevertheless equally accessible. Wise men would seek the friendship of the gods and make them regular gifts in the form of sacrifices. The basic canon of Greek religion owed much to Homer, who may have lived in the eighth century BC (although some elements in the poems ascribed to him, the *Iliad* and the *Odyssey*, are certainly earlier in date), but it continued to appeal to men and women until the end of the classical world and even beyond, as Jean Seznec demonstrates in his *Survival of the Pagan Gods* (1953). Life on Mount Olympus mirrors that on earth. Its ruler Zeus (Jupiter) is 'father of gods and men'; his wife Hera (Juno) is a noble consort but somewhat given to jealousy when Jupiter falls in love with a beautiful boy (e.g. Ganymede) or girl (e.g. Europa). Apollo has all the grace and artistic accomplishment of an ideal Greek ephebe. Hermes (Mercury) is especially friendly to men looking after flocks and herds as well as taking care of financial dealings, and furthermore is the guide of the souls of the dead. Dionysus (Bacchus) is the bearer of life-giving wine and the saviour from death.

Not even Christianity had the power to destroy such powerful images. Instead, saints such as St Dionysios acquired the attributes of the gods. We may note that St Christopher who bears the infant Christ is none other than Hermes who carried the saviour Dionysus, for example in Praxiteles' famous statue at Olympia. It may be remarked that the Virgin Mary is invoked with especial fervour in those areas of Europe where mother goddesses were especially important: the medieval church at Capaccio Vecchio near Paestum is dedicated to the 'Madonna of the Pomegranate', who is none other than Hera (Juno) in Christianised form. As is well known the iconography of the Virgin and Child found universally amongst Catholic and Orthodox congregations is taken from that of the Egyptian deity Isis holding the infant Horus.

For a few men the ordinary conception of the gods was too limited. Philosophers with such elevated conceptions of the divine as Pythagoras (sixth century BC), Plato (fourth century BC) and Plotinus (third century AD) could not reconcile themselves to a belief in gods who behaved like men and were guilty of acts of lust, cruelty or revenge. The rare vision of these men was of course highly individual, but it might have taken very different forms in a non-classical milieu. For the Hebrew prophets the motivating force in the world was an absolute monarch; the Greek philosophers were guided by an aesthetic ideal, a conception of beauty without which Dante would have been unable to write of love 'moving the sun and the other stars' or Shakespeare have presented the good and beautiful Perdita as the bringer of forgiveness and reconciliation to Leontes in *The Winter's Tale*.

The archaeologist is in a good position to show how ideals which may be broadly labelled platonic or neo-platonic arose. Graeco-Roman art is representational in character. To us, imbued by classical and Renaissance ideals, such a way of seeing and describing the world may appear commonplace, but it is evident from comparative ethnology that the dominant modes in world art are not descriptive. The Greek attempt to delineate the natural world correctly must be qualified in one respect: there was a tendency to simplify and reduce discordant elements to a minimum, so that the real became the ideal. It was only a short step from here to the platonic theory of form and the coherent description of this vision:

Imagine someone living in the depths of the sea. He might think that he was living on the surface, and seeing the sun and the other heavenly bodies through the water, he might think that the sea was the sky. . . . Now we are in just the same position. Although we live in a hollow of the earth, we assume that we are living on the surface, and we call the air heaven, as though it were the heaven through which the stars move . . . If someone could . . . put on wings and fly aloft, when he put up his head he would see the world above, just as fishes see our world when they put up their heads out of the sea; and if his nature were able to bear the sight, he would recognise that that is the true heaven and the true light and the true earth. For this earth and its stones and all the regions in which we live are marred and corroded, just as in the sea everything is corroded by the brine. . . . (Plato, *Phaedo*, trans. H. Tredennick, Penguin, Harmondsworth 1954, 146–7.)

As the most cursory examination of classical art or reading of classical literature will suggest, the human body and especially the male body was admired as an ideal form. Some art historians, for example John Boardman, are cautious about reading too much into 'the Greek "cult of the nude", which reflects rather the popular and uncritical attitude of a hundred years ago to anything classical' (Boardman 1964, 143). But Professor Licht's assessment of the strong homosexual bias in Greek society has much to recommend it and is supported by wealth of literary references (Licht 1932, 365–437). In addition, very many painted cups show boys playing games, bathing or taking part in banquets; often there is an accompanying inscription: 'Memnomos is beautiful', 'Santhes is beautiful', to cite two examples in the Ashmolean Museum, Oxford. Occasionally the erotic intentions are made even more explicit and we find scenes of men fondling boys (Vermeule 1969). Youths are compared with flowers which soon wither away: 'Isias, though thy perfumed breath be ten times sweeter than spikenard, awake, and take this garland in thy dear hands. Now it is blooming, but as dawn approaches thou wilt see it fading, a symbol of thine own fresh youth.' (*Palatine Anthology*, trans. W. R. Paton, v: 118.) This poem was written in Roman times but the same sentiments can be found earlier.

The Greeks and Romans hungered for a beauty that would not fade. For Plato, the love of beauty may have *begun* with the body of a fair youth but it certainly did not end there:

And the true order of going, or being led by another, to the things of love, is to begin from the beauties of earth and mount upwards for the sake of that other beauty . . . a beauty which if you once beheld, you would see not to be after the measure of gold, and garments, and fair boys and youths, whose presence now entrances you. . . . Remember how in that communion only, beholding beauty with that by which it can be beheld, [a man] will be enabled to bring forth, not images of beauty, but realities (for he has hold not of an image but of a reality), and bringing forth and nourishing true virtue will properly become the friend of God and be immortal, if mortal man may. Would that be an ignoble life? (Plato, *Symposium*, trans. B. Jowett, 211–12.)

It is not far from here to Plotinus' vision of God 700 years later: 'No eye that has not become like the Sun will ever look upon the Sun; nor will any that is not beautiful look upon the beautiful.' (*Enneads* 1: 6.)

For the Greeks and Romans physical values led onwards and upwards to spiritual ones. In Antiquity men did not fear sexual desire as an enemy to the soul as did medieval Christians, but rather welcomed it as a divine gift. This is no mere academic statement: without this realisation of a sensuality allied to religious awe, the archaeologist may fail to perceive the significance of many a beautiful statue, painting or engraved sealstone.

A little gem from the fort of Chesters depicts Alexander the Great holding his weapons but otherwise nude (Henig 1970). This brings to mind a passage of Plutarch which describes Alexander's veneration for Achilles (whom he resembled in his beauty and prowess): 'He anointed the gravestone of Achilles with oil, and ran a race by it with his companions, naked as is the custom.' (Plutarch, *Alexander* xv.) Again, the idealised face-masks which form the visors of a group of parade helmets, found in the western provinces of the Roman Empire at such sites as Ribchester and Straubing, and used by the auxiliary cavalry in manoeuvres based on the battles of the Trojan War, remind us that heroes are of their nature beautiful. One of the most striking paintings from Herculaneum shows Theseus after he has slain the Minotaur, with the children who were the intended victims of that monster clasping his arms and legs in gratitude. Theseus is nude and the beauty of his body seems to tell us immediately that he is no ordinary person.

Before leaving this topic, we must mention one more example. The Emperor Hadrian had a boy-friend called Antinous who was drowned in the Nile in AD 130 during an imperial progress. The aftermath was that the youth, aged about eighteen at the time of his death, became 'the last god of the classical world', as Francisco de la Maza subtitles his fine study (1966). A keynote of the many beautiful statues which depict Antinous is the blend of spirituality with sensuality, seen to best advantage in the Antinous Farnese (at Naples) and the Antinous Mondragone (in Paris), which are surely the greatest sculptures of their age. Sometimes Antinous is identified with the gods – Hermes guide of souls, the saviour god Dionysus, or Silvanus who supervised the growth of trees and plants. Antinous' beauty was allowed to transcend the physical. For many of his contempories factors such as these were enough to bring the promise of immortality to men.

Chapter 10

MATERIAL EVIDENCE

The preceding pages will already have demonstrated that there is a profound difference of approach between the classical archaeologist and the prehistorian. Both attempt to arrive at the truth about the past, but their sources of information are very different.

One change is the widespread use of writing. Most of the important surviving texts have been transmitted through the agency of medieval copies. A high proportion of the books written in Antiquity are lost, but from what survives we can build up an extensive knowledge of history and daily life as well as of thought and artistic taste. To take a few examples from Roman imperial times – military works can be associated with specific campaigns by reference to sources (e.g. Josephus' account of the siege of Masada (AD 72–3) in the Jewish War of AD 66–73 can be checked against the surviving remains at the site (Richmond 1962), while for the Flavian conquest of north Britain excavation must take note of Tacitus' biography of Agricola). The way in which a Roman country house was planned and functioned is clear if the writings of such literate owners as Cicero and the Younger Pliny are read as well as modern descriptions of sites. Equally life among the *nouveaux riches* of a companion town (Pozzuoli) is vividly portrayed in Petronius' *Satyricon*, and the objects his characters possess or admire – paintings, silver plate, bronzes – can be compared with finds from Pompeii and Herculaneum. Furthermore, the descriptions of food here and elsewhere (e.g. in the cookery book attributed to Apicius) supply a wealth of factual information which the excavator can supplement from his own discovery of food remains, but never replace. Finally, the characters of the men who shaped events and dominated their own times are evident from their own writings (in the case of Caesar, Augustus, Marcus Aurelius and Julian), or from those of their contemporaries and near contemporaries (one thinks of Tacitus on Tiberius, Claudius, Nero, Galba, Otho and Vitellius; of Ammianus Marcellinus on Constantius II, Julian, Valens and Valentinian I).

Thanks to the preservative properties of a dry climate, papyri have survived in great number in Egypt (especially at Oxyrhynchus) and elsewhere in the Middle East. There are literary texts (some of them unknown from medieval manuscript sources), but the majority are private letters and financial documents which often tell us things that no historian would have thought it worth his while to record.

There is little chance of finding a papyrus elsewhere (e.g. in Britain), although some documents written on wooden tablets (*tabullae ceratae*) have been preserved in waterlogged conditions. However, inscriptions on stone do last, whatever the climatic conditions. One of the key branches of classical archaeology everywhere is epigraphy, for it illuminates the written sources and expands on them in a way that the usual sort of archaeological evidence cannot hope to do.

Tacitus (*Ann.* XIV: 38) writes of the man sent to replace Catus Decianus as procurator (i.e. high financial official) of Britain in the aftermath of the Boudiccan revolt. His tone is sarcastic. 'Julius Classicianus [the procurator] . . . was on bad terms with Suetonius [Suetonius Paulinus, the governor] and permitted his private animosities to interfere with the public interest. He gave out that it would be well to wait for a new Legate, free from feelings of hostility, or triumph, who would deal gently with our conquered enemies . . .' (Translated by G. Ramsay.) Light is thrown on this passage by an inscription on a tombstone found re-used in one of the bastions of Roman London. The upper stone discovered in the nineteenth century gives the man's name, 'Dis Manibus Gai Iuli Gai fili Fabia tribu Alpini Classiciani', and the lower part revealed in 1935

(Plate X) reads, '*procuratoris provinciae Britanniae Iulia Indi filia Pacata Indiana Uxor fecit.*' This shows that Classicianus was married to the daughter of Julius Indus, a Celtic chieftain from Trier friendly to Rome (who had opposed the rebellion of Julius Florus and Julius Sacrovir in AD 21), and we can thus presume that Classicianus felt a closer affinity to the natives of Britain and their aspirations than did a man like Suetonius Paulinus whose family came from Italy.

Again, in a well-known passage of the *Agricola* (ch. 21), Tacitus describes how his father-in-law inaugurated a programme of public works in the winter of AD 79: 'In order that a population scattered and uncivilised, and proportionately ready for war, might be habituated by comfort to peace and quiet, he would exhort individuals, assist communities, to erect temples, market-places, houses: he praised the energetic, rebuked the indolent, and the rivalry for his compliments took the place of coercion.' (Translated by M. Hutt.) Excavation on the site of the forum at St Albans has revealed a fragmentary inscription which may be reconstructed to read as a dedication of the basilica by the Municipium of Verulamium. It carried the name of the Emperor Titus who reigned between AD 79 and AD 81 as well as of the governor (Legatus Augustus Pro Praetore), Agricola. 'As Titus is called *Cos. design* (*Consul designatus*) and as he was not consul in AD 81, this designation must fall in AD 79. Although Vespasian died on 24 June 79, an inscription for the new emperor could not have been planned and executed in a distant province in his first week of rule and must fall between 1 July and 31 December 79, in the ninth year of Titus' tribunician power.' (R. P. Wright in *JRS* XLVI (1956), 147.)

Very occasionally works of major importance are inscribed on stone, such as Augustus' *Res Gestae* which can be seen on the walls of a temple at Ancyra in Turkey; or Diocletian's *Edict of Maximum Prices*, so useful to the economic historian of the late Empire (AD 302), portions of which have been found in several cities of the Empire. There are many other stories of a more or less literary character, like this official account of the building of Hadrian's Wall found re-used as a building stone in Jarrow Church but originally part of some war memorial: 'Son of all the deified emperors, the Emperor Caesar Trajan Hadrian Augustus, after the necessity of keeping the empire within its limits had been laid upon him by divine precept . . . [and] . . . after the barbarians had been dispersed and the province of Britain had been recovered, he added a frontier-line between either shore of the ocean for 80 miles.' (Cf. Collingwood and Wright, *RIB* 1051.) Or again an inscription from Normandy dating from the third century (AD 220) contains a letter from the governor of lower Britain, Tiberius Claudius Paulinus, to his friend Sennius Sollemnis in Gaul, offering him a staff appointment with Legio VI (when one became vacant) and also describing a number of gifts which Paulinus was sending him. Sollemnis had his own reasons for having the letter carved on stone, but he has thereby given us a splendid example of a semi-official letter dispatched from a centre of provincial government. (*CIL* XIII: 3162.)

The majority of inscriptions are more humdrum, but they too yield information to the skilled epigrapher about the people and deities mentioned. At Bath dedications and gravestones show the presence of legionaries, auxiliaries, a town councillor of Gloucester, and a number of Gauls; here we are reminded that spas, shrines of healing gods and goddesses, were centres of pilgrimage to which people came from far and wide. A tombstone from South Shields reading '*Dis Manibus Regina liberta et coniuge Barates Palmyrenus natione Catuallauna annorum XXX*' and followed by a line of Palmyrene, 'Regina, the freedwomen of Barates, Alas!' (*RIB* 1065), tells us that a Syrian merchant from Palmyra had bought a slave whose home was in south-eastern Britain (Essex or Hertfordshire), and afterwards freed and married her. The stone also demonstrates the relative frequency of early death in the Roman Empire, a factor not always appreciated from political histories which record many men and women of advanced age.

The use of coinage as a medium for exchange instead of barter was probably a Lydian invention of the seventh century BC. In the course of time the medium became almost universal in the states of the classical world. Coins struck by the authority of Greek cities generally exhibit devices appropriate to their respective states. These devices are, indeed, official seals guaranteeing the quality of the metal. Sometimes they are very beautiful but economic factors acted as a brake on aesthetic ones. Thus Athens, pre-eminent in the arts, continued to strike a currency that employed an archaic head of Athena and an owl as its symbols until the third century BC. People trusted the quality of the silver from the Laurium mines far beyond the borders of the Greek world, in Gaza and in Arabia, and Athena and the owl identified it.

Often political allusions are found but they are difficult for the non-specialist to evaluate. For example Diodorus tells us that after the battle of Himera (479 BC) the Carthaginians presented a gold crown to Demarete, wife of Gelon the ruler of Syracuse. From this was struck the gold Demareteion. However, no such coin has ever been found, although there are fine silver ten-drachma pieces that depict the head of Arethusa on one side and a quadriga (four-horsed chariot) crowned by a Nike (Victory) on the other. Numismatists still argue about whether this is the coin referred to or not. Similar problems confront the attempt to connect the decadrachm issues signed by the engravers Cimon and Euaenetos with the Athenian defeat of 413 BC.

The Hellenistic monarchs had their portraits engraved on their coin dies. Apart from the tradition of idealised naturalism so deeply embedded in the Greek consciousness (cf. above), the kings wished to see themselves glorified in the eyes of their subjects. These portraits can be used to identify persons shown on gems and statuary but they have an intrinsic interest as well. The coins of Bactria, for example, are the best evidence we have of the Greeks in north-west India.

Portraiture was slow in establishing a hold on the Roman

IX. (a) One of a pair of bronze flagons found in a tomb at Basse-Yutz in Lorraine

(b) Bronze shield dredged from the Thames at Battersea

Facing page 240

X. (a) Part of the tombstone of Gaius Iulius Classicianus (*RIB* 12) as discovered re-used in a fourth-century bastion in Roman London in 1935. First-century AD. Length of stone 155 cm. Now in the British Museum

(b) Reverse of Aureus of Claudius, showing the arch commemorating the conquest of Britain, AD 43

Facing page 241

coinage – indeed coinage itself did not appear until the early third century BC with Romano-Campanian coins closely modelled on the Greek. However, the coiners of the second and first centuries BC recognised the propaganda potential of coins to a degree unheard of in the classical world before this date. Thus C. Mamilius Limetanus, whose family claimed descent from the grand-daughter of Ulysses and Circe, showed Ulysses on his coins. L. Titurius Sabinus struck coins that figured the rape of the Sabine Women from whom his forbears took their cognomen; the tyrannicide M. Brutus had his illustrious forbear L. Junius Brutus, who expelled the Etruscan dynasty of the Tarquins, depicted on some of his issues. Sulla was blatantly advertising his own *auctoritas* when he struck coins showing Bocchus surrendering the rebel Jugurtha to him, and Julius Caesar, a master of propaganda, had a number of coins issued that concerned the conquest of Gaul. The head of Vercingetorix appears on one coin and an elephant trampling on a serpent (or, perhaps, a war-trumpet or *carnyx*) upon another.

The emperors found that coinage was an ideal way of disseminating information about their policies, for almost the entire population of the Roman world made use of money. The meaning of the devices shown on imperial coins is frequently 'pointed' by means of short legends. Thus the defeat of Cleopatra and the absorption of Egypt into the Empire is marked by means of a commemorative *denarius* showing a crocodile (typical of the Nile's fauna) and with the legend *Aegupto Capta*. Similarly Claudius' conquest of Britain gave rise to coins that figure (on their reverses) a triumphal arch with the words *De Britann[is]* over the lintel in each case (Plate X (b)). Nero advertised his Hellenism with coins that depict him in the persona of Apollo, and also informed the people of his building programme with bronzes that show his meat-market and the port of Ostia. Other emperors were proud of their programmes of public works and amongst famous surviving buildings shown on coins are the Colosseum (coin of Nero) and Trajan's column.

Concord with the armies is signified by clasped hands and the words *Concordia Exercituum*, and between two emperors (e.g. Lucius Verus and Marcus Aurelius) by the legend *Concord[ia] Augustor[um]*. The gods on whom the prosperity of Rome depended are shown with appropriate emblems as are the members of the Emperor's family (*Domus Divina*) who, if not in the same class as the great state deities, were also deemed worthy of veneration. The coinage reflects the anarchy of the third century by the multitude of emperors and usurpers who produced it, and the economic uncertainty of the time by its debasement and the widespread occurrence of forgeries. It is not surprising that the British usurper Carausius (AD 287–93) struck a coin which showed him being welcomed to Britain and has the legend (taken from Virgil) *Expectate Veni*, even if the long wait for a man who would restore prosperity to the world could not be totally fulfilled in one island; any more than Constantius Chlorus' claim to be the *Redditor Lucis Aeternae* on a gold medallion minted in Trier was the full truth.

In the late Empire fancy increasingly takes the place of fact. The boasting legends *Gloria Romanorum*, *Fel Temp Reparatio*, *Triumfato Gent Barb*, are, as Mattingly shows in his general study of the Roman coinage (Mattingly 1960, 232), part of the decay in moral standards which so weakened the state.

More serious [than this fault in taste] is the element of savagery, which the conflict with a barbarian world introduced. The Emperor is portrayed, with a special complacency, as the 'Conqueror of the whole world', the 'Conqueror of the barbarian nations', and is shown setting his foot in triumph on a crouching captive. The famous '*Fel Temp Reparatio*' of Constantius II shows a Roman legionary about to transfix with his spear a fallen Persian; in the 'Gloria Romanorum' of Valentinian I the Emperor drags a captive by the hair.

It is a melancholy fact that these excesses were perpetrated in an Empire which, officially at least, had embraced Christianity.

Engraved gems are another useful source of evidence, being

much more personal than coins. Men chose their signet-rings with care and intended them to reflect their aspirations. This is clear from several ancient texts. Cicero tells us that the portrait of Epicurus appeared on the seals of his followers (*De finibus* v: 1, 3), and there are indeed a number of stones extant that show philosophers. Augustus employed at various times a sphinx which symbolised wisdom and also elusiveness, the portrait of Alexander the Great (who we have already suggested above was the exemplar of the emperors), and finally his own portrait. (Pliny, *Naturalis Historia* XXXVII: iv, 10; Suetonius, *Augustus* L; Dio Cassius, LI: 3, 4 ff.) Clement of Alexandria's advice to the Christians in his flock is of great interest, not only because it shows how the new religion absorbed pagan imagery but because it demonstrates that attention to subject matter was still a major concern in the choice of stones as late as the second century AD:

And let the engraving upon the gem be either a dove or a fish, or a ship running before the wind, or a musical lyre, which was the device used by Polycrates, or a ship's anchor, which Seleucus had cut upon his signet. And if it represent a man fishing, the wearer will be put in mind of the Apostles, as well as of the little children drawn up out of the water. But we must not engrave on it images of idols, which we are forbidden even to look at; nor a sword nor bow, for we are followers after peace; nor a drinking goblet, for we are sober men. Yet many of the licentious world wear engravings of their naked minions or mistresses in their rings, so that not even if they wish it can they at any time enjoy a respite from the torments of desire. (*Paedagogium* II: 11)

I have noted the relatively large number of gems depicting legendary heroes which must have been lost in the years immediately following the conquest of Britain and are probably to be assigned to members of the Roman army. The insular evidence probably holds true for intaglios found on the Continent. It seems that the deeds of prowess performed by the great figures of the past would act as examples for their successors. This point is made more certain by the occurrence of mythological scenes on items of military equipment (e.g. Oedipus and the Sphinx on a sword scabbard from Vindonissa in Switzerland). Our illustration (Plate XI (a)) shows Diomedes stealing the Palladium from Troy and is cut on a sard from Verulamium (Henig 1970).

A garnet engraved with the representation of a dramatic mask and set in a gold ring was found in the latrine of the *Praetorium* (commandant's house) at the fort of Housesteads, Northumberland (Plate XI (b)). Now the gold ring was the prerogative of members of the second rank of Roman society, the *Ordo Equester* or knights, and the commanding officer of an auxiliary regiment was an Equestrian. So this ring is certainly the personal signet-ring of the Housesteads commandant; the subject reflects his cultivated tastes (and we must bear in mind the fact that several gems of high quality showing dramatic themes have been found in military contexts), which he would have found difficulty in indulging in northern Britain.

Engraved gems invited amuletic interpretation. Just as a St Christopher medallion may be thought by some people today to protect them on journeys, so for example would an intaglio depicting Hermes (Mercury) have been regarded as a lucky charm for one's financial transactions; and a victory such as the one depicted in Plate XI (c) (from Sandy Lodge, Hertfordshire) would naturally imply success against the vagaries of fortune. True magical amulets come into a different category and belong to the world of eastern thought. Magical legends and devices, the figures of Egyptian deities and the unspoken name of the Jewish God possessed miraculous powers; carved on stones or inscribed on pieces of gold and silver they were secreted about one's person and enabled one to fight the 'powers and principalities' of the demonic world successfully. Our frontispiece shows a remarkable amulet carved on a neolithic stone axe which the ancients would have interpreted as a thunderbolt. The figure is Bes, the god of fertility and joy, who in the Ptolemaic and Roman period was identified with Horus (Harpocrates), venerated as a saviour god. The inscription contains the Hebrew words *Jahweh Sabaoth, Adonai* transliterated into Greek combined with more or less nonsensical sounds and the name of the sun as it occurs in the 'Ephesian Spell'. This may be no coincidence as the stone is alleged to have been found at Ephesus.

After our brief consideration of gems, it may be useful to turn to silver plate and jewellery. These are not the commonest of finds on excavations, but like gemstones they can be extremely informative about the aspirations of their owners. Both body ornament and fine vessels are well known in the 'barbarian' world of the Celts. We know from classical writers (and can assume from graves like those at Vix in France and Klein Aspergle in Germany) that this love of magnificence had a social purpose. The import of classical metalwork into northern Europe, together with wine and other southern luxuries, prepared their owners for the advent of Rome.

The rich in Greek and Roman society liked to boast of their wealth in the same way but with greater sophistication. Trimalchio in Petronius' *Satyricon* pretended to be able to throw away vessels that dropped to the floor as though they were mere pottery vessels, other owners, more circumspect, at least liked to have a display of plate on a sideboard. One such is shown on a Pompeian wall-painting, and a large hoard of silver vessels has been found in the house known as the 'Casa del Menandro'. Sometimes silver vessels were plain or decorated with floral devices, but we find cups with mythological scenes (e.g. at Pompeii, and cups taken from the grave of a chieftain at Hoby in Denmark, where they had arrived by means of trade, loot, diplomatic gift – who knows?) or historical scenes (Boscoreale). A cup which must have been made to satisfy the personal whims of its owner shows youths engaged in sodomy. Perhaps the most important category of plate is religious. A hoard from a temple at Berthouville in France is dedicated to the local manifestation of Mercury. The great silver dish from Corbridge (now in Alnwick Castle) shows a group of deities worshipped on Delos and may commemorate Julian the Apostate's visit to the island in AD 363. Even the 'Neptune Dish' from the Mildenhall Treasure with its lively representation of Bacchus with his followers, satyrs and nereids was probably a piece of temple plate. Illustrated here is the lid of a silver casket (which contained a ceremonial strainer) from the temple of Mithras in London (Plate XI (d)). It depicts men escaping from boxes (? coffins) that are being attacked by griffins, symbolic of destruction and death. We also see an elephant and two panthers: both are animals connected with Bacchus and perhaps they are intended to bring to mind this saviour god who was amongst the Greek deities invoked alongside the 'Persian' Mithras at his temple.

Jewellery could include figured scenes. In recent excavations in London, a gold-worker's studio dating from the reign of Nero was discovered. Some of the pieces of clay with which the crucibles were sealed had impressions executed from the moulds used for stamping out gold plaques. The lion confronting a boar (Plate XII (a)) may have had a symbolic importance although in all probability it reflects the Roman love of wild beast fights. Very rich jewellery is worn by the men and women portrayed in Palmyrene portrait busts. Although such opulence was uncommon elsewhere, we may note the central hair-clasp on the pottery face mask from Toot Baldon (XII (b)). One or two gold frontlets of this sort are known. Bracelets are much commoner and we may note one from Rhayader in Radnorshire which includes Celtic curvilinear scrolls, demonstrating a certain conservatism in fashion amongst the aristocracy of Roman Britain. A common form of bracelet, found at Castlethorpe in Buckinghamshire amongst other places, has snake-head terminals, and this is likely to have some quasi-amuletic significance, for snakes were frequently worshipped (or at the very least held to be sacred) in Greek and Roman times. We need only recall Alexander of Abontoneichos' famous hoax as told by Lucian to see what a hold snake cults had on the popular imagination.

Finally amongst the small objects, with which this section is concerned, we come to ceramics. For the prehistorian pottery has a primary significance, and many archaeologists ascribe an equal value to it in Greek and Roman times – especially in Britain and Germany. Without in any way decrying the excellent work of a large number of scholars on this material, it does seem to me of limited value in assessing classical civilisation as a whole. There are exceptions of course: Greek painted wares must always comprise one of the more important aspects of world art, the more so as almost all Greek mural painting is lost to us (at least in the original); Roman Arretine, and to some extent later Gaulish red wares ('samian') such as the piece illustrated in Plate XII (c), reflect the form and subject matter of the silverware discussed above. That scene of homosexual love-making mentioned earlier finds quite a close parallel on Arretine of the late first century BC. In Britain we may note the necks of certain flagons moulded into the forms of masks (like the Toot Baldon example (Plate XII (b)) discussed in another connection, above), or the lively free-flowing representations of stags and hounds on pots from the factories at Castor, Northamptonshire, which carry a suggestion of the survival of pre-Roman, Iron Age forms.

The more ordinary 'coarse' vessels are often better made than their prehistoric forbears and are usually factory produced: very often in their simple, prosaic forms we feel a sense of timelessness which is the converse of the dynamism that characterises classical civilisation in general. It is salutory to remember that life remains hard and fairly basic for the peasant. His ancestors and descendants observe the rise of empires and their decline, and one culture succeeded by another.

The so-called 'major arts' of painting, mosaic, sculpture and architecture have naturally received the bulk of the classical archaeologist's attention. Indeed it is only by studying such monumental remains as these that we can form an authoritative judgement on the physical context in which life was lived in the ancient world. Both Greeks and Romans appreciated splendour as an expression of the qualities and power of the state. Thucydides in a famous 'archaeological' comment wrote:

Suppose that Sparta were to be deserted and only the temples and foundations of buildings remained, I think that future generations would find it very difficult to believe that the place had really been as powerful as it was represented to be. . . . If on the other hand the same thing were to happen to Athens, one would conjecture from what one saw that the city had been twice as powerful as in fact it is. (I: 10)

Athens was superior to Sparta precisely because of buildings such as the Parthenon and the Erechtheion. Augustus' boast that he had transformed Rome visually in that he had 'left in marble that which he found made of brick' receives the accolade of Suetonius' praise. (Suetonius, *De Vita Caesarum*, XXVIII: 3.) Dio praises Trajan's building mania especially as he did not impoverish anyone and showed singular modesty – 'when the Circus had fallen into decay, he restored it on a greater scale and in a much more beautiful fashion and then added an inscription saying only that he had made it adequate for the Roman people'. (Dio, LXVIII: 7, 1–2.) Ammianus Marcellinus tells an instructive anecdote about Constantius II's wish to emulate Trajan in his building programme, a desire grossly beyond the skill and resources of the fourth-century Empire (Amm., XVI: 10, 15–16).

Although private displays of wealth might have appeared to be hubristic in classical Greece, the Romans encouraged noble ostentation as a sign of one's personal *dignitas*. The same idea was, of course, current in the Renaissance. It is true that Nero broke the bounds of good taste with his enormous *Domus Aurea* (Tacitus, *Ann.* XV: 42–3; Suetonius, *Nero* XXXI), but other emperors indulged in palace building. Hadrian's villa at Tivoli is constructed on a grand scale and employs several idiosyncrasies of plan which reflect the wide travels of its builder. Palaces are rare outside Italy but we may note the residence of (?) the client king Cogidubnus at Fishbourne near Chichester (see Figure 24) in Britain and Herod's palaces in Judea as buildings intended to overawe the subjects of their respective domains. Of course, people other than emperors and kings constructed lavish houses for themselves. The Younger Pliny has left a full description of his mansion at Laurentum (Pliny, *Ep.* II: 17) where he loved to retreat from the heat of Rome. Although the house seems to have been large, it is clear that many of his contemporaries were building on an even more opulent scale. The aristocracy expected to dwell in style and great houses, such as those revealed by archaeology at Sirmione in Italy, Chiragan in Gaul and Woodchester in Britain, were evidently scattered throughout the Empire. Their owners were no doubt frequently *patroni* of their local communities, in which they endowed fountains, statues, baths, theatres and other useful amenities.

In the second century, Herodes Atticus, a very wealthy Greek, embellished the famous Peirine fountain at Corinth and built a concert hall (*Odeion*) in Athens. Documentary evidence from north Africa suggests that the wealthy vied with one another in such acts of munificence. We hear for example of a woman flamen from Calama, Annia Aelia Restituta, who promised 400,000 sesterces for the construction of a theatre, and expenditure on this scale cannot have been unique (Duncan-Jones 1962).

In all Roman building enterprises, decoration played a very large part in achieving a suitable effect. Brick was faced with marble, walls were painted with frescoes or ornamented with stucco, mosaics covered floors and colonnades were lined with statuary. The modern observer viewing a Roman building robbed of these features is likely to regard the architecture of the time as unduly utilitarian. The fantastic caprices of the Pompeian 'third style' paintings or the marble caryatids surrounding 'Canopus' at Hadrian's palace at Tivoli show us how false this impression would be.

Our knowledge of ancient painting owes much to two and a half centuries of excavation in the Campanian cities overwhelmed by the eruption of Vesuvius in AD 79 (Maiuri 1953). However some important frescoes are preserved in Rome, such as the scenes from the *Odyssey* in the Vatican, set in a strange, almost Claude-like, landscape, or the idyllic garden which occupies the walls of a room of Livia's house at Prima Porta. Even in Britain, thanks to areas of plaster falling away from the daub of the house walls in slabs, a surprising amount of wall-painting survives. The illustration shows a detail from a fresco found at Leicester (Plate XIII (a)).

Paintings were often adapted from masterpieces of Greek classical and Hellenistic times. As Pfuhl says, 'actual copies can seldom be pointed to with absolute confidence, but many famous old pictures are undoubtedly preserved to us in their main features' (Pfuhl 1955: 89). Thus Timanthes was probably the originator of the type of the *Sacrifice of Iphigenia* in which Agamemnon is hiding his face, for the Elder Pliny tells us that this artist felt unable to give adequate expression to the king's grief (*N.H.* xxxv: 73). *Perseus and Andromeda* is assigned to Nikias, who worked in the fourth century BC. Of course not all ancient paintings are frescoes. Panel paintings and illuminated manuscripts were known, and the wooden shields from Dura Europos are adorned with painted scenes from mythology that could only have been taken from such small-scale compositions. The famous Virgil manuscripts in the Vatican are not much later than these shields, one of which depicts the fall of Troy (Plate XIII (b)), and are certainly not the first illustrated books to have been produced in the Roman world.

Mosaics, which are merely pictures executed in small pebbles or clips of cut stone, first appear in the fifth and fourth centuries BC at Olynthus and Pella (pebble mosaics). The art reached great refinement in the Hellenistic age both in Italy (e.g. the Nilotic pavement at Palestrina and the Alexander mosaic from the House of the Faun, Pompeii, now in the National Museum at Naples) and in the east Mediterranean (notably on the island of Delos). Mosaic floors are very durable and often survive when the walls of the buildings in which they were laid are reduced to rubble; hence fine examples are to be found throughout the Empire. The best figured pavements are probably the north African series, distinguished by their rich colours and wealth of detail, but even mosaics from Germany (one thinks of the floor depicting Bacchus with maenads and satyrs at Cologne), Gaul (the Circus, shown on a mosaic from Lyons) and Britain (e.g. the fourth-century mosaic from Hinton St Mary, Dorset, with its central emblem of the head of Christ, and that at Low Ham, Somerset, telling the story of the Trojans at Carthage) can be of fine quality.

It is possible to assign mosaic floors to specific workshops, as David Smith has done in the case of Britain. (Smith, 'The Mosaic Pavements', in Rivet 1969: 71–125.) These presumably operated with the help of pattern books that allowed intending patrons to select schemes of decoration before the craftsmen moved in to begin work.

Statues – both copies of Greek masterpieces and new compositions based on them – were executed in bronze and stone. The market was a large one and embraced works of all types, from the larger-than-life size head of Hadrian found in London, perhaps the centre-piece of some public monument, to the miniature figurine of a lar made of bronze and inlaid with silver (recently purchased by the Ashmolean Museum), evidently an ornament from a private Lararium. In Roman times statues were frequently disposed in groups (Vermeule 1968). Good examples of such arrangements are known from Italy (e.g. the Horti Lamiani, Rome and the Grotto of Tiberius, Sperlonga and above all Hadrian's villa, Tivoli). Sculpture galleries are however also recorded elsewhere, for instance at Olympia (Nymphaeum of Herodes Atticus) and in the villa of Chiragan near Toulouse; the latter site has yielded no fewer than seventy marble heads or busts.

Chapter 11

ROMAN BRITAIN

The literary sources for Roman Britain are few in number and of variable quality. It is certain that if study had been limited to the surviving texts or even to inscriptions, Britain would be a relatively little-known province. Instead, thanks to the patient work of classicists, historians, epigraphists, excavators, art historians, geographers and natural scientists, it is a part of the Empire from which many deductions can be made about life in other areas where only the occasional spectacular artefact is ever published.

It has been fortunate for Romano-British archaeology in the twentieth century that it has attracted scholars of the ability of R. G. Collingwood, I. A. Richmond, J. M. C. Toynbee, S. S. Frere and Eric Birley, but the tradition they have been called upon to uphold dates back at least to the time of Camden (1551–1623). Research continues at a faster rate than ever and the recent foundation of a new journal, *Britannia*, augurs well for the future state of scholarship in this field.

In his valedictory lecture as Professor of European Archaeology at Oxford, Christopher Hawkes spoke of the shadowy period that lies between prehistory and history. He claimed, with justice, that much of this disputed ground was the proper subject for the historian. Certainly in the last decades of the pre-Roman Iron Age in Britain, we can perceive dynastic rivalries as bitter and as full of consequence as any in history.

The two most important tribes in south-eastern Britain were the Catuvellauni, whose territory lay north of the Thames in the counties of Hertfordshire and Essex, and the Atrebates, on the south coast in Hampshire and Sussex. The first tribal capital of the Catuvellauni was Wheathamstead (stormed by

Map 9. Roman Britain.

Julius Caesar in 54 BC), but it was later moved to Verulamium (St Albans). Under Cunobelin, the territory of the Trinovantes was captured and the *oppidum* of Camulodunum (Colchester) became the chief city of the kingdom, although a mint continued to operate at Verulamium. The Atrebatic kingdom seems to have been founded by Commius, at one time an ally of Caesar's in Gaul but later his enemy. He fled to Britain resolving never to come into the sight of a Roman again (Caesar, *De Bello Gallico* VIII: 23, 48; Frontinus, *Strategemata* II: XIII,

11). Commius' sons Tincommius (*c.* 20 BC–AD 5) and Verica (*c.* AD 10–AD 40) are the two most important rulers of the dynasty whose capital may have been at Selsey, a site now largely washed away by the sea.

Much of the rivalry between the two peoples was diplomatic and not until a year or so before the Roman conquest was the balance of power seriously overthrown. It is possible that the Atrebates were more favourably inclined to the Roman Empire than their rivals. Verica issued a gold coin depicting a vine leaf, interpreted as a reference to wine which came from Roman provinces. Cunobelin portrayed an ear of barley on his staters signifying home-brewed beer. A few coins of the Catuvell-aunian house are inscribed *Ricon*, probably the Celtic equivalent of *Rex*, the Latin title displayed by kings of the Atrebates. However, as other coins of the Catuvellauni adopt the same name for the ruler, it is somewhat stretching a point to cite this as evidence for nationalistic feeling. Certainly from the time of Tincommius of the Atrebates and Tasciovanus of the Catuvel-launi, the devices on coins were often taken from Roman issues. A few types were evidently inspired by glyptic art (Plate XIV (a) and (b)) which suggests that the cutters of coin dies had access to discarded clay sealings from letters sent to the king or even to actual signet-rings (Henig 1972). Knowledge of how to write and speak Latin cannot have been entirely lacking in pre-Roman Britain.

Roman luxuries certainly circulated. They included wine amphorae, silver drinking-cups, bronze vessels, glass and figurines. The best-preserved and most spectacular items come from tombs, for example those at Welwyn, Hertfordshire, Lexden in Essex, and Aylesford in Kent, but Roman material is also found on occupation sites such as the *oppidum* of Camulodunum.

How long a group of independent but increasingly Romanised states might have survived on the borders of the Empire if the balance of power had not been upset is uncertain. Britain had been officially subjugated by Julius Caesar and both Augustus and Gaius 'Caligula' had been tempted to make this theoretical conquest an actuality. For Claudius, a man who had been placed on the throne in a somewhat undignified fashion in AD 41 and who furthermore suffered from personal disadvantages such as a stammer, there was every reason to prove himself in some military campaign. Britain could offer more than glory. It was thought to abound in metals and it was obviously a source of raw material such as slaves and animal skins.

Cunobelin had been sensible. Although he had expanded his kingdom into Essex, he had carefully refrained from annexing the realm of Verica. On his death *c.* AD 40 his foolhardy sons Caratacus and Togodumnus attempted to do just this. In the first volume of the report on the Fishbourne excavations edited by Professor Cunliffe, Richard Bradley has combined archaeology, topography and history with great brilliance in order to explain a group of earthworks near Chichester. The Chichester Dykes were constructed in three phases and represent the progressive contraction of a system of defence thrown up by the aged Verica against the invaders of his kingdom. In the end he was forced to flee to Rome where his arrival gave Claudius the *casus belli* he needed.

The conquest of Britain was entrusted to Aulus Plautius who commanded four legions (II Augusta, IX Hispana, XIV Gemina, and XX Valeria), each consisting of about 5,000 men. There were also a corresponding number of auxiliaries, non-Roman units generally raised in the frontier regions of the Empire. Both categories of soldier can be illustrated from tombstones found at Colchester. Marcus Favonius Facilis, a centurion of the twentieth legion whose home was probably in Italy, is depicted frontally. His neat hair-style and smart uniform (tunic, breast-plate, belt and cloak) epitomise the discipline and turn-out of the regular units in the Roman army. Longinus, son of Sdapezematygus, mounted on a horse which rides down a nude barbarian, was a member of a cavalry regiment of Thracians. He is clad in scale armour, a form of armour evolved in the Eurasian steppe.

Plautius established the main invasion base at Richborough in Kent and from here the various units fanned out to subdue much of the lowlands. One of the first tasks of the Second Legion under the direct command of Vespasian (the future Emperor) must have been to restore Verica to his throne. Geoffrey of Monmouth may have preserved an account of this in his notoriously inaccurate *History of the Kings of Britain*, written in the twelfth century. The story of King Lear is given a Roman setting. Two wicked princes (Maglaunus and Henvin) drive the king to take sanctuary with Aganippus, surely a corruption of the name Agrippa, ruler of the Franks. The two invade Britain together and are completely successful. However, Lear dies three years after this event. It is now thought that there may have been a considerable rearrangement of civil and military government *c*. AD 48 when the legionary fortress of Camulodunum was replaced by a *colonia*. The friendly Atrebates were evidently confirmed in their status as clients of the Empire, and Verica was succeeded as ruler by Cogidubnus. He is attested by an inscription from Chichester (*RIB* 91) which gives his titles as '*Rex*' and '*Legatus Augusti in Britannia*'. Thus he was both native king and Roman governor. Tacitus (*Agricola* 14) informs us that 'certain states were presented to King Cogidumnus (i.e. Cogidubnus), who maintained an unswerving loyalty right up to our own times'. The palace at Fishbourne, Sussex, with its sophisticated, Italianate plan (Figure 24) was presumably a product of Cogidubnus' last years. The construction and decoration of the palace is remarkable, and although the courtyard, bath suite, frescoes and mosaic floors can be paralleled in ordinary town houses from the Mediterranean area, for example the House of the Exedra at Italica (Figure 25), in Britain we have to turn to the partially excavated Governor's Palace in London for architecture of a similar sort at this early date.

Archaeological evidence for the conquest is found at native sites, such as Maiden Castle, Dorset, where a skeleton from the war cemetery has the tip of a javelin lodged between two of its

(a) Sard intaglio showing Diomedes about to seize the palladium at Troy. From Verulamium (St. Albans) Herts, perhaps second century BC. Scale 4:1

(c) Red jasper intaglio showing victory in a quadriga, from a building at Sandy Lodge, Herts, second century AD. Scale 4:1

(b) Garnet intaglio depicting a dramatic mask in profile. The stone is set in a gold ring, found in the latrine drain of the praetorium at Housesteads, Northumberland, Late first or early second century AD. Length of intaglio 9 mm

(d) Lid of silver casket with figure ornament cast in relief and chased. Designs include wild beasts (e.g. elephant and panther) as well as griffins attempting to prize open coffins with their beaks. From the Temple of Mithras, London. Guildhall Museum, third century AD. Dia. 7.8 cm

XII. (a) Clay luting from goldsmith's workshop, Bush Lane, London, with impressed design of lion and boar. Guildhall Museum, first century AD

(b) Front view of pottery face mask found at Toot Baldon, Oxfordshire. Probably fourth century AD. Scale c. 1:2.

(c) Samian bowl (form: Déchelette 7 with decoration *en barbotine* a appliqué designs, from New Guy House, Southwark. Guildhall Museum, second century AD. Heig about 19 cm

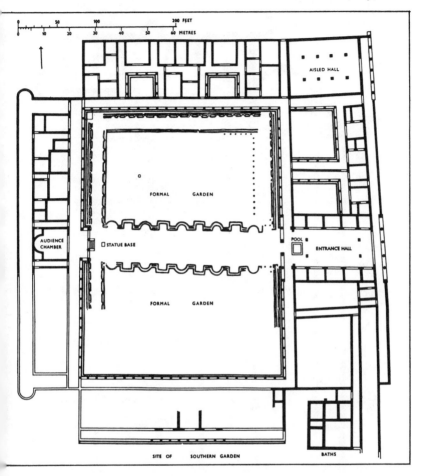

Figure 24. Roman palace at Fishbourne, Sussex.

vertebrae, but the most copious source is from the actual forts of the invading army, for example Hod Hill in Dorset, or Great Casterton in Rutland. These were defended by turf ramparts and the internal buildings were of wood. Simple as these timber structures were, they represented a major advance on native building methods and influenced the design of

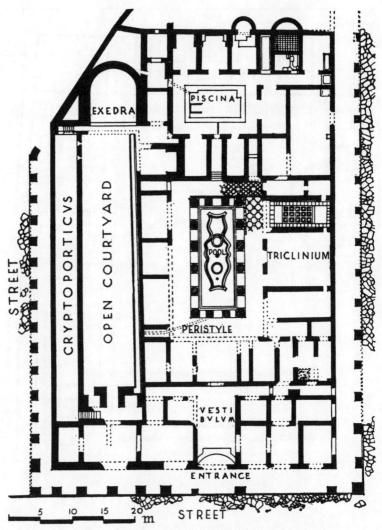

Figure 25. House of the Exedra, Italica, Spain.

commercial and domestic developments in such towns as
London and Verulamium. The status of London, which does
not seem to have had any pre-Roman antecedents, is uncertain,

but Verulamium (as we have seen, an ancient Catuvellaunian capital) became a *municipium*, and Colchester received a new settlement of legionary veterans and was dignified with the name of *colonia*.

The conquest of south-eastern Britain was rather too smooth. Outside the Atrebatic *regnum*, the Romans were both arrogant and self-confident. If the administration had had more sympathy with the native Britons and a more cautious attitude to Romanisation, the rebellion of Boudicca which cost so many lives might have been avoided. Colchester was the 'flash-point' for the revolt (AD 60).

The *colonia* had been founded at the expense of the native Trinovantes who were driven from their land or enslaved. To them the temple of Claudius seemed to be the 'citadel of their eternal domination'. Further north in East Anglia the client kingdom of the Iceni had been incorporated into the province without ceremony and against the wishes of its former king Prasutagus. His wife Boudicca claimed that she had been flogged and her daughters raped; whether this atrocity story was true or not, it was believed. A grasping and unsympathetic procurator Catus Decianus antagonised the Britons by his rapacity, forgetting Tiberius' good advice on such matters: 'A good shepherd shears his sheep, he does not flay them.'

Boudicca and her followers destroyed Colchester, London and Verulamium. Tacitus writes that 'close upon seventy thousand Roman citizens and allies fell in these places. For the enemy neither took nor sold captives. . . . He was hasty with slaughter and the gibbet, with arson and the cross.' (Tacitus, *Ann.* XIV: xxxiii.) Of the Roman forces in the province, one legion (IX Hispana) was badly defeated and another (II Augusta) had its honour stained through the timidity of its temporary commander, Poenius Postumus, who kept the unit in camp. We need not wonder that the governor Suetonius Paulinus pursued a policy of repression after the Boudiccan revolt had been stamped out.

At this point we can see how archaeology can correct the

distortions of aristocratic writers like Tacitus or Suetonius Tranquillus. Nero sent a new procurator, Julius Classicianus, to Britain and accepted his advice about the necessity for conciliation. Classicianus' tombstone, which was found in London (cf. above and Plate X (a)) shows that he was married to a Celtic aristocrat, and it is likely that he came from a similar background himself. Above the layer of ash and burnt daub that marks the Boudiccan sack of London, a new city arose.

The great public buildings of the Romano-British cities date in the first instance from Flavian times and the succeeding age. Although the Tacitean account of Agricola's actions in the winter of AD 79 gives especial prominence to one particular governor in this work of Romanisation, it seems to have begun before Agricola reached Britain and certainly continued for many years after he had left. The forum and basilica as the administrative and commercial centre of a Roman city must always have been a major architectural undertaking (cf. Figure 26) but some, notably those at London and Cirencester were

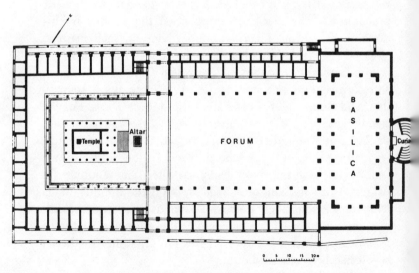

Figure 26. Forum at Augst, Switzerland.

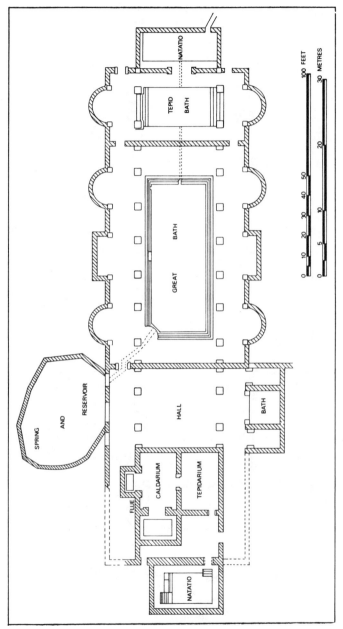

Figure 27. The Roman Baths at Bath, Somerset, in the Flavian period.

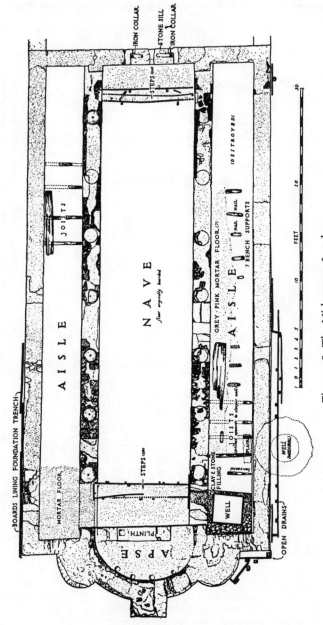

Figure 28. The Mithraeum, London.

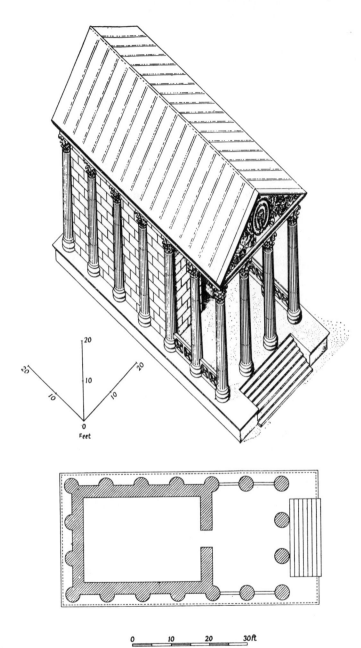

Figure 29. Temple of Sulis Minerva at Bath.

very large indeed by any standard. The baths at Bath (Figure 27) seem to have been built in the late first century, as were those of Silchester. The baths of Leicester were constructed in the Hadrianic age and those at Wroxeter belong to the late second century. It is probable that many of the public buildings found in Romano-British towns were privately financed and this must have been so in the case of temples dedicated to deities not venerated in the state cults, for example the Persian god Mithras or native Celtic gods and goddesses. The illustration shows a plan of the second-century Mithraeum in London, one of the largest known (Figure 28), and also a plan and reconstruction of the temple built in regular classical style at Bath and dedicated to Sulis Minerva (Figure 29). Theatres, as we have seen above, might be private benefactions, and an inscription dated to AD 140/144 from Brough-on-Humber records that Marcus Ulpius Januarius presented a new stage to the Vicus of Petuaria at his own expense (*RIB* 707).

Private houses were given mosaic floors for the first time in the second century. Before that we must assume that simple paving, crushed chalk or limestone (*opus signinum*) or even beaten earth were considered enough. These mosaics are frequently decorative patterns like the one from Bucklersbury in the Guildhall Museum, London, but some show figured devices. A lion holding the head of a stag from Verulamium is particularly fine. In recent years frescoes from walls have been recovered from various sites – Verulamium, Dover, Catterick and Leicester (Plate XIII (a)) – where slabs of plaster have fallen onto the ground to await the skills of the modern archaeologist. Paintings such as these show that the Pompeian third and fourth styles did not cease at the time of the eruption of Vesuvius in AD 79, but continued to be employed in the provinces of the Empire.

Several of the plates have been chosen to illustrate aspects of life in the towns. The fragment of clay luting from a gold-smith's workshop in London (Plate XII (a)) is a reminder that one of the most important functions of an urban community is the manufacture and distribution of consumer goods. Sir Ian Richmond ('Industry in Roman Britain', in Wacher 1966: 76–86) has given a memorable account of the type of manufacture involved:

The stock of goods was not large and many purchases were the result of special orders, the goods being manufactured on the spot. Thus the metal-workers of the Verulamium shops operate their furnaces and smelting-pits in the front part of the premises open to public view, exactly as was seen in medieval towns and as may be seen in a Middle-Eastern town today.

One such special order might have been the pewter spoon from Princes Street with its engraved device on the bowl (Plate XIII (c)). Pewter (an alloy of tin and lead) was a distinctively British product in Roman times and is not found in other provinces. There is nothing local in the device, however, and Bacchus' bird, the parrot, standing on a crater, is certainly an allusion to the god of wine. It is just possible that this Bacchic imagery, which brings the saving, life-giving attributes of the god to mind, was interpreted in a Christian sense. Christian art certainly borrowed many of its forms from other cults that preached salvation, and the bowl of another spoon from London which exhibits three fish is suggestive of Christianity, for the *ichthys* was a common Christian motif.

It is almost certain that there were Christians in Britain in the second century and the Cirencester acrostic – '*Rotas Opera tenet Arepo Sator*' – was probably scratched on plaster at this time (words whose letters can be arranged in the form of a cross together with the letters *alpha* and *omega*, as in the illustration below). But the interpretation of the London spoons must remain doubtful. The silver casket whose lid is shown in Plate XI (d) was certainly associated with religious practice, for not only was it found hidden in the London Mithraeum, but, as we have seen, the scenes shown symbolise the battle between good and evil.

A final object from London, a Samian ware bowl made in

```
      A
      —
      P
      A
      T
      E
A | P A T E R N O S T E R | O
      N
      O
      S
      T
      E
      R
      —
      O
    Acrostic
```

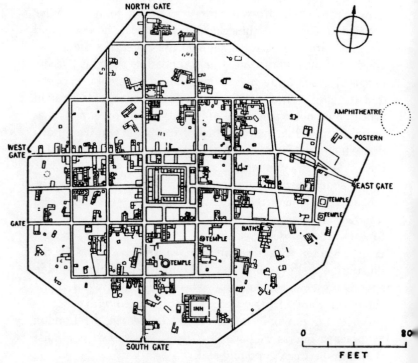

Figure 30. Plan of Calleva Atrebatum, Silchester, Hampshire.

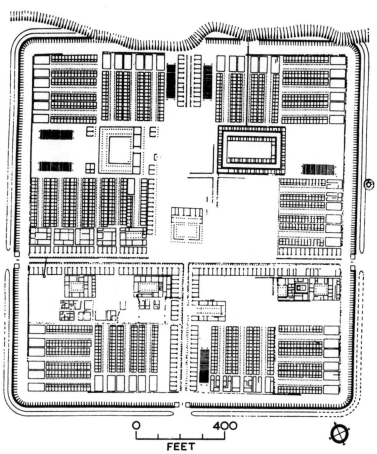

Figure 31. Legionary fortress at Inchtuthil, Perthshire.

central Gaul (Plate XII (c)) has been selected to show that trade with other provinces had great importance in Roman times. A ship carrying Samian ware was wrecked near Whitstable in Kent, and the number of complete pots that have been dredged up from it have given the area the name Pudding Pan Rock. Inscriptions from the Continent show British factors engaged in the importation of pottery and wine to Britain.

The plan of Silchester (Figure 30) shows all the essential

features of a Romano-British city. Within the walls (a third century feature which will be mentioned in due course) there are great public buildings such as the baths, forum and official guest house; a number of temples dedicated mainly to local deities, although a small fourth-century church and a temple dedicated to the Egyptian deities are known as well; and a great many private houses, workshops and shops. Outside the city is an amphitheatre used mainly for wild-animal baiting although gladiators doubtless made an occasional appearance. The Silchester amphitheatre retains its high earth-banks but the internal features are uncertain. It would have looked something like the military *ludus* at Caerleon (Plate XV).

But we have run ahead of our political survey. The story of Agricola's campaigns in northern England and Scotland is enshrined in Roman literature, but it is left to archaeology to fill in the details of the campaigns he conducted between AD 77 and 83. There have been spectacular finds like the fortress at Inchtuthil, Perthshire (Figure 31) excavated by Sir Ian Richmond. It was never finished, for there is no 'palace' for the legionary legate. Agricola's plan to hold down the inhabitable area of Scotland by blockading the Highland passes was abandoned by order of Domitian: '*Perdomita Britannia et statim omissa*' is Tacitus' bitter comment (*Historiae:* I, II). Nevertheless such buildings as were erected, barracks, officers' houses, granaries and hospitals teach us much about the military architecture of the age. There is much to be said for the idea that the period of Agricola's governship in Britain sees the apogee of Roman fort design. Certainly the auxiliary fort at Fendoch, Perthshire (Figure 32), exhibits the same rationality of layout as the legionary fortress.

After Agricola, the next important figure in Romano-British history is the philhellene emperor Hadrian. He came to Britain in AD 122 and it would have been strange if he had not given considerable encouragement to the arts. It is possible that the beautiful relief of a boy charioteer from Lincoln (Toynbee 1962) dates from about this time. It would certainly

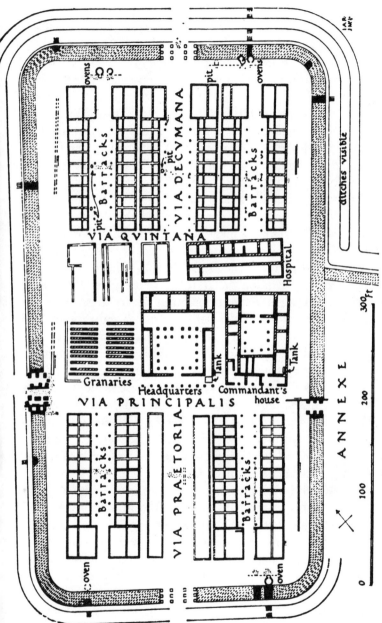

Figure 32. Fort at Fendoch, Perthshire. Scale 1:1800.

be apt, for if on the one hand we are made to think of the ideal-isation of human beauty and the classical heritage of Greece, on the other we are reminded of military organisation, for the boy was probably a member of the *iuventus*, a cadet force which trained the local aristocracy for their service as officers.

Of course, Hadrian's most famous work in Britain was the great wall which forms a barrier across the Tyne-Solway isthmus, a distance of some eighty Roman miles. The frontier consists of a curtain-wall with mile-castles and turrets, a large ditch known as the *vallum* about thirty yards behind, creating a zone of complete military control in order to rule out the possibility of unauthorised crossings, and a small ditch in front of the Wall. Originally forts were constructed well to the rear of the frontier line, but the plan was quickly changed and they were erected on the curtain itself. We have already mentioned the Jarrow inscription (*RIB* 1051) which gives the official account of Hadrian's enterprise, but if we are to get nearer to the full story of the Wall's construction we must rely on the piecing together of many scraps of archaeological and epi-graphic evidence. C. E. Stevens (1966) has written an ingenious but by its very nature speculative book on this very subject.

Hadrian's Wall survived with varying viscissitudes until the fourth century. For a time in the second century (AD 142 onwards) it was replaced by another linear barrier in southern Scotland, only thirty-seven miles across, between the estuaries of the Forth and the Clyde. However the Antonine Wall was not a success and was abandoned by the Severan dynasty in the early third century. The abandonment of Hadrian's Wall meant that on its reoccupation it had to be refurbished, and indeed throughout its history we find individual structures suffering from neglect, accidental fire and perhaps hostile action. The political historian reading inscriptions that are usually all too brief will be tempted to group together de-scriptions of buildings 'fallen down through age' (*vetustate conlabsum*) as a circumlocution covering military disaster (cf. *RIB* 1465, 1738, both from the third decade of the third century), but this is probably wrong. The history of medieval town walls provides perfectly good analogies for the collapse of defensive works through neglect and their subsequent rebuilding.

Hadrian's Wall and its short-lived successor are not the only walls that need to be considered in a discussion of provincial defence. In AD 196 the governor of Britain, Clodius Albinus, withdrew troops to make a bid for the rule of the Roman Empire. It appears that he gave permission for at least certain towns to defend themselves with walls – the wall of London is earlier than the third century – to compensate for the greater vulnerability of lowland Britain. Despite his failure and the victory of his rival Septimus Severus, the programme of fortification was not seriously disrupted. The town walls of Britain surely contributed to the relative security of the province in a time of general lawlessness.

Britain was only marginally affected by barbarians and by civil strife in the third century. She lent support to the Gallic usurpers (*c*. AD 259–74) because they were the nearest effective power, and of course the coasts were troubled by pirates to a greater degree than before. Probably the most serious crisis which had to be faced was the collapse of the currency which could not be avoided by any province however remote or well defended. Local production of coins and downright forgery (the distinction at this time is perhaps not great) were rife.

In AD 287, M. Aurelius Mausaeus Carausius, commander of the Classis Britannica, seized Britain. He attempted to deal with the pirates by systematising the line of defence, known as the Saxon shore, in south-eastern Britain. He did not build all the Saxon shore forts, which are different one from another in construction, shape and date, but it is not until the end of the third century that we can discern the operation of a regular *limes* (frontier) in this area. Carausius also attempted to reform the currency. He reintroduced silver coins and struck bronze *antoniniani* of a larger size than was current in the central Empire. The legends found on his coins are fascinating examples of imperial propaganda. *'Expectate Veni'* echoes Virgil's *'Quibus Hector ab oris exspectate venis'* (*Aeneid* III: 282–3). *'Restitutor Britanniae'*, *'Romano Renova'* and *'Aequitas Mundi'* herald a break with the past and the beginning of a new era. However Carausius attempted to conciliate Diocletian and Maximian by striking coins in their names as well as one issue showing three conjoined heads, *'Carausius et fratres sui'*.

Carausius was murdered by his chief finance officer Allectus in AD 293. Little is known about this man, who perhaps lacked Carausius' flair. His coins were interesting because they seem to depict the actual types of vessel employed by the British fleet (Dove 1971).

Constantius Chlorus managed to invade Britain from Gaul in 296 and Allectus was defeated and killed. The famous gold medallion from the Arras hoard which depicts Constantius being welcomed by a personification of London has the legend *'Redditor Lucis Aeternae'* and bears witness to the relief of the central government at the turn of events. Constantius spent a considerable amount of time reorganising the provincial government of Britain as well as sponsoring various building schemes. The river wall of the fortress of the Sixth Legion was rebuilt with six projecting interval towers and two corner towers on the south and west (the 'Multangular Tower'), and this enhanced grandeur perhaps signified the fact that York was to be headquarters of the *Dux Britanniarum*. British building workers were sent to restore the ancient walls of Autun in AD 298 so the province cannot have lacked skilled craftsmen.

In AD 305 Constantius died at York and was succeeded by his son Constantine the Great. Although the main events of Constantine's reign (and the Emperor's conversion to Christianity) took place outside Britain, there is some reason to believe that the province felt an especial loyalty to his family. On his death in AD 337, his eldest son who was also called Constantine became ruler of the western provinces of the Roman world, but in 340 Constans his brother slew him in the battle of Aquileia. For some reason, and it *may* have been the

XIII. (a) Detail from Roman wall-painting, showing a tragic mask and actor's staff. Found in a second-century town house near the Basilica at Leicester (Ratae Coritanorum). Height of mask 23 cm

(b) Painted wooden shield from Dura Europos, reconstructed by H J Gute. Third century AD. Height 107 cm

(c) Pewter spoon with engraved design in bowl, showing a parrot on a cantharus, from the site at the National Provincial Bank, Princes Street, London. Second or third century AD

Facing page 272

XIV. (a) Silver coin of Cunobelin (reverse) depicting
a griffin. Mint of
Camulodunum (Col-
chester) first century
AD

(b) Silver coin of Cuno-
belin (reverse) depict-
ing Apollo. Mint of
Camulodumum, first
century AD

(c) Bronze statuette of a hound from Lydney Park, Gloucestershire.
Third or fourth century AD. Length about 10 cm

stirrings of revolt, Constans had to hurry to Britain in the winter of 343.

Whatever the truth about the events of 343 – and the part of Ammianus Marcellinus' history which would have told us about it is lost – Britain was deeply involved in AD 350 in the rising of Flavius Magnentius, who was possibly of British origin and certainly very popular in the province. An interesting find from Richborough is a casket attachment showing Magnentius holding the imperial *labarum*, in the form of the Christian *Chi-Rho*. Certainly after the defeat of Magnentius in AD 353, there is good evidence for pro-Magnentian feeling in Ammianus' account of how Constantius II sent the notorious agent Paulus (known as 'the chain' (*catena*) because of his skill in discovering almost endless chains of treasonable talk) to carry out investigations in Britain. Ammianus says (XIV: 5, 6) that 'like a flood he suddenly overwhelmed the fortunes of many, making his way amid manifold slaughter and destruction, imprisoning freeborn men and even degrading some with handcuffs'. He goes on to record 'the impious crime, which fixed an eternal stain upon the time of Constantius' – the way in which Paulus drove the vicar (governor) of Britain to commit suicide.

For Tacitus the Britons were a native people new to civilisation, but Ammianus is able to see the upper classes at any rate as fully equal to the landowning class in other provinces. This should not surprise us if we take time to examine the remains of the 'villa culture' of Britain. Some of the country houses were very large and possessed a number of expensive, mosaic floors, but villas as opulent as those at Woodchester, Gloucestershire, Bignor in Sussex or Brading in the Isle of Wight cannot have been usual. Most were comfortable working farms like that at Sparsholt, Hampshire (Figure 33).

The pattern of life was similar to that described by Ausonius in the Moselle valley during the same period, or by Sidonius Apollinaris in central Gaul around the middle of the fifth century. We have seen that Carausius expected the literate

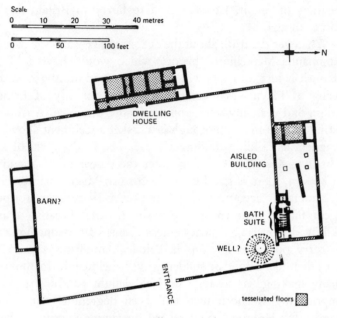

Figure 33. Roman villa, Sparsholt, Hampshire.

classes in Britain to understand a Virgilian reference, so it is no surprise to find a fragment of wall plaster from the villa at Otford, Kent, with the painted legend, '*Bina Manu L[ato crispans hastilia ferro]*' (AEN: I, 313; XII: 165). Nearby at Lullingstone we find further evidence of the high culture to which the British aristocracy aspired. There a mosaic shows Europa sitting on a bull (which is in fact Jupiter in disguise), and it is accompanied by a legend alluding to the first book of the *Aeneid* in which Juno asks the wind god to stir up the elements against the Trojan fleet:

> Invida Si Ta[uri] Vidisset Juno Natatus
> Iustius Aeolias Isset Adusque Domos.

A mosaic from Low Ham, Somerset (now in the museum at Taunton) tells the story of Aeneas' flight from Troy and his infatuation with Dido. In the centre of the floor Venus is shown controlling the destinies of men.

Many of the mythological scenes shown on mosaic floors suggest a knowledge of literature. We find the myth of Lycurgus and Ambrosia at Brading, Ganymede and the eagle at Bignor, and Acteon savaged by his own hounds on the floor of a house in Cirencester. The *Metamorphoses* of Ovid provide a possible source for these.

The use of Latin verse, of which we see one example above, is itself suggestive of a secure, self-confident civilisation. A mosaic at Frampton, Dorset, presumably has a Christian significance for it exhibits the *Chi-Rho*. However the pagan past could not be altogether rejected, for the head of Neptune figures as well, and the legend in heptameters alludes to him:

> Neptuni vertex regmen sortiti mobile ventis
> Scutum cui caerula es[t frons] delphinis cinota
> duob[us].

It should be noted that Christianity and paganism did not always coexist so easily in the fourth century. An inscription (in hexameters) from Cirencester (*RIB* 103) shows the governor of Britannia Prima restoring a Jupiter column originally set up under the 'Old Religion'. This implies former desecration and presumably the inscription dates from the pagan reaction under Julian (AD 360–3). However, the ancient cults enjoyed great prosperity throughout much of the fourth century, and indeed the great shrine at Lydney (Figure 34) was mostly built *after* the reign of the last non-Christian emperor. A mosaic from the site was inscribed with a dedication to the Celtic god Nodens by 'Titus Flavius Senilis, officer in charge of the supply depot of the fleet'. This is now lost, but a splendid bronze figurine of a hound in the site museum (Plate XIV (c)) is evidence of the taste and sophistication of one worshipper at the temple.

Christianity is attested most notably on a mosaic at Hinton St Mary, Dorset. Here the head of Christ himself is shown with

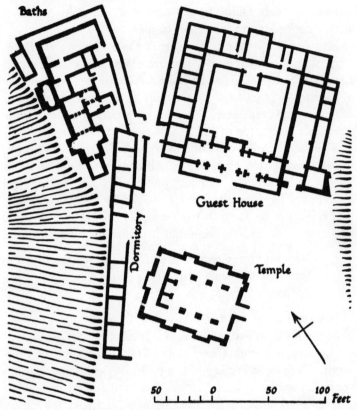

Figure 34. Shrine of Nodens at Lydney Park, Gloucestershire.

the *Chi-Rho* behind his head to make the identification clear. Possibly this room was used as a church. It is of some interest that an adjoining panel depicts Bellerophon slaying the Chimera, a subject which is also found at Frampton and at Lullingstone. The Lullingstone villa has provided the clearest evidence for a 'house-church' in Britain in the form of frescoes that depict the *Chi-Rho* and '*Orans*' figures, praying with raised arms. It is evident that for Romano-British Christians, the Bellerophon theme was thoroughly acceptable as an allegory of the victory of good over evil.

Here we have a clue about the end of Roman Britain, which is far more complex than the familiar and preposterous story of the army of occupation leaving in the year 410. The ancient virtues of self-help appealed to the Britons and to one Briton in particular. Pelagius (and several of his supporters, notably the writer of *De Vita Christiana*) was born in Britain, where sheltered from the harsh realities of barbarian invasion and civil unrest, the quietist doctrines of St Augustine must have seemed like a betrayal of all that the Roman Upper classes held most dear. In particular the idea of divine 'grace' with its overtones of court favouritism (the word *gratia* meant 'influence' in the imperial court) was obnoxious. Zosimus tells us bluntly that in the early fifth century the Britons 'revolted from Rome and lived on their own without obeying Roman laws' (Zosimus VI: 5). A description of this rebellion seems to be preserved in the tract *De Vita Christiana* written in about the year AD 411. Pelagianism was still in the ascendant in 429 when St Germanus came to Britain in order to aid the Catholic faith against the 'heresy'. He found a flourishing state of affairs at Verulamium where the local aristocracy still maintained the forms of Roman town government. Recent archaeological research has demonstrated that this city was indeed thriving until at least the middle of the fifth century.

If we take this as our background the history of the second half of the fourth century can no longer be seen as one of decline. The excavations at Dorchester, Oxfordshire, are especially instructive. Many small coins of the house of Theodosius have been found, showing that Dorchester was a important market town. There are also some pieces of 'Saxon' metalwork, but these belonged to friendly mercenary troops who formed the town's guard. There is no real evidence for a revolt of the *foederati*, and whether or not they are described as 'barbarians' they are not the destroyers of Roman civilisation but its defenders.

Attacks from outside the Empire were another matter. In AD 367 bands of Saxons, Irishmen and Picts swept down on

Britain from the north, ambushed and took prisoner the *Dux Britanniarum* and killed the *Comes Litoris Saxonici* (Ammianus, XXVII: 8, 1). The situation although serious was restored by Count Theodosius, father of the later emperor (Ammianus, XXVIII: 3, 1 ff.,),

In AD 383–4, Magnus Maximus, who made his bid for the imperial throne from Britain (where he was presumably governor), seems to have abandoned Hadrian's Wall (but not before he had led a punitive expedition against the Picts and Scots). This was fatal to the security of northern Britain, and although Stilicho came to remedy the situation in the last years of the fourth century, his primary purpose was to draw off troops for his continental campaigns. The failure of the Roman armies obviously had a marked effect in the unromanised military zone, but, as we have seen, its significance in the civilised lowlands must not be overrated.

CONCLUSION

An exercise too many scholars have attempted is to define the break between the Ancient World and the medieval civilisation that followed it. The question takes too simple a view of history, demonstrating the organic way in which institutions grow and undergo metamorphosis. Thus the authoritarian rule of Septimius Severus (early third century) prefigures the absolution of the fourth century 'dominate', which in its turn foreshadows the Holy Roman Empire of Charlemagne. The rise of the mystery cults in the Antonine Age, the worship of Sol Invictus under Aurelian and the Christianity of the court of Theodosius follow one another as a natural progression.

The excavator sees the buildings he uncovers undergo changes from age to age. Churches such as St Séverin (Cologne) or the cathedral at Xanten in Germany had Roman antecedents. Many Roman buildings were certainly used in the middle ages and beyond. The Praetorium at York was still standing in Saxon times when perhaps it served as a church; the fort of

Portus Adurni (Portchester) became in succession a Saxon burgh and a Norman castle.

If a point must be found at which the civilisation of Antiquity seems to be replaced by something new, I would opt for the second half of the fourth century, when paganism suffered eclipse and Christianity triumphed, for this entailed more than religion: the aesthetic basis of life was shaken.

When St Jerome questioned the necessity for taking baths he was attacking one of the cornerstones of Roman life. Paulinus of Nola, a man marked out for high public office, entered a monastery to the bewilderment of his old tutor Ausonius (whose Christianity was probably no more than nominal). In Egypt and Syria men left the city and its hinterland to fight demons in the desert; the Roman gods demanded civic service.

The reign of Julian shows us the tensions underlying this crisis of the Ancient World. Through his own writings and those of his admirer, the historian Ammianus Marcellinus, we perceive the heroic but doomed struggles of a ruler who rejected the changes in Roman society, and whom we can imagine crying out with Hamlet,

> The time is out of joint; O cursed spite
> That ever I was born to set it right!

As Caesar (i.e. junior colleague) to Constantius II in Gaul (AD 355–60) he defeated the Alamanni and Franks and reduced taxation. Later when he became Augustus and undisputed master of the Roman world (AD 360) he reduced the size of the bureaucracy and tried to counter the oriental pomp of the court with the quiet dignity associated with the philosopher-emperor of the second century, Marcus Aurelius. Above all his reforming zeal was levelled against Christianity, which he regarded as a blasphemous superstition that (unlike Judaism) did not even have the merit of being a national cult. Literature was pagan and a man who did not believe in Homer had no right to teach him. Julian forbade Christians to teach the classics and in so doing almost succeeded in his aims. The aristocracy, pagan or carrying the new faith lightly, would always prefer Cicero to Christ if they had to choose.

If this *had* happened, of course, the Christian middle ages could not have taken place. However Julian decided to emulate Alexander the Great and marched against Persia where he was killed in AD 363. His death-bed speech, which Ammianus records, displays the ideals that Antiquity valued so highly: moderation, faith in the gods, virtue and above all renown. Like Socrates he talks with friends about the nobility of the soul. (Ammianus, XXV: 3, 15–21.) Ammianus says 'he was a man truly to be numbered with the heroic spirits, distinguished for his illustrious deeds and his inborn majesty.' (XXV: 4, 1.)

Compare this with the troubled end of St Augustine, seventy years later:

He ordered the four psalms of David that deal with penance to be copied out. From his sick-bed he could see these sheets of paper every day, hanging on his walls, and would read them, crying constantly and deeply. And lest his attention be distracted from this in any way, almost ten days before his death, he asked us that none should come in to see him. . . . This was duly observed: and so he had all that stretch of time to pray. (*Vita* XXXI: 1–3; quoted by Peter Brown 1967, 432.)

The easy confidence of the last pagan emperor is very remote from the fears of one of the founding fathers of medieval Christendom.

PART IV

MEDIEVAL EUROPE FROM THE FIFTH TO THE TWELFTH CENTURY

David Whitehouse

Chapter 12

THE TRANSFORMATION OF EUROPE

The years between the late fourth and the seventh centuries in Europe are usually known as the Migration Period, because one of their most prominent features was folk movement on a dramatic scale. Peoples from eastern and northern Europe migrated into the Roman provinces; the Roman administration, hamstrung by problems of manpower, inflation and the lack of a regular succession, relinquished province after province. Whereas in the third century Rome governed large parts of Europe, the Near East and north Africa, by 500 the Empire had split into eastern and western sectors and the

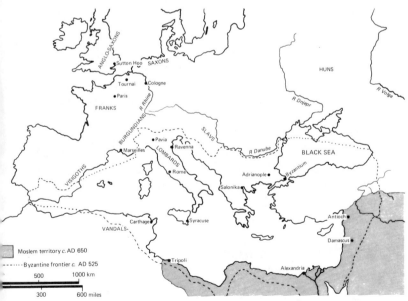

Map 10. Europe in the Migration Period.

283

western part had been reduced to its Mediterranean nucleus. Western Europe no longer consisted of imperial provinces, but of more or less autonomous chiefdoms and states.

By any standard this was a spectacular transformation, and for generations scholars have debated the course of events and the causes that lay behind them. Today it is abundantly clear that the collapse of the western Empire was a long process, for Rome had been labouring under heavy pressure since the third century. On the Danube frontier, the Emperor Decius died with his legions fighting the Goths in 251. In the east, the Sasanian ruler Shahpur I defeated the Romans in a series of frontier wars, culminating in the capture of the Emperor Valerian and his army in 260. A few years later, the Emperor Aurelian felt compelled to build new defences round the city of Rome. Diocletian (284–305) (Plate XVI) made a vigorous – but unsuccessful – attempt to stabilise the situation by political and monetary reforms. The Emperor Constantine (306–36) made a realistic assessment of conditions in the west – and removed his administration to the security of the east Mediterranean.

Meanwhile in the west barbarian pirates had begun to menace shipping in the North Sea and the extent of their activity is indicated by the scale of the Roman response. In Britain, a chain of coastal fortresses was erected from the Isle of Wight to the Wash. Farther north, on the Yorkshire coast, signal stations and naval patrols gave early warning of enemy raids. The *Classis Britannica*, or British Fleet, became a powerful force – so powerful, in fact, that it served as a springboard from which its commander, Carausius, usurped a share in imperial power in 287. On the Continent, bands of rebellious peasants, *bagaudae*, fanned outbreaks of guerrilla warfare. In the confused conditions of the late third and fourth centuries provincial defences were reorganised. Towns were provided with massive walls, and barbarian soldiers and settlers were encouraged to occupy potentially vulnerable areas, thus forming buffers against aggression from beyond the frontiers. The

Franks, for example, first entered Gaul as *laeti* (farmers who formed a peasant militia), and later as *foederati* (larger groups of immigrants) with the permission of the provincial government. At a later date, Hengest and Horsa arrived in Kent at the invitation of Vortigern, a warlord operating in the confused conditions of sub-Roman Britain. In short, by no means all the barbarians were invaders bent on destruction. Many had arrived by invitation and borne the brunt of subsequent attacks on the Roman frontier. In the changing circumstances of the fourth century they often played an important role in local defence. Indeed, by the year 400 the distinction between daily life in the outermost provinces, such as Britain and northern Gaul, and in the lands beyond the frontier, was irrevocably blurred. Long before the incursions of the Goths, the Migration Period was effectively under way.

Thus the Roman frontiers had been under pressure since the third century; in the 350s the barriers broke. On the Iranian border, Shahpur II captured two legions when he stormed the garrison town of Singara in 360. In the far west, a concerted barbarian attack caused heavy damage in 367–9. And in 378 the Goths invaded the Empire, defeated a Roman army and threatened Constantinople itself.

The Goths inhabited the northern shores of the Black Sea, forming two principal groups: the Ostrogoths in the Crimea and the Visigoths, who had defeated Decius, in the Danube basin. To the north and east of the Goths lived the Huns, a semi-nomadic people who were thrown into turmoil in the fourth century by folk movements on the steppes between the Volga and the Dniepr. In a process comparable with the 'domino' effect of the modern political strategist, movement among the Huns unsettled the Goths, who migrated south – into the eastern provinces of the Empire. The army defending Constantinople moved forward to meet the threat. The two forces clashed at Adrianopolis (modern Edirne), only 230 km from the capital. The Romans were defeated and the Emperor Valens was killed. The threat to Constantinople was averted only when Valens' successor, Theodosius I, negotiated a settlement with the Gothic leaders. When Theodosius died, the agreement lapsed and the Goths migrated westwards under the command of Alaric. The Ostrogoths invaded Italy and Alaric sacked Rome in 410. The Gothic rulers in Italy apparently aspired to creating an empire in the west. The last Roman emperor of the west, Romulus Augustulus, was deposed by a Gothic ruler in 476. Under Theodoric (493–526) the churches of their capital, Ravenna, were embellished with splendid mosaics. Throughout Italy, the Roman nobility learnt to live with barbarian overlords; Roman institutions survived; Roman field systems were farmed in the traditional manner, sometimes surviving to the present day (Figure 35).

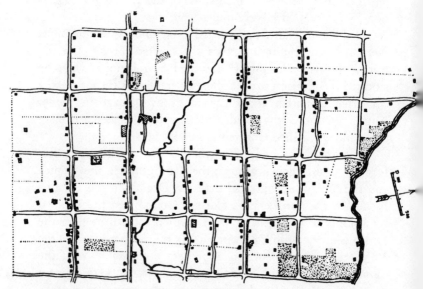

Figure 35. Continuity in the Po valley: the pattern of Roman centuriation surviving as modern roads and field boundaries near Padua.

Meanwhile, the Visigoths established a kingdom in south-west France and parts of Spain. Their authority in France was cut short in 507, when they were defeated by the Franks, but the Spanish kingdom survived for more than two centuries, until the Moslem invasion of 711.

The Franks themselves, who as *laeti* had begun to settle in the provinces of Gaul before *c.* 200, emerged as a political entity and replaced the tottering Roman administration in the later fifth century. Under their first great ruler Clovis (482–511), the Franks defeated the last organised Roman opposition at Soissons in 486. In a series of campaigns the Franks then defined their frontiers. In 534 Theodobert brought the powerful state of Burgundy into the Frankish realm and when he died in 548 the kingdom had reached its greatest extent.

Like the Gothic rulers, the Frankish administration assimilated many features of Roman government and society. Christianity, for example, flourished in the Frankish kingdom. Clovis had adopted Christianity as the 'official' religion and when the Irish monk Columbanus visited the Continent in 588 no fewer than two hundred monasteries existed in Frankia; a century later the number had doubled. Gregory of Tours (d. 594), one of the finest historians of early medieval Europe, describes ambitious ecclesiastical architecture, and we are told that Bishop Nicetus (526–66) rebuilt the huge fourth-century double cathedral at Trier. In the monastic *scriptoria*, a distinctive style of manuscript illustration emerged, based on late Roman prototypes.

Despite their taste for Roman titles – the Byzantine Emperor Anastasius confirmed their right to the term *consul* – and their tolerance of Roman institutions, such as the church, the Frankish rulers did not forget their non-Roman origin. They retained, for example, their traditional code of laws. Frankish nobles dressed in traditional style, wearing flamboyant polychrome jewellery. The earliest royal burial known to us in Frankia is that of Childeric (d. 482), which was found at Tournai in 1653. Most of the rich grave goods have vanished, but engravings made shortly after the discovery show that by 480 a distinctive style of Frankish gold and garnet cloisonné jewellery existed. Rich jewellery also accompanied the burial

OUTER HEBRIDES

IONA

STRATH

DALRIADA

GALLO

ULSTER

WHITE

ARMAGH ●

ISLE OF
MAN

KELLS ●

IRISH SEA

TARA ●

CLONMACNOISE ●

DURROW

● DUBLIN

HOLYHEAD

?

CASHEL ●

SKELLIG
MICHAEL

CORK ●

ST DAVIDS

?

TINTAGEL

TREWI

0   100   200 km

GWITHIAN

.0   50   100 miles

SCILLY ISLES

Map 11. The I

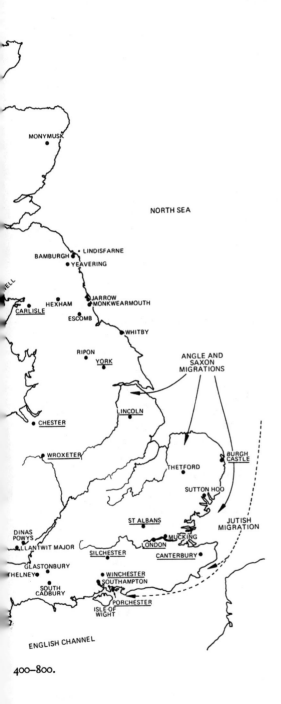

MONYMUSK

NORTH SEA

BAMBURGH • LINDISFARNE
• YEAVERING

HEXHAM •JARROW
CARLISLE •MONKWEARMOUTH
ESCOMB

WHITBY

RIPON
YORK

ANGLE AND
SAXON
MIGRATIONS

LINCOLN

CHESTER

WROXETER

THETFORD
BURGH
CASTLE

SUTTON HOO

ST ALBANS

JUTISH
MIGRATION

DINAS
POWYS
LLANTWIT MAJOR
MUCKING
LONDON
SILCHESTER
CANTERBURY

GLASTONBURY
THELNEY
WINCHESTER
SOUTHAMPTON
SOUTH
CADBURY
PORCHESTER
ISLE-OF-
WIGHT

ENGLISH CHANNEL

400–800.

of a princess and a boy prince found under Cologne cathedral in 1959 and the royal grave, possibly that of Queen Arnegunde (died c. 570) at St Denis near Paris (Plate XVII (a)).

In Britain, we have evidence for several migrations in the fifth and sixth centuries (Map 11). Bede maintained that the invaders from Europe consisted of Angles, Saxons and Jutes; the Byzantine historian Procopius mentioned Frisians; groups from Ireland settled in Scotland, Wales and Cornwall; finally, emigrants from south-west England, perturbed perhaps by the Irish and Anglo-Saxon advances, settled in France. With the collapse of the provincial administration Britain, with its long coastlines inviting settlement and attack from outside the Empire, was even more vulnerable than the provinces on the Continent.

By the early fifth century, Germanic soldiers and settlers were probably installed in many areas of Roman Britain (Hawkes and Dunning 1967). We learn of a 'king' of the Alemanni, Fraomar, commanding a detachment of mercenaries in Britain in the 370s. Several types of late Roman military equipment – distinctive chip-carved buckles and buckle-plates, strap tags, etc. – almost certainly of continental manufacture, and apparently representing continental troops, occur in cemeteries outside towns and military sites. 'Romano-Saxon' pottery, which combines the Roman technique of throwing on a wheel with Germanic styles of ornament, such as stamped motifs and bosses, again occurs in late Roman towns and garrisons. We have an impression of regional governments arranging their own defence in a fast-deteriorating situation.

It was in this confused situation that leaders like Arthur emerged. Behind the hero of later medieval romance we catch glimpses of a native soldier, perhaps the leader of a mercenary band, who fought a series of battles against the Anglo-Saxon invaders. His greatest exploit was the victory at Mons Badonicus, somewhere in southern England (perhaps at Badbury Rings in Dorset), which temporarily halted the Saxon advance.

Without doubt the battle of Badon was an historical event; it is described by Gildas, a polemical Welsh writer (who flourished *c.* 540), and the later medieval *Annales Cambriae* place it in 516 or 518. Arthur, we are told, died at the battle of Camlann, which the Annals date to 537 or 539. In recent years discussion of Arthur has revived, thanks largely to Leslie Alcock's excavations at South Cadbury in Somerset. In 1542, the antiquary John Leland reported that the local inhabitants knew the Iron Age hill fort at South Cadbury as Camallate – Arthur's Camelot. Excavations in 1966–70 (discussed in Alcock 1972) revealed that the hill fort was reoccupied *c.* 460. The old defences were brought back into commission. A spacious timber hall, 19 m long, was built in the interior (Figure 36), and late Roman table wares, imported from the Mediterranean, indicate a prosperous community, perhaps the war band of an

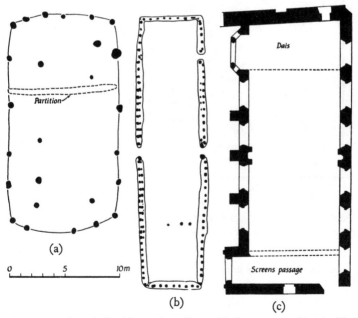

Figure 36. Three halls: (a) South Cadbury (sixth century), (b) Cheddar (ninth century), (c) Exeter College, Oxford (seventeenth century).

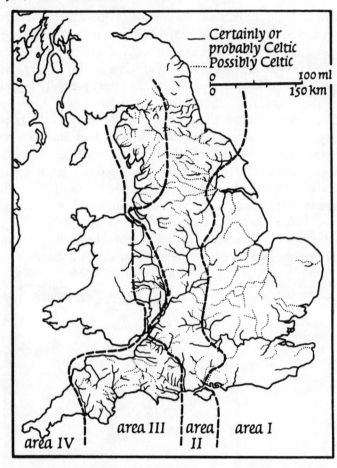

Certainly or
probably Celtic
.......Possibly Celtic

0   100 ml
0   150 km

area III area area I
area IV   II

12(a)

'Arthurian' chief. Leland apart, we have no evidence that South
Cadbury *was* Arthur's stronghold – indeed, as Professor
Charles Thomas (1971) insists, the weight of the evidence
places Arthur in the *north* of England, not the south. Nevertheless, South Cadbury provides a clear example of British defence
in the face of the Anglo-Saxon invasions.

The course of the migrations that overwhelmed the late and

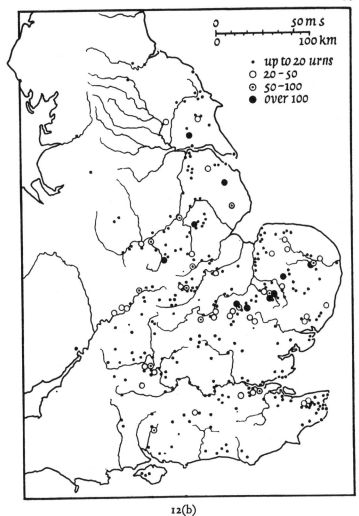

12(b)

Map 12. The impact of Germanic settlement in England: (a) the disappearance of Celtic river names in the east (b) the distribution of Anglo-Saxon cemeteries.

sub-Roman communities of Britain is illustrated by the distribution of archaeological discoveries and by the evidence of place names and language. The most striking evidence of the

Germanic settlement is provided by the philologist. Latin disappeared and was replaced in most areas of England by Germanic languages. Anglo-Saxon provided the roots of the majority of English place names. The map of river names prepared by Professor Kenneth Jackson (Map 12 (a)) shows England and Wales divided into four distinct zones, from the east, where very few Celtic names survive – *Thames* being a notable exception – to the far west, where few Saxon names occur. In eastern England (Area I) Celtic names are rare, but further west, Celtic survivals are much more frequent and many more rivers are shown. (Almost all the rivers of Scotland, Wales and Cornwall of course have Celtic names because they lay outside the area of Anglo-Saxon settlement.) If we consider the spoken language, we find that the transformation was even more dramatic, with literally fewer than two dozen words, *ass*, *brock* (meaning badger) and the colour *dun* among them, surviving from the Romano-British vocabulary.

Archaeology plays a vital part in any attempt to distinguish the various groups of Germanic immigrants. Thus a distinctive type of ornament, known as Jutish Style A, occurs on brooches and other metal objects found in the areas of Jutish settlement in Kent, parts of Wessex and the Isle of Wight. Among the standard features of Jutish Style A are sheet silver inlays, friezes of animal ornament and individual animals with double outlines and spotted bodies, seen to advantage on the famous quoit brooch from a cemetery at Sarre (Figure 37 (b)). Associated with the Saxons, who occupied the Thames valley, Wessex and parts of the Midlands (the county names Essex, Middlesex and Sussex recall the east, middle and southern areas of Saxon penetration), are equal arm relief brooches (Figure 37 (a)), small saucer brooches (Figure 37 (c) and (d)), and other types of jewellery, together with distinctive pottery, notably the so-called *buckelurnen* and 'window' urns. Cruciform brooches represent Anglian settlement in East Anglia, Lindsey, Yorkshire and the east Midlands. Finally, types of pottery and certain East Anglian institutions are thought to

a

b

c   d

Figure 37. Migration Period jewellery in England: (a) equal arm relief
brooch (length 9·4 cm) from Haslingfield, Cambridgeshire; (b) silver
quoit brooch (dia. 7·8 cm) from the Jutish cemetery at Sarre, Kent; (c) and
(d) Saxon gilt bronze saucer brooches (dia. of larger brooch 4·5 cm).

show influence from Frisia, the nearest point of departure for continental settlers moving to England. We find, therefore, that the 'Anglo-Saxon' settlers came from several areas on the North Sea coast: Jutland, Angeln (the land of the Angles, between Jutland and Saxony), north Germany and the Low Countries. They began to arrive in the Roman period, came in growing numbers in the fifth century, and by the end of the sixth century they dominated large parts of a country known thereafter not as Britannia, but England, the Land of the Angles.

We are accustomed to viewing these events as the beginning of a Dark Age, in which civilisation was snuffed out by barbarian hordes. In a sense, this is an understandable assessment; cities disappeared, the market economy collapsed, literacy became a rare accomplishment, imported consumer goods, such as Rhenish glass (Plate XVII (b)), were rare. On the other hand, Anglo-Saxon institutions formed the basis of life in medieval England; Anglo-Saxon farming, with its intensive cereal production, changed the face of the country; Anglo-Saxon technology, though restricted, was far from incompetent; and Anglo-Saxon craftsmen were by no means insensitive. In short, although the contrast between Britain the outpost of Rome and Anglo-Saxon England was great, it was *not* a contrast between light and darkness, civilisation and savagery.

Let us examine two archaeological discoveries: Yeavering and Sutton Hoo. At Yeavering (Northumberland), Dr Brian Hope-Taylor examined the site of a royal residence, evidently the *villa regalis* of Gefrin mentioned by Bede (see below, p. 301). It was at Gefrin that the missionary Paulinus was received by Edwin, king of Northumbria, in 627. Among the major structures found at Yeavering were the post-holes of a spectacular timber hall, 25 m long and a wedge-shaped building, apparently with banked seats like one segment of a Roman amphitheatre – perhaps the meeting-place of the king's council. Throughout the site, Hope-Taylor detected the use of a standard unit of length and careful planning. Clearly, the builders of Gefrin were skilled carpenters prepared to work on a lavish scale, and

XV. (a) General view of the military amphitheatre (*ludus*) at Caerleon

(b) *Ludus*. View of chamber with shrine of (?) Nemesis below
entrance D. First century AD and later

Facing page 296

XVI. The Roman Emperor Diocletian (283–305) and his colleagues. A porphyry sculpture outside St Mark's, Venice

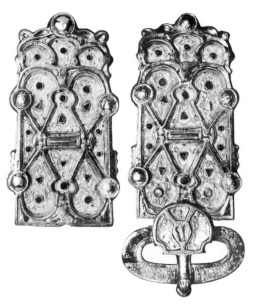

XVII. (a) Jewellery from the tomb of a Frankish queen, possibly Arnegunde, (died *c.* 570), at St Denis, near Paris

(b) The Castle Eden vase, a claw beaker made in the Rhine valley in the sixth century and exported to Anglo-Saxon England

(b) St Mark: a full-page picture from the Lindisfarne Gospels, created in a Northumbrian monastery c. 698

XVIII. (a) The gold belt buckle (length 13.2 cm) from Sutton Hoo, the seventh-century ship burial of an East

the planning and execution of the great hall called for technology of a high order. At Sutton Hoo (Suffolk), C. W. Phillips and a distinguished team of excavators, hastily assembled in 1939, excavated the burial ship of a seventh-century East Anglian king. The grave goods are sumptuous: royal regalia and personal possessions, Frankish gold coins, a Byzantine silver dish and many other imported objects. It is an immense treasure, illustrating the wealth of some of the early Anglo-Saxon rulers. Above all, however, the finds illustrate the skill and sophistication of Anglo-Saxon craftsmen. Most of the jewellery from Sutton Hoo – buckles (including the great gold buckle (Plate XVIII (a)), clasps, etc. – together with the purse mounts, all carried out in gold, with inlays of garnet and glass, was made in south-east England in the first half of the seventh century. It displays a remarkable expertise and sense of design.

Chapter 13

THE END OF THE 'DARK AGES'

On Christmas Day 800 Charles, king of the Franks, was crowned emperor in Rome by Pope Leo III, the first emperor in the west since the Goths toppled Romulus Augustulus in 476. The kingdom of the Franks had developed enormously since the campaigns of Theodobert in the sixth century. Indeed, the whole of western Europe had changed. The new 'barbarian' states were kingdoms. A stratified society had emerged in which the aristocracy and those freed from the land by special skills or responsibilities – notably soldiers – were clearly separated from the peasants: in short, the germ of the feudal system. In many areas, Christianity had become the majority religion and the church was beginning to find new roles, political, social, cultural and economic, in national affairs. Long-distance contacts were renewed by traders, pilgrims and political emissaries.

ANGLO-SAXON ENGLAND, c. 600–800

Let us take as a case history England in the seventh and eighth centuries. In the mid-seventh century – the period of Sutton Hoo – Anglo-Saxon England contained some seven states (the Heptarchy), among which the most powerful were Wessex, Mercia and Northumbria. In each state, a hereditary king occupied the throne, surrounded, even in the seventh century, by his *eorls*, or noblemen. The most famous of all Anglo-Saxon poems, the epic *Beowulf*, describes just such a society. King Hrothgar resides in Heorot, his splendid timber hall (one thinks immediately of Yeavering), surrounded by noblemen and retainers. His kingdom is tightly organised, with coastguards who conduct the hero to Hrothgar's court. The *Laws of Ine*, a document written in the reign of Alfred the Great (876–99) but based on a late seventh-century original, provides us with valuable information on the early society of Wessex. Much is expressed in terms of *wergeld*, the blood money payable by a murderer or his family to compensate the family of the victim. The Wessex aristocrats had a high price on their heads (1,200 shillings), while the *ceorls*, or peasantry, were valued at only one-sixth of that amount.

Within a century, the political situation had changed. Just as the Franks had formed a powerful kingdom by annexing the territory of local rivals, such as the Burgundians, so too in England a larger power emerged. Under Offa (757–96), the Midland kingdom of Mercia expanded, first gaining control of East Anglia and Essex and later embracing Wessex, Sussex and the Isle of Wight. The Mercians held London, and minted coins at Canterbury. In 770 Offa proclaimed his *de facto* position; he was now *Rex Totius Anglorum Patriae*, king of all England – the first man to claim authority over the whole country since the governors of Roman Britain. During Offa's reign, the English currency was reformed and the silver penny (the *Laws of Ine* contain the word *paening*) came into use. This reorganisation was a direct response to Frankish monetary reforms and we know that Offa was in frequent contact with the Franks. Indeed, he clashed with Charlemagne more than once over commercial disputes. In the 790s, it appears, Offa complained to Charles about the size of the 'stones' (presumably lumps of Tournai marble destined to be carved into fonts) exported from Frankia, and Charlemagne retaliated by criticising the short length of the *palliola* ('mini-cloaks') imported by the Franks. From the English point of view, the horizons were certainly broader in the eighth century than the seventh, a development which Offa unconsciously symbolised when he struck a coin in direct imitation of a Middle Eastern *dinar*: even the date, written in Arabic and giving the year 176 after the Hegira, was carefully copied. On the ground, how-

ever, the most imposing monument to Mercian expansion is
the massive earthwork known as Offa's Dyke. The Dyke,
which ran almost without a break from the Severn to the Dee,
protected the western border of Mercia against raiders from
the marches of Wales.

During the period *c*. 600–800 the church became a powerful
element in Anglo-Saxon England. The conversion of the
English was initiated by Pope Gregory I (590–604) and the
first mission, led by Augustine, arrived in Kent in 597. Although the Anglo-Saxons themselves were pagan, the British
Isles as a whole contained numerous Christian communities.
In the fourth century, Roman Britain contained several
Christian dioceses and in the Migration Period Christianity
survived in the monasteries of Ireland, Scotland and Wales.
Indeed, in the seventh century, a major part in the conversion
of the English was played by monks from the 'Celtic' monasteries of Iona and Lindisfarne, while in the eighth century
Irish missionaries travelled to the Continent in large numbers.
During their long separation from Rome, the British com-
munities had developed their own (almost heretical) views on
matters of doctrine. In 663 delegates of the Roman and Celtic
churches thrashed out their differences at the Synod of Whitby.
Rome prevailed and subsequently Theodore of Tarsus,
Archbishop of Canterbury (668–90), organised the English
church into fifteen dioceses, distributed from Northumbria to
Kent.

The church that emerged was governed by two archbishops,
Canterbury and York (although Lichfield had an archbishop
for a short period in the ninth century). Bishops, elected by
their clergy under varying degrees of pressure from the king,
administered the dioceses. Full priests were celibate, usually
literate and, generally speaking, of some social standing. The
poet Caedmon, who became a monk despite his peasant
origins, was thought remarkable.

In England, as on the Continent, Christianity was a *literate*
religion. Monastic libraries were the centres of learning and the

monastic *scriptoria*, in which manuscripts were copied, were in effect the printing houses of Anglo-Saxon England. Bede completed his *Ecclesiastical History* (in Latin) in the monastery at Jarrow in 731; Aedfrith illustrated, or supervised the task of illustrating, the Lindisfarne Gospels in the monastery of Lindisfarne *c.* 696–98. Indeed, the monasteries of Northumbria created a brilliant cultural 'renaissance' in the late seventh and early eighth centuries, combining the traditions of Celts and Anglo-Saxons with the new culture of Rome. Thus the designer of the Lindisfarne Gospels drew on Anglo-Saxon animal art, employing interlocking animals such as occur on the gold buckle from Sutton Hoo; he drew on the 'Celtic' repertoire of curvilinear abstract designs; and finally he incorporated portraits of the evangelists (see Plate XVIII (b)) carried out in Mediterranean fashion – all to illustrate a text based partly, if not wholly, on a Neapolitan original.

CHARLEMAGNE'S RENEWAL

The developments we have just described were of immense importance, for they consolidated the foundations of Anglo-Saxon England. The developments we shall discuss next effected the political and cultural development of the whole of western Europe, for under Charlemagne (768–814) the Frankish kingdom became a powerful empire, which no one in the west could afford to ignore (Map 13). Charles had inherited half of the kingdom from his father Pépin III – it was Frankish custom to *divide* the kingdom among the sons of the deceased ruler. Pépin had been a staunch supporter of the papacy and Charles continued this pro-Roman policy. In the late eighth century, the Pope came into open conflict with the Lombards (the last 'barbarian' group to enter Italy in the Migration Period), who had established a kingdom based on Pavia. In 773 the Franks besieged Pavia, which capitulated a year later. Flushed by this success, Charles assumed the title *Rex Longobardorum* and entered into an even closer relationship with

Map 13. The Carolingian Empire in 814.

Rome. Effectively, the Frankish king was now the champion of the Pope. In 800, Pope Leo III took the unprecedented step of crowning Charlemagne emperor in the basilica of St Peter at Rome.

Charlemagne's Renewal (his biographer Einhard uses the latin *renovatio*) came as a direct result of his strong contacts south of the Alps. What the renewal comprised was this: a deliberate cultural revival in Frankia, based on current

Mediterranean usage. It was *not* a 'renaissance' in the sense of a classical revival; it was a transplant of recent and contemporary culture (Beckwith 1964). The focal point of the movement was Aachen, which Charlemagne chose as his permanent residence in 794. Although the status of Aachen remains in doubt (was it a town or simply a royal residence?), the adoption of a fixed capital was in itself a Mediterranean feature; Charlemagne's predecessors had spent the year in a royal progress through the kingdom, from one centre to the next. The palatine chapel at Aachen (probably dedicated in 805) was built in the style of a polygonal Mediterranean church, reminiscent of the sixth-century church of San Vitale at Ravenna (Figure 38). Else-

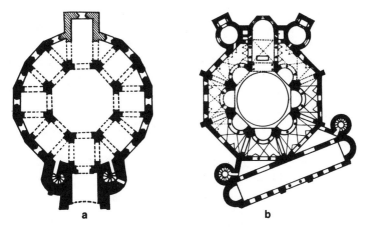

a   b

Figure 38. A Carolingian building and its Mediterranean forerunner: (a) the Palatine Chapel, Aachen (late eighth century); (b) S. Vitale, Ravenna (consecrated in 547).

where in Frankia, the major buildings were planned after Mediterranean originals. The great abbey church at Fulda (dedicated in 819) was based on the basilica of St Peter at Rome, while Theodulf's oratory at St Germigny des Prés (dedicated in 806) has a cruciform plan and is decorated with mosaics of Byzantine type.

Meanwhile, Charlemagne encouraged a literary revival, bringing to Aachen distinguished scholars from all over Europe, among them the Anglo-Saxon Alcuin from York and the historian Paul the Deacon from Lombard Italy. Charlemagne himself, Einhard tells us, made a desperate effort to learn to read, but never succeeded. In the monastic *scriptoria*, a new Carolingian style of lettering and manuscript illustration developed. Indeed, the court style of Charlemagne's Frankia formed the basis of developments in western Europe for generations to come.

WESSEX IN THE NINTH CENTURY

Despite the considerable achievements of Offa, the first English king to create a legend – indeed, the only English king to receive the epithet 'Great' – was Alfred of Wessex (876–99). Nor does Alfred's fame rest on the tale of the cakes alone. In his foreign policy, he made a viable peace with the Danes, who had been campaigning with success in England since 865. At home, he not only created (or so it seems) the first Anglo-Saxon towns (see below, p. 313), but also initiated a programme of educational reform.

The spearhead of Alfred's cultural programme was the English language. When he came to the throne, he tells us, there was hardly a cleric in England who understood the Latin services he conducted. The continued Scandinavian raids had taken a heavy toll on English monastic life and intellectual attainments had suffered accordingly. Alfred's response was severely practical. If the Latin services were incomprehensible, they should be translated. Key works by Augustine and Gregory the Great, selections from Bede's *Ecclesiastical History* and the late Roman philosopher Boethius' *De Consolatione Philosophiae* were all translated into the west Saxon dialect. Alfred himself translated Gregory's *Pastoral Care*. The *Laws of Ine* were revised and the *Anglo-Saxon Chronicle* was assembled from scattered texts and traditions. Meanwhile, the clergy were encouraged to acquire a working knowledge of Latin. Alfred's intention was to foster a *literate* society in which all free men could read their own language.

One artefact is closely associated with Alfred the Great: the so-called Alfred Jewel in the Ashmolean Museum, Oxford. The jewel was found in 1693 near Athelney (Somerset), the scene of Alfred's victory over the Danes and the site of a monastery which he founded. It consists of an oval enamelled plate depicting a half-length figure, the identity of which has given rise to lengthy debate. The enamel is covered by a piece of rock crystal and the jewel is surrounded by a gold mounting which contains the openwork inscription AELFRED ME HEHT GEWYRCAN: 'Alfred had me made.' The function of the object, which ends in a ferrule to receive some kind of rod or pin, is unknown. Its identification as the property of Alfred the Great is generally agreed.

The Alfred Jewel has more than sentimental importance. The style of workmanship, which is matched on a smaller but similar gem from Minster Lovell (Oxfordshire), also in the Ashmolean, shows influence from Carolingian Europe. Other English metalwork, notably the later Saxon disc brooches, including the Fuller Brooch (Plate XX (a)), also reveals Carolingian features, and it is clear that continental influence was felt in England from the ninth century onwards. At the same time, especially in northern and eastern England, Scandinavian motifs appeared – a reminder of the strong influence of the Danish and Norwegian settlers who arrived in Britain in the ninth and tenth centuries (see below, p. 316).

Chapter 14

TOWNS AND TRADE

In the last two chapters we reviewed the 'Dark Ages', during which western Europe was transformed from an integral part of a Mediterranean empire into a group of independent, largely self-sufficient states. For the ancient historian, concerned with the achievements of Roman civilisation, the period was indeed a dark age, for western Europe abandoned the Roman social and economic systems, Roman law and classical literature. For the medievalist, however, it was an essential formative period during which the foundations of medieval society were laid on a basis of more efficient agriculture – and perhaps a higher general standard of nutrition – than had existed under the colonial administration of Rome. Feudal society and the church emerged as potent forces in the life of Everyman. In this chapter, we shall discuss the revival of the European economy, the growth of towns and the resurgence of international trade.

While western Europe underwent a radical change in the period c. 400–800, the east was also changing, although here urban life, a vigorous market economy and international trade continued (Brown 1971). Despite crushing defeats in the seventh century, Byzantium survived; for centuries, westerners were to regard it as a byword for luxury and power. Under Justinian (526–65) (Plate XIX (a)) a partial revival had taken place; Italy was reconquered and north Africa was brought partly under Byzantine control. But in the seventh century, first the Iranians and later the Arabs invaded the Byzantine Empire. Under the last great Sasanian ruler, Khusro II, the Iranians sacked Antioch (in 613), Jerusalem (614) and Alexandria (619), before suffering a decisive defeat at the hands of Heraclius in 627. The war between Byzantium and Iran crippled both combatants. Seizing their chance the Arabs, marching under the new banner of Islam, invaded both empires. The Sasanians were defeated at Qadissiyah (637) and at Niha-vand (640) in the Zagros Mountains, and Iran became a Moslem possession. The Byzantines were defeated at the Yarmuk in 636; Antioch fell in the following year and the Arabs occupied Palestine and Syria. Meanwhile, Moslem troops had invaded Egypt and advanced across north Africa. By 645 they held the whole coast from Tripoli to Suez. Within a century of the Hegira (622), when Mohammed fled from Mecca to Medina and proclaimed a new religion, Islamic rulers administered an empire that spread from Spain to the Indus valley. A concise history of Moslem expansion can be found in Hitti (1953).

But Byzantium survived. The city itself, built on a promon-tory between the Sea of Marmora and the Golden Horn, was almost impregnable (Plate XIX (b)). In the middle ages it was taken only twice: by the Latins in 1204 and the Ottoman Turks in 1453. Although the Empire had been considerably reduced by the Arab conquests and the administration of the surviving areas (now the responsibility of military governors) was con-siderably weakened, a powerful fleet ensured that maritime trade continued. Caravans still crossed the deserts of Syria and the Arabian peninsula, bringing merchandise from Mesopo-tamia, the Persian Gulf and beyond. Byzantium remained the most formidable power in Europe: still the largest, most wealthy individual city; the most tightly governed empire; the *only* state to issue gold currency without a break from Roman times to the Turkish conquest.

THE PIRENNE THESIS

Things were very different in the west. Perhaps the most influential discussion of the early medieval development of western Europe comes from the Belgian historian Henri Pirenne (1862–1935). In a series of books and articles, notably *Medieval Cities* (1925) and *Mohammed and Charlemagne* (1939),

Pirenne put forward a revolutionary view of Dark Age history. The Roman world, he argued – and he was thinking in terms of economy – survived the barbarian incursions of the fourth and fifth centuries, only to collapse under the impact of Moslem expansion. For Pirenne, Islam tipped the balance of power in the west Mediterranean, cut the main commercial arteries and thereby created a vacuum into which the Frankish Empire expanded. 'Without Mohammed,' ran Pirenne's aphorism, 'Charlemagne would be inconceivable.'

The 'Pirenne thesis' had a huge impact on the study of medieval history and, despite numerous objections, his views are still discussed after nearly forty years. Nevertheless, as new evidence accumulates, notably from archaeological research, the Pirenne thesis comes to require greater and greater revision. Pirenne maintained that maritime trade continued in the west Mediterranean until the Moslems in north Africa, refusing to trade with infidels, made the sea lanes impassable. He listed four commodities, previously available in the Frankish kingdom, which went out of use as a result of the Moslem blockade: papyrus, oriental textiles, spice and gold currency. In a critical counterblast, R. S. Lopez (1943) agreed that these items became unobtainable, but disputed Pirenne's explanation. Papyrus, for example, was made in Egypt and the Moslems had conquered Egypt by 641; yet the Franks were still using papyrus at the *end* of the seventh century. Again, gold coins were still minted in Frankia in the eighth century and in Italy *c.* 800. Moreover, Moslems certainly did not refuse to trade with unbelievers on principle; they were trading with Naples in 722 and had colonies in the ports of south China in the ninth century. Thus, instead of a catastrophic rupture of international trade in the west, we see a gradual decline, beginning long before the Moslem invasion and continuing after the conquest of Spain. In the west Mediterranean, population declined, central government collapsed and trade was dislocated by successive barbarian migrations. On the Continent, town life survived under the Franks, but in a modified form. In Britain, the most 'provincial' of all Rome's western provinces, the towns virtually disappeared.

In the Mediterranean, the most vigorous trading state was Byzantium and the survival of international trade in the west owed much to Byzantine enterprise. In Italy, Naples, Amalfi and Gaeta on the west coast, and Bari in the south-east, all thrived under Byzantine governors. In Sicily, Syracuse and Palermo were rich Byzantine ports until the Moslem conquest of the eighth century. After the conquest, Naples and Amalfi traded freely with Islamic cities both in Sicily and north Africa, where the chief city, Qairovan (founded in 671) became a leading commercial centre. Goods might arrive via the ports of Tunis or Mahdiya (founded in 912), or by caravan along the desert route from Egypt. A vivid picture of the scale and intensity of medieval trade in the Mediterranean is emerging from Professor S. D. Goitein's monumental study of the documents from the *geniza* of a synagogue in Cairo. We read of traffic between the Moslem states and Christendom, of fluctuating prices and rates of exchange and of leading bankers, merchants and shippers. (For other documents illustrating the Mediterranean world, cp. Lopez and Raymond (1955).)

Farther north, three cities which later dominated the maritime trade of the Mediterranean – Venice, Pisa and Genoa – emerged as international ports in the ninth and tenth centuries (Luzzatto 1961). Venice, the most cosmopolitan of the three, was already important in the early ninth century. The will of the *doge* (the Venetian head of state) Justinian Partecipazio, who died in 829, reveals him as an ambitious merchant. Venetian supremacy over her competitors was confirmed by the so-called Golden Bull of 992, and in 1082 the Byzantine Emperor Alexius I granted Venetian merchant venturers trading rights throughout his empire. Venice depended wholly on trade. Without the profits of international shipping, the city would have starved; marooned among the salt flats of the lagoon, the Venetians were compelled to buy provisions (grain, wine, etc.) as far afield as Pavia, only 30 km south of Milan.

Meanwhile, Genoa and Pisa were seeking markets in the west. The Pisans sacked the great Moslem port of Palermo in 1072, an event that enlarged their sphere of activity and was celebrated by the construction of a magnificent new cathedral (Plate XXI (a)). In 1088 they renewed the offensive and, with assistance from Genoa and Amalfi, sacked Mahdiya on the African coast. By the end of the middle ages, Genoese captains were visiting the English Channel and the Crimea.

For Pirenne (1925 etc.), the re-emergence of cities north of the Alps was a localised phenomenon. In the tenth century the towns of the Low Countries became the home of a new class of society: the professional merchants, who derived their wealth from long-distance commerce. The weekly market might provide profits of a sort, but the volume of trade was small, and the income proportional; it was the *international* trade in costly merchandise that yielded incomes large enough to finance the new merchant class.

Pirenne's model, with its emphasis on the role of international trade, goes a long way towards explaining the *growth* of cities; it does not explain their birth. Long-distance trade was not the only ingredient in the establishment of urban life in the middle ages. Furthermore, it is clear now that towns did not develop at an early date exclusively in the Low Countries, as Pirenne believed, but in many areas of Europe north of the Alps. Today, historians and archaeologists see the following broad pattern of events (Hensel 1970: Biddle (ed.) 1971). We find first *incipient towns*: settlements, often no larger than agricultural villages, in which some of the occupants lived by specialised non-agricultural pursuits. Such settlements existed in many areas by the ninth century. In Poland and Czechoslovakia, for example, incipient towns, often with earthwork defences, sometimes developed in the shadow of castles. Poznan, Prague and, in Russia, Kiev, all sprang up outside castles. In western Europe, excavations at Duurstede, one of the North Sea ports of the Carolingian period, revealed a large settlement with a surprisingly 'rural' aspect. Size apart, the only indication that Duurstede had a special, non-agricultural function was the discovery of concentrations of imported pottery in particular areas of the site.

The next stage of development north of the Alps saw the emergence of *towns with local rights*: that is, settlements which had a well-defined economic relationship with the surrounding region. They were market centres, supported by their hinterlands, which supplied the region with manufactured and imported goods. Remove the local buyers and suppliers, and the town would collapse. Prague, as described by the traveller Ibrahim b. Jacob in 965–6, was a flourishing centre with a market and a community of specialist craftsmen.

Finally, we have the *developed towns* (towns in Pirenne's sense of the word), each with a particular place in the wider network of national rights and duties and an interest in international trade. The towns of Norman England fall into this category, as perhaps does pre-Conquest London.

It is instructive to compare the sequence of development of towns in early medieval Europe with the emergence of the first towns of all in western Asia (see above, p. 169), where intensive agriculture made it possible for communities to support what were by the standards of medieval Europe large cities, specialist craftsmen and merchants.

URBAN ORIGINS: ENGLAND

But what of urban origins in England where, as we saw on pp. 290–7, the majority of Roman institutions disappeared in the upheavals of the Migration Period? Ten years ago, the conventional view was that town life ceased in Britain in the fifth century; the Anglo-Saxons and their colleagues, arriving from north-west Germany, the Low Countries and Denmark – mostly areas outside the frontiers of Rome's 'urban' provinces – introduced a rural economy in which villages were the focal points and towns were redundant. Today the picture has changed. Although the fifth century remains one of the darkest periods of the so-called Dark Ages, excavation and re-evaluation of the written evidence have shed a glimmer of light on the end of urban life in the former provinces of Britain. At Canterbury, for example, Professor Frere discovered fifth-century *grübenhauser* (huts with sunken floors) built on the same alignment as the Roman streets. Associated with the huts was the 'Anglo-Frisian' pottery of the Germanic settlers. In a brilliant review of the evidence for Anglo-Saxon towns, Martin Biddle (1971) suggested that here we have evidence of the cantonal capitals of Roman Britain falling into the hands of Germanic immigrants, perhaps the *foederati* who arrived at the invitation of local commanders. The evidence of the Romano-Saxon pottery (see p. 290), which occurs on urban and strategic sites, seems to support such a view.

Granted, however, that life in some of the towns of Roman Britain continued after 400, what was the scale of the occupation and how long did it last? When in 596 Augustine met the king of Kent, he did so at Canterbury; according to Bede, in 628 Paulinus was received within the walls of Lincoln by the *praefectus* of the town; we hear of Frisian merchants in London in the seventh century and Bede calls the place an *emporium*. Should we assume that here, if nowhere else in Britain, some semblance of urban life survived? In the case of Canterbury, Biddle's answer is no. Augustine encountered a royal centre, broadly comparable with the royal and religious centre that existed at Winchester between the seventh and the ninth centuries; he did *not* encounter a town with a market economy. Although the site of Canterbury may have been occupied continuously from Roman to medieval times, it was not always occupied by a town. Certainly this is the direction in which the present evidence points. We may wonder, however, whether the germ of urban institutions did not survive in some of the towns of eastern England, such as Canterbury, London, Lincoln and York.

Be that as it may, the general pattern is clear: from the fifth century England was a rural society. At the same time, it is

XIX. (a) The Emperor Justinian (527–65). From a sixth-century mosaic in S. Vitale, Ravenna

(b) The land walls of Constantinople, built by Theodosius II (408–50)

XX. (a) The Fuller Brooch, an Anglo-Saxon disc brooch of nielloed silver made in the ninth century

(b) The prow of the Oseberg ship, designed c. 800 for coastal voyages and buried with the possessions of a Norwegian queen, possibly Åse, shortly before 900

XXI. (a) Pisa: the cathedral, begun in 1063 to celebrate the sack of Palermo, which opened the way to Pisan expansion in the Mediterranean. In the background the Campanile (begun in 1137)

(b) Norman cavalry in action: a scene from the Bayeux Tapestry, embroidered in southern England or Normandy in the late eleventh century

(b) The Palatine chapel, Palermo (begun in 1132), an amalgam of Byzantine mosaics and Islamic architecture and decoration

XXII. (a) The White Tower, keep of the Tower of London, begun by William the Conqueror in 1066 to protect

equally clear that in 1066 towns were common. The view that towns were reintroduced *after* the Norman Conquest, disputed by James Tait in his classic *Medieval English Borough* (1936), is now known to be wrong. Indeed, by the time of the Domesday survey at least 10 per cent of the English population lived in towns. What happened between 400 and 1066; when was urban life re-established in England?

Although 'incipient' towns may have existed before the ninth century – we hear of markets in London and Rochester, for example – the establishment of true towns throughout southern and eastern England apparently dates from the reigns of Alfred (876–99), his son Edward the Elder and his daughter Aethelflaed, and her husband Ethelred. In response to the Scandinavian invasions of the ninth century, the rulers of Wessex established a network of *burgs*, or fortified settlements, which served as the focus of local defence. The majority of burgs had earthen defences, but some, such as Cricklade and South Cadbury, were fortified in stone. Much of our information on the original function of the burgs comes from a document known as the *Burghal Hideage*, an assessment of the manpower necessary to defend the strongholds of Wessex in the period 911–19. In the Midland kingdom of Mercia, other documents provide information on a similar programme of defence: Aethelflaed built earthworks at Tamworth, Stafford and at least eight other centres, while the decaying Roman walls of Chester were restored.

Charters and other late Saxon documents reveal something of the institutions which the burg might contain. Some of the strongholds, such as Oxford and Wallingford, seem to have been 'urban' from the beginning and, after defence, an important function of the burg was to provide the setting for an expanding market economy. Thus the charters speak of markets; in 858 we hear of the first recorded guild, the *cnihtengild* at Canterbury; we hear of the role of the church in promoting urban affairs – and we hear of the mints. For the burgs housed the mints of late Saxon England. More than

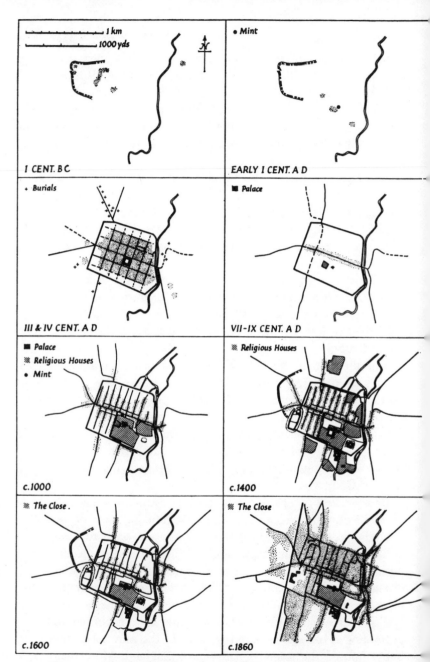

Figure 39. The development of an English town: Winchester from the Iron Age to the nineteenth century.

sixty in all, the mints were rigidly controlled by a central authority responsible for issuing new dies and maintaining a fixed standard of purity. After the monetary reforms of Edgar (959–75) the English *penny*, struck in silver, displayed the name of both the mint and the moneyer, in addition to a portrait of the king.

THE ARCHAEOLOGY OF TOWNS

All over Europe – from Bergen to Byzantium, literally – medieval archaeologists are turning their attention to towns and the problems of urban origins and development. This flurry of interest comes partly as a result of the growing importance of archaeology in medieval studies and partly because of the pace of modern urban renewal. Whole quarters of our medieval towns are demolished for redevelopment and the loss of information is incalculable. Fortunately, archaeologists are now making strenuous efforts to repair the situation; urban archaeology is an established aspect of the archaeological scene in Britain, and even areas in which medieval archaeology of any kind was slow to develop now boast urban excavations. Italy, for example, has inquiries under way in Genoa and other towns.

In Britain, the most ambitious excavation of a medieval town carried out to date is at Winchester, where the Winchester Research Unit, directed by Martin Biddle, has combined the results of careful excavation, architectural survey and historical research to assemble an account of the development of the town from the pre-Roman Iron Age to the present day (Figure 39). Among the medieval areas investigated are the Anglo-Saxon minster, a Norman palace, the castle and a large area of dwellings, workshops and a church. Another ambitious project began recently in York, potentially one of the most informative sites in Britain, and among many smaller excavations one should mention Thetford, Southampton, Norwich and Stamford.

Chapter 15

THE IMPACT OF THE NORTH

In the preceding chapters, we discussed some of the developments of the early medieval period: the emergence of a new social order, the growth of independent states in western Europe, the 'renaissance' of the Carolingian period and the re-establishment of an urban economy. In this chapter, we shall look at the changes that followed the expansion of the Vikings and of one of their settlements, Normandy. We take up the story towards the end of the eighth century and leave it c. 1100, when Norman rulers held territory as far apart, and as different, as northern England, Sicily and Antioch in Syria.

THE AGE OF THE VIKINGS

Suddenly, in the late eighth century, a new power entered the arena (Wilson 1970; Foot and Wilson 1970). From their homeland in Scandinavia, the Vikings – raiders, settlers and merchants – ventured farther and farther afield until their influence extended from Greenland to the Volga (Map 14). The Vikings comprised not one but several cultural groups, and they never became a unified state. Nevertheless, many of their activities were broadly similar whether they originated in Denmark, Norway or Sweden, and we may discuss the Vikings in general terms, with only occasional reference to regional variation.

The Vikings appeared first as brigands. Beginning c. 780, Viking fleets conducted a series of raids on the coastal settlements of the North Sea and Ireland. Alcuin of York, writing at Charlemagne's court c. 800, was only one of the witnesses who recorded these raids: 'Never before has such terror appeared in Britain. . . . Behold the church of St Cuthbert spattered with the blood of the priests of God, despoiled of all its ornaments [Lindisfarne had been sacked in 793]; a place more venerable than all in Britain is given as prey to pagan peoples.' Alcuin, of course, was a Christian, and the Vikings were notorious pagans. The *Anglo-Saxon Chronicle* contains a long list of raids on Britain, beginning in 789 and growing in frequency after 835. On the Continent, Viking flotillas raided the ports of the Carolingian Empire and the Cordovan caliphate in Spain. Duurstede was burnt in 834, Quentovic in 842; in 844 Vikings attacked Lisbon, Cadiz and Seville. Even farther afield, a Viking fleet operated in the Mediterranean in 859–62, raiding the coasts of Provence, Liguria and Tuscany. They ravaged Pisa and occupied Luni, mistaking the small town for Rome and one of its priests for the Pope!

Despite their reputation in Christian Europe, the Vikings were not simply pirates. Indeed, it was Viking merchants and colonists who made a more lasting contribution to European development. In the west, land hunger compelled would-be emigrants to explore the north Atlantic, equipped with the most sophisticated ships then available in north-west Europe. In the east, Viking merchants created trade routes between the Baltic, Russia and western Asia.

At their best, the Viking ships were superb (Plate XX (b)). The vessels interred with the rich burials at Gokstad, Oseberg and Tune, all on Oslo Fjord in Norway, and the block-ships scuttled in Roskilde Fjord, Denmark, tell us much about Viking ships, which enabled colonists to visit regions that hitherto had lain beyond the reach of European sailors. The Gokstad ship, buried *c.* 900, was made of oak, with decking, mast and oars of pine. It was clinker-built and measured 23·3 m long by 5·25 m in the beam. The keel was a single baulk of oak, and a massive block contained the mast. Although only the lower part survives, it appears that the mast was about 10 m high. It had a single yard, which carried a striped woollen sail. The ship was built for thirty-two rowers. The Viking ships

GREENLAND

ICELAND

ARCTIC CIRCLE

NORTH
ATLANTIC

FAEROE IS

SHETLAND IS

ORKNEY IS

BALTIC
SEA

OSLO-
FJORD

BIRKA

NORTH
SEA

LINDISFARNE

GOTLAND

ROSKILDE

DUBLIN

YORK

WISKIAUTE

HEDEBY

LONDON

TRUSO

WOLLIN

QUENTOVIC

ROUEN

CAROLINGIAN

EMPIRE

VENICE

CORDOBA

ROME

PALERMO

KAIROUAN

MEDITERRANEAN SEA

TRIPOLI

0   1000 km

0   500 miles

Map 14. The

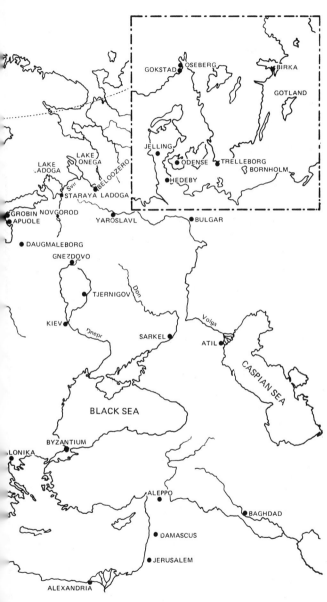

GOKSTAD OSEBERG BIRKA

GOTLAND

JELLING

ODENSE TRELLEBORG
BORNHOLM
HEDEBY

LAKE
ONEGA
LAKE
LADOGA BELOOZERO

Svir
STARAYA LADOGA

GROBIN NOVGOROD
APUOLE
YAROSLAVL BULGAR

DAUGMALEBORG

GNEZDOVO

Don

TJERNIGOV

Volga

KIEV
Dnepr
SARKEL
ATIL

CASPIAN SEA

BLACK SEA

BYZANTIUM

LONIKA

ALEPPO

BAGHDAD

DAMASCUS

JERUSALEM

ALEXANDRIA

ne Vikings.

were markedly superior to their forerunners in northern Europe. The fourth-century Nydam ship, for example, sunk as an offering in a Danish swamp, had only a rudimentary keel, as apparently did the boat from Sutton Hoo. In 1893 a replica of the Gokstad ship was sailed from Europe to America under an experienced master, Magnus Anderson. The crossing took twenty-eight days and Anderson reported that the boat handled well at speeds of 10 or 11 knots.

Viking expeditions began to penetrate the coastal kingdoms of western Europe in the ninth century. Settlers from Norway founded a 'kingdom' in Ireland, with the capital at Dublin, in the 850s, and in 851 a Danish army first wintered in England. In 867 the Danes occupied York and in the following year they invaded Mercia. In 869 they advanced into East Anglia and in 870 attacked Wessex. Six years later they annexed Northumbria. Large areas of northern and eastern England now contained Viking settlers and even in the eleventh century much of the region was known as the *Danelaw*, for Danish laws and customs were prominent. Although we have surprisingly little material evidence of the Danish settlement, its extent is revealed clearly by the wide distribution of place names containing Danish elements. The suffixes -*by* (as in Derby) and -*thorpe* (Scunthorpe) are Danish, and at the time of the Domesday survey, described on p. 329, 40 per cent of the place names in the East Riding of Yorkshire were Scandinavian.

In an attempt to buy their safety, the English paid an annual tribute, the proverbial *Danegeld*, to the invaders. However, it was not until 886 that peace was obtained when Alfred, king of Wessex (870–99), made terms with Guthrum, securing his own frontiers at the cost of northern and eastern England, which he ceded to the Danes.

Viking activity in the more remote regions of the north Atlantic followed a different course, and we are fortunate to possess not only archaeological evidence but also the detailed historical or quasi-historical information preserved in the *sagas* – epic poems describing places, personalities and events

(Jones 1968). Compared with western Europe, the Faeroes, Iceland, Greenland and the coast of North America were sparsely populated, and as a result the Viking settlement was much more peaceful than in Britain. The first Scandinavians probably reached the Faeroes *c.* 800, a century after their discovery by Irish monks. The Irish writer Dicuil (*c.* 825) and the Icelander Are Frode (*c.* 1130) maintain that anchorites from Ireland also discovered Iceland, where the first Viking explorers landed *c.* 860. Clearly the Irish colonies were small, for the Vikings found Iceland abundant in fish and game. Farming, whaling and hunting seal offered a good living and by *c.* 930 Scandinavian colonists, mostly from Norway, had occupied most of the habitable areas. The names of the leading settlers are preserved in *Landnámabók*, an Icelandic work of the thirteenth century.

According to the sagas, Greenland was sighted first *c.* 980, and in 985, after exploring the coast, Erik the Red, a Norwegian exile, led an expedition of twenty-five ships carrying colonists from Iceland. They established two main settlements, centred on Eriksfjord and Godhåb on the south-west coast. The settlement in Eriksfjord, known as Brattahlidh (modern Qaqssiarssuk) is one of several excavated sites in Greenland, where Viking communities survived in increasingly isolated and impoverished conditions until the fifteenth century. It was from Brattahlidh that Lief, the son of Erik the Red, set out *c.* 922 to make the first European landfall in America. According to the sagas, the new continent had been discovered in 986 by Bjarni Herjolfsson. Blown off course west of Iceland, Bjarni sighted a low forested coast, completely unlike the glaciers of Greenland. Lief Eriksson revisited this coast, which he named *Markland*, landed and then wintered farther south, in an area which he named *Vinland* after its vines. For forty years it appears that Viking expeditions attempted to explore and colonise the coast, but after indifferent success and skirmishes with the Indian or Eskimo inhabitants the project was abandoned. Until recently, no plausible object of Viking origin was known in America. However, excavations at L'Anse aux Meadows in northern Newfoundland have revealed a settlement with houses of apparently Scandinavian type, dated by C14 to the eleventh century, and it seems likely that we have here the first tangible evidence of Viking settlement in America.

Although Viking merchants operated in Atlantic waters and in the North Sea, they established their most ambitious trading network in the east. During the ninth century, Viking merchants, mostly from Denmark and Sweden, established a trade route through Russia to the Black Sea and the Caspian. Merchants from Baltic entrepôts, such as Hedeby in north Germany and Birka on Lake Mälar in Sweden, travelled first to Staraya Ladoga, east of Leningrad. Thence two routes were available. The first led to Novgorod and Gnezdovo (modern Smolensk), where it met the river Dniepr, which flowed past Kiev to the Black Sea. Travellers along the Dniepr were usually bound for Byzantium, which the Vikings knew simply as *Miklegarthr*, the Great City. Here, the Scandinavians had obtained special trading concessions, and until the eleventh century the prestigious Varangian Guard was recruited almost exclusively from Viking mercenaries. The second route to the south took merchants down the Volga to the Caspian Sea, whence roads led eastwards to the great caravan cities of central Asia – Bokhara, Samarqand and Balkh – to Chorezm and south to Baghdad.

A Moslem writer, Ibn Fadlan, has left us a detailed account of a Viking ship burial on the Volga in 922. The man was placed in a boat, lying on a bier draped with silk. He was dressed in fine clothes and equipped with food, drink, his weapons and a lyre. The women of his household were slaughtered and placed on the ship, as was his dog. The whole assemblage was burnt. The Vikings then raised a barrow over the ashes and marked it with a pole bearing the name of the deceased.

According to the *Nestorian* or *Primary Russian Chronicle*, which was compiled at Kiev in the twelfth century, the Russians originally invited Scandinavian overlords to settle in Novgorod and other towns *c.* 860. This statement has given rise to fierce debate, with some scholars regarding Novgorod as virtually a Viking town and others consistently emphasising its local character. Certainly, as excavation has shown, Novgorod was essentially a Slav town by the eleventh century and Viking influence – if it was ever profound – must have been short-lived.

No such dispute surrounds the importance of Viking trade in the east. In Scandinavia, finds of more than 85,000 Islamic coins – Byzantine pieces are strikingly rare – attest the volume of furs, walrus ivory, slaves and other merchandise dispatched to the south, while the graves at Birka have yielded fragments of Chinese or central Asian silk, a vivid reminder that international trade was one of the Vikings' most solid achievements.

THE NORMANS

Despite their activities in the north Atlantic and their distant trade connections in the east, perhaps the most astonishing of the Vikings' achievements was the success of one small settlement in western Europe. For Normandy, carved out of Frankish territory by settlers from Norway or Denmark in the early eleventh century, underwent a phenomenal phase of expansion *c.* 1050–1100 (Map 15). During this period, the Normans not only conquered Anglo-Saxon England, but also created a kingdom (Sicily) and a principate (Antioch) in the Mediterranean (Douglas 1969). Indeed, it is arguable that Norman influence in the political and cultural life of the Mediterranean was greater than that of the Carolingians, five centuries earlier.

In 911 Hrolf, a Norwegian or Danish adventurer who had previously campaigned in Ireland, raided the coast of France, pressing inland to Chartres. Here he was defeated by the Emperor Charles III. In return for their formal submission, Charles granted the Vikings land in the lower Seine valley, below Rouen – a move which the Franks were soon to regret.

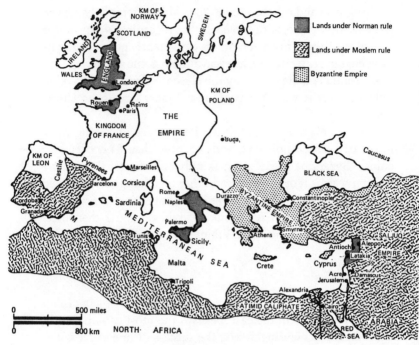

Map 15. Norman expansion, c. 1050–1100.

By 918 the Vikings had captured Rouen; by 932 they had advanced to the river Couesnon, which remained the boundary between the Norman duchy and Brittany throughout the middle ages. Later chroniclers maintain that the Viking expansion was accompanied by a reign of terror and we know that the Frankish church was disrupted. Nevertheless, numerically the Viking element was small, few Scandinavian place names exist in Normandy and the Viking aristocracy quickly absorbed the Latin learning of the Franks. Indeed, by 1050 the rulers of Normandy had adopted Christianity as their official religion, established a close relationship between church and state and organised their country on a feudal basis. They spoke French and used a Frankish title, *duke*, to distinguish their leader.

Between 1050 and 1100 Norman magnates came to power in England, Italy and Sicily, and played an important role in the first Crusade. They were ruthless, opportunist and extremely efficient. The brutal 'harrying of the north' by William the Conqueror had echoes in Sicily, Calabria and in the sack of Rome (1084), when Norman soldiers massacred many of the inhabitants. In the north, the Normans had long-standing connections with Anglo-Saxon England. In 991 the two states had signed a kind of mutual defence treaty and in 1002 King Ethelred II married Emma, daughter of Duke Richard I. When between 1016 and 1042 the Danes acquired temporary control of the Anglo-Saxon kingdom, members of the English royal family fled to Rouen. In 1051 Edward the Confessor appointed a Norman, Robert of Jumièges, as archbishop of Canterbury. Norman writers even maintain that Edward nominated Duke William II to succeed him as king.

When the Confessor died in January 1066, the most powerful English earl, Harold of Wessex, was acclaimed his successor. William was not the only ruler to dispute Harold's accession, for Harold Hardraada, king of Norway and the most influential ruler in Scandinavia, also claimed the throne, conscious (no doubt) of the large Scandinavian element in the English countryside.

The crisis of 1066 moved to a rapid climax, in which timing was an important factor. Hearing of Harold's coronation, William prepared a Norman fleet and the Anglo-Saxons prepared to defend the south coast. Then on 18 September Hardraada landed at the mouth of the Humber and was joined by rebels from the north. On the twentieth, the English were defeated at York. Learning this, Harold drew his crack troops from the south coast and the home counties and by forced marches reached Yorkshire by the twenty-fifth. On that day the English won a crushing victory at Stamford Bridge; the *Scandinavian* threat had been averted. Two days later, William made a night crossing and on the twenty-eighth the *Normans* landed unopposed. William disembarked an army of some

7,000 men, including cavalry and archers. Harold returned to the south. He was in London by 5 October and after an abortive delay awaiting reinforcements (which never came) he advanced to the south coast. Instead of waiting for the Normans' supplies to run out, Harold immediately prepared for battle; he probably feared defections from his battle-weary troops if he delayed too long. On 14 October, making full use of his archers and cavalry – detachments which the Anglo-Saxons did not possess – William won a decisive victory at Battle near Hastings. The English resistance collapsed.

Meanwhile, the Normans had established themselves as a growing force in southern Italy, where the Byzantines (based in Bari), the papacy, the Moslem emirate of Sicily and the duchy of Benevento were all jockeying for power. Norman mercenaries appeared on the scene first in 1017, fighting for the Beneventans against Byzantium. In 1029 they received a grant of land at Aversa from the ruler of Naples and with this as a base steadily consolidated their foothold in south-west Italy. Soon afterwards a second group of Norman adventurers arrived in the south, led by Guillaume d'Hauteville. In 1041 the newcomers seized Melfi, a Byzantine frontier town on the east side of the Apennines. By 1043 d'Hauteville was the most powerful man in Apulia, a position shortly recognised by the creation of a Norman duchy. Four years later, Robert Guiscard, a younger brother of Guillaume d'Hauteville, came to Italy and from this moment Norman activity took an even more determined direction. In 1053 the Normans defeated a papal army at Civitate in northern Apulia, but some years later, having made themselves the virtual rulers of the south, they agreed terms with the Pope. In 1061 Guiscard invaded Sicily, transporting his army, equipment and cavalry across the Strait of Messina in a naval operation that foreshadowed William's invasion of England, five years later. Palermo, the capital and richest port of the Sicilian emirate, still recovering from the Pisan attack (see above, p. 310) fell in 1072, taken from the Moslems by Norman troops urged on in the name of the church. In the words of Professor David Douglas, Palermo was now 'with the single exception of Constantinople, the largest and richest city in the world under Christian government'. A year previously Bari, the Byzantine headquarters in Italy, had fallen after a protracted siege. With the cities of Bari, Palermo and Syracuse and ports on the west coast of Italy such as Salerno and Amalfi in their possession, the Normans now controlled an extremely rich and powerful state. Indeed, their only rivals were the Byzantines and the Fatimids and their allies in north Africa.

The Normans, who in Normandy had welded church and state and in Italy had made an alliance with the Pope, were prepared – when the circumstances suited them – to espouse the cause of a Holy War. They had stormed Palermo in the name of God and in 1096 they took part in the first Crusade. Bohemond, a half-brother of Robert Guiscard's son Roger, emerged as a brilliant crusader general. In 1098 he led the assault on Antioch, taking personal possession of the city and installing a Norman garrison. Once more, the papacy adopted a realistic approach to Norman affairs and in 1100 the papal legate invested Bohemond with the title Prince of Antioch, establishing a dynasty which outlasted the Norman dynasties of England and Sicily. Thus at the end of the eleventh century, Norman kings ruled in England and Sicily and a Norman prince governed a crusader state in Syria.

Without doubt, an important ingredient in the Normans' success was their military strength. Norman armies were efficient and well equipped – and not only by the standards of north-west Europe. The Byzantine Empress, Anna Comnena, described Bohemond's troops in tones of considerable respect. Characteristically, the Normans were well disciplined; they co-ordinated land and naval movements with confidence and skill, and in the field they were masters of the feigned flight, a ruse demanding the firmest control. In their cavalry, they possessed some of the most devastating shock troops in Christendom, for at Civitate, Hastings and Antioch, the

Norman cavalry was decisive. The Bayeux Tapestry, a pictorial account, 70 m long, of the battle of Hastings and the events that led up to it, is an unconscious – or perhaps half-conscious – celebration of Norman cavalry. From the moment the Normans take the field, the Tapestry is full of their cavalry; a quarter of the whole embroidery depicts Norman horsemen (Plate XXI (b)). After victory, the Normans policed their new territory ruthlessly, planting castles at key points throughout the country. They learnt this strategem in Italy in the 1050s and applied it to England immediately after the Conquest; the Tower of London was begun in 1066 (Plate XXII (a)).

With Norman rulers in western Europe, the Mediterranean and the Near East, it is hardly surprising that many of the intellectual developments which make up the 'twelfth-century renaissance' took place in areas of Norman domination. This is not to claim that a *Norman* renaissance occurred – Normandy itself provided few important intellectuals – but rather that frequent communications between one Norman state and another probably created a climate in which ideas were rapidly diffused. In Italy, the great abbey of Montecassino underwent a revival during the rule of Abbot Desiderius (from 1058 to 1087, when he became Pope Victor III). The monks of Monte-cassino were in touch with the Byzantine world and added Greek learning to their considerable Latin scholarship. Farther south, in the Norman city of Salerno, a university and pioneer medical school developed. In Sicily, Norman rulers commissioned buildings and architectural ornament from Italian, Moslem and Byzantine craftsmen (Plate XXII (b)). The moslem scholar Edrisi worked under the patronage of a Norman king, and many western scholars first came into contact with Islamic science and literature in Norman Sicily. In England, an ambitious programme of building, both ecclesiastical and secular, followed hard upon the Norman Conquest, and scholars like Lanfranc and Anselm (both north Italians) were imported to revitalise the church according to the Norman pattern.

NORMAN ENGLAND: THE DOMESDAY SURVEY

At Christmas 1085 William I held a Council at Gloucester. The most important outcome was the so-called Domesday Book, a detailed survey of the king's possessions and income, and all other land, livestock and wealth. The purpose of the survey was practical; in order to rule efficiently, William needed to know exactly what his kingdom contained, and what income he might expect in both goods and services. The Domesday commissioners examined the kingdom shire by shire, noting the situation in the time of Edward the Confessor, in 1066 and again in 1086. The surveys were then sent to a central registry, perhaps at Winchester, where they were rearranged so that analyses of each shire showed who held the land. The survey is incomplete. We have, for example, no return for London, the largest town in the realm; we have no figure for the population of England – Domesday was not a census in the strict sense of the word – although we do have sufficient evidence to estimate a total of about one and a half million. Nevertheless, the Domesday Book represents the most ambitious survey of people and property attempted anywhere in medieval Europe. It is a mine of information on the population, society and economy of Norman England. The paragraphs that follow describe conditions in England under the Norman kings in the light of the Domesday returns.

England in the eleventh and twelfth centuries was a rural society. Indeed, to modern eyes, the country would seem almost empty, with large areas of woodland, scrub and swamp separating the villages, for settlements (though numerous) were small and scattered. In many cases, these areas were ripe for settlement. H. R. Loyn (1962: 332) makes the point: 'The expanding frontier lay not in the wide open spaces, but in the heart of the long-settled shires.' Expansion certainly occurred, though on a smaller scale than during the surge of population growth in the thirteenth century. The moated farmsteads of East Anglia, the south and the Midlands, dating from the twelfth century and later, represent new settlement in marginal land which was previously uncultivated.

Most of the population – an estimated 90 per cent in 1086 – lived on the land, usually in small settlements where production revolved round the manor. By no means the whole of England was organised on a manorial basis and in many areas, such as the eastern counties, the manor was a much looser organisation, with lords holding land in several settlements, than it was in Wessex, where most villages had a single lord. The English manor had evolved gradually during the Anglo-Saxon period from the royal or noble estate, which offered protection in return for such duties as bearing arms or tilling the fields. A comparable development affected the lands of the church, strengthened by the doctrine of obedience which St Benedict had enjoined. In the troubled times of the Scandinavian invasions, the bond between the protector and the protected became still stronger. Thus by 1086 the manor (*manerium*) was already assuming some of the rigid features it contained in the thirteenth century: a distinct territory, a lord with prescribed rights of jurisdiction and a bound peasantry.

What was the position of the peasantry, the great mass of the English population, in 1086? There is no short answer to the question, as the analysis by R. Lennard (1959) indicates. Indeed, as Lennard states, we find four principal categories of peasant, with diminishing degrees of personal freedom. At the top of the scale are the *liberi homines*, the free men, followed by the *villani*, then the cottagers, and last of all the slaves (*servi*). In 1086 the great majority of peasants (some 75 per cent) were classified as *villani*. These were not the 'villeins' of the thirteenth century; they were a heterogeneous class, many of whom were prosperous farmers with 30 or 40 hectares of land and a team of oxen for ploughing. They rendered goods and services to their lords, but retained a fair measure of freedom. At the bottom of the ladder were the slaves, a diminishing class, perhaps because the Normans found it more expedient to call on free peasants than to support totally dependent slaves. The

Anglo-Saxons had been unrepentant slave-owners and ports like Bristol were notorious markets for human cattle. In 1066 fully 9 per cent of the recorded population were slaves; by the thirteenth century, slavery had vanished.

In the country, the Domesday commissioners were concerned primarily with arable land, for in most regions villages derived a living from the fields. Bread was the staple diet and a large part of the arable land was devoted to growing corn. The Domesday Book records more than 5,600 mills, many of which earned handsome revenues by grinding flour for the neighbouring settlements. The mills were driven by water. Tide mills were built in some of the estuaries, but most mills derived their power from carefully contoured leats which drew water from a river, higher up the valley. At Old Windsor, Dr Brian Hope-Taylor excavated a pre-Conquest mill with three vertical wheels turned by water from a leat more than a kilometre long.

The countryside contained other sources of wealth. In some areas, fishing provided an important part of the diet. The Fens yielded rich harvests of eels and the village of Doddington (Cambridgeshire) rendered no fewer than 27,150 eels a year. Off the south and east coasts herrings were equally abundant; Sandwich in Kent yielded 60,000 herrings per year to the abbey of Christchurch, Canterbury, while Beccles rendered a mere 40,000 to the monks of Bury St Edmunds. The Domesday Book records 65 fisheries at Tidenham (Gloucestershire), and although these may have been small basket weirs, they represent a considerable potential catch.

Throughout the country, woodland provided three vital ingredients of the rural economy: firewood, timber for building and – above all, in 1086 – pannage for swine. The manor might boast sufficient oxen for several plough teams, but it possessed few dairy cattle and in the lowlands, which were still extensively wooded and poorly drained, swine were a valuable source of meat. The chase, of course, also provided meat, but hunting rights were restrictive and jealously preserved. Poaching was a dangerous pastime and most people probably obtained only rabbits and other small game.

Locally, a valuable raw material might provide the basis for industrial development. Quarries provided millstones and stone for building, for with the introduction of ambitious building on a nation-wide scale masons were demanding special materials for jambs, moulding and weight-bearing elements. In the weald of Kent and Sussex, the Forest of Dean and other regions, a regular iron industry developed. Derbyshire mines were already rendering the archbishop of Canterbury a yearly quota of lead valued at 300 shillings in 835. Droitwich and other centres marketed salt. Cornwall produced that rare commodity, tin.

And what of the towns? As we saw in Chapter 14, the towns of late Saxon England were small, but viable – indeed, centres like London, Lincoln and York flourished. In 1066 many of the towns suffered serious damage. Although London was spared, Lincoln lost some 250 houses; in 1066 Domesday Book records 1,150 inhabited houses, 166 were demolished to make way for the castle and in 1086 the number was down to 900. It was by no means exceptional. The Norman army was ruthless in its creation of castles to pin down the country, dominate the towns and control the roads, fords and rivers. Nevertheless, the towns recovered, and grew. In 1086, London probably had a population of about 10,000; Lincoln, York and Norwich may have contained 6,000–7,000 inhabitants; Ipswich, Oxford and Thetford were slightly smaller, each with about 5,000 occupants. Most of the towns held regular markets, as did many smaller settlements. The Domesday survey records numerous *burgesses*, who rendered dues in the borough, presumably from the proceeds of trade. Rural manors, too, might play a part in the market trade of the town by acquiring a house, which served as business premises or a store. In Chichester, for example, 142 houses were owned by manors. This was just one aspect of the close connection between town and country in Norman England; all towns possessed arable and housed large numbers of agricultural workers. Towns committed wholly to commerce (like medieval Venice) or to industry (like nineteenth-century Manchester) had yet to appear on the English scene.

BIBLIOGRAPHY

PART I. EARLY MAN

This list comprises those books referred to in the text, with a few useful references added. Simpler books are marked with an asterisk.

* Bordes, F., *The Old Stone Age* (London 1968)
   Bourdier, F., *Préhistoire de France* (Paris 1967)
* Brace, C. L., *The Stages of Human Evolution* (Englewood Cliffs 1967)
   Breuil, H., *Les Subdivisions du Paléolithique Supérieur et leur Signification* (International Congress of Anthropology and Prehistoric Archaeology, Geneva 1912)
   Butzer, K., *Environment and Archaeology* (London 1964)
   Campbell, B. G., *Human Evolution* (London 1966)
   Clark, J. D., *The Prehistory of Africa* (London 1970)
   Collins, D. M., *Culture Traditions and Environment of Early Man* (Chicago 1969)
   Coon, C. S., *The Origin of Races* (London 1963)
   de Beer, Sir G., *Embryos and Ancestors* (Oxford 1958)
   de Mortillet, G., *Musée Préhistorique* (Paris 1881)
   Garrod, D., 'The Upper Palaeolithic in the Light of Recent Discovery', *Proceedings of the Prehistoric Society* 4:1 (1938)
   Giedion, S., *The Eternal Present* (Oxford 1963)
   Jolly, C., 'The Seed Eaters', *Man* 5:1 (London 1970)
   Leakey, M. D., *Olduvai Gorge*, vol. 3, (Cambridge 1971)
   Leroi-Gourhan, A., *The Art of Prehistoric Man in Western Europe* (London 1968)
* Life Books, *Early Man* (New York 1966)
* Oakley, K. P., *Man the Toolmaker* (London 1961); *Frameworks for Dating Fossil Man* (London 1964)
   Oakley, K. P., and Campbell, B. G., *Catalogue of Fossil Hominids* (London 1967, 1972)
   Penck, A. and Bruckner, E., *Die Alpen im Eiszeitalter* (Leipzig 1909)
   Peyrony, D., 'La Ferrassie', *Préhistoire* 3:1 (Paris 1934)
* Pfeiffer, J., *The Emergence of Man* (London 1970)
* Pilbeam, D., *The Evolution of Man* (London 1970)
   Robinson, J., 'The Genera and Species of the Australopithecinae', *American Journ. of Phys. Anth.* 12:181 (1954)
   Tauber, H., *The Scandinavian Varve Chronology and C14 Dating* (Nobel Symposium 12, Stockholm 1970)

Washburn, S. L., *Classification and Human Evolution* (New York 1963)

West, R. G., *Pleistocene Geology and Biology* (London 1968)

West, R. G., 'Pleistocene History of the British Flora' (in *Studies in the Vegetational History of the British Isles* (Cambridge 1970)

Wymer, J., *Lower Palaeolithic Archaeology in Britain* (London 1968)

PART II. LATER PREHISTORY

For general reading

Childe, V. G., *What Happened in History* (Harmondsworth 1964); *New Light on the Most Ancient East*, 5th edn (London 1954); *The Dawn of European Civilisation*, 6th edn (London 1957); *The Prehistory of European Society* (Harmondsworth 1958)

Clark, G. and Piggott, S., *Prehistoric Societies* (London 1965)

Clark, J. G. D., *Prehistoric Europe. The Economic Basis* (London 1952)

Lamberg-Karlovsky, C., *Readings in Old World Archaeology* (New York 1972)

Piggott, S., *Ancient Europe* (Edinburgh 1965)

Renfrew, C., *The Emergence of Civilisation. The Cyclades and the Aegean in the Third Millennium BC* (London 1972)

Renfrew, C. (ed). The Explanation of Culture Change. Models in Prehistory. (London 1973)

Ucko, P. J. and Dimbleby, G. W. (eds), *The Domestication and Exploitation of Plants and Animals* (London 1969)

Ucko, P. J., Tringham, R. and Dimbleby, G. W. (eds), *Man, Settlement and Urbanism* (London 1972)

More specialised reading

Braidwood, R. J. and Reed, C., 'The Achievement and Early Consequences of Food Production: A Consideration of the Archaeological and Natural-Historical Evidence' in *Cold Spring Harbour Symposia on Quantitative Biology*, 22 (1957): 19–31

Braidwood, R. J. and Willey, G. R. (eds), *Courses Toward Urban Life* (Edinburgh 1962)

Clark, J. G. D., 'Radiocarbon Dating and the Spread of the Farming Economy', *Antiquity* 39: (1965) 45–8

Deevey, E. S., 'The Human Population', *Scientific American* 203: 195–204

De Navarro, J. M., 'Massilia and Early Celtic Culture', *Antiquity* 2 (1928): 423–4

Hole, F. and Flannery, K. V., 'The Prehistory of South-Western Iran. A Preliminary Report', *Proceedings of the Prehistoric Society* 33 (1967): 147–206

Masson, V. H., 'The Urban Revolution in South Turkmenia', *Antiquity* 42 (1968): 178–87

Mellaart, J., *Çatal Hüyük. A Neolithic Town in Anatolia* (London 1967)

Murray, J., *The Origins of European Agriculture* (Edinburgh 1971)

Renfrew, C., 'The Autonomy of the South-East European Copper Age', *Proceedings of the Prehistoric Society*, N.S. 35 (1969): 12–47; 'The Tree-Ring Calibration of Radiocarbon: An Archaeological Evaluation', *Proceedings of the Prehistoric Society* N.S. 36 (1970): 280–311

Thom, A., *Megalithic Sites in Britain* (Oxford 1967)

Trewartha, G. T., *A Geography of Population World Patterns* (New York 1969)

Wynne-Edwards, V. C., 'Social Organisation as a Population Regulator' in Brothwell, D. and Higgs, E. (eds), *Science in Archaeology*, 2nd edn (Bristol 1969)

Yengoyan, A. A., 'Demographic and Ecological Influences on Aboriginal Australian Marriage Sections' in Lee, R. B. and De Vore, I. (eds), *Man the Hunter* (Chicago 1968)

PART III. ARCHAEOLOGY AND THE CLASSICAL MIND

All Ancient authorities are potentially useful and translations of most of them are to be found in the Loeb Classical Library. A number of texts have also been translated for Penguin Classics.

The great *Corpus Inscriptionum Latinarum* (abbreviated *CIL*) will doubtless never be superseded in its entirety, although some volumes can be replaced by more recent works (e.g. R. G. Collingwood and R. P. Wright, *The Roman Inscriptions of Britain* I (abbreviated *RIB*) (Oxford 1965).

The following list is a selection of useful studies dealing with the ancient world and more particularly with Roman civilisation. Easier works are asterisked.

For general reading

* Balsdon, J. P. V. D., *Life and Leisure in Ancient Rome* (London 1969)

* Boardman, J., *Greek Art* (London 1964)

  Boëthius, A. and Ward Perkins, J. B., *Etruscan and Roman Architecture* (Harmondsworth 1970)

  Brown, P., *Augustine of Hippo: A biography* (London 1967); *The World of Late Antiquity* (London 1971)

  Charbonneaux, J., *L'Art au Siècle d'Auguste* (Paris 1948)

  Collingwood, R. G. and Richmond, I. A., *The Archaeology of Roman Britain*, 2nd edn (London 1969)

Cook, R. M., *The Greeks until Alexander* (London 1961)

Cunliffe, B. W., *Fishbourne. A Roman Palace and its Garden* (London 1971)

de la Maza, F., *Antinoo el Ultimo Dios del Mundo Clásico* (Mexico 1966)

Ferguson J., *The Religions of the Roman Empire* (London 1970)

Frere, S. S., *Britannia: A History of Roman Britain* (London 1967)

* Grant, M., *The World of Rome* (London 1960); *The Climax of Rome* (London 1968)

Grimal, P., *Les Jardins Romains*, 2nd edn (Paris 1969)

Higgins, R. A., *Greek and Roman Jewellery* (London 1961)

Lawrence, A. W., *Greek and Roman Sculpture*, revised edn (London 1972)

* Licht, H., *Sexual Life in Ancient Greece* (London 1932)

McDonald, A. H., *Republican Rome* (London 1966)

* Maiuri, A., *Roman Painting* (Geneva 1953)

Mattingly, H., *Roman Coins* 2nd edn (London 1960)

Merrifield, R., *Roman London* (London 1969)

Momigliano, A. (ed.), *The Conflict between Paganism and Christianity in the Fourth Century* (Oxford 1963)

* Reece, R., *Roman Coins* (London 1970)

* Richmond, I. A., *Roman Britain* (Harmondsworth 1955)

Richter, G. M. A., *The Engraved Gems of the Greeks, Etruscans and Romans*, 2 vols (London 1968, 1971)

Rivet, A. L. F. (ed.), *The Roman Villa in Britain* (London 1969)

Strong, D. E., *Roman Imperial Sculpture* (London 1961); *Greek and Roman Gold and Silver Plate* (London 1966)

* Syme, R., *The Roman Revolution* (Oxford 1939)

Toynbee, J. M. C., *Art in Britain under the Romans* (Oxford 1964); *The Art of the Romans* (London 1965)

Wacher, J. S. (ed.), *The Civitas Capitals of Roman Britain* (Leicester 1966)

Webster, G., *The Roman Imperial Army* (London 1969)

White, K. D., *Roman Farming* (London 1970)

Wightman, E. M., *Roman Trier and the Treveri* (London 1970)

* Zimmern, A. E., *The Greek Commonwealth*, 4th edn (Oxford 1924)

More specialised reading

Dove, C. E., 'The First British Navy', *Antiquity* XLV (1971) 15–20

Duncan-Jones, R., 'Costs, Outlays and Summae Honoriae from Roman Africa', *Papers of the British School at Rome* XXX (1962): 47–115

Henig, M., 'The Veneration of Heroes in the Roman Army: The Evidence of Engraved Gemstones', *Britannia* I (1970): 249–65; 'The

Origin of some Ancient British Coin Types', *Britannia* III (1972): 209–23

Pfuhl, E., *Masterpieces of Greek Drawing and Painting*, 2nd edn (London 1955)

Richmond, I. A., 'The Roman Siege Works of Masada, Israel', *JRS* LII (1962): 142–55

Seznec, J., *The Survival of the Pagan Gods* (New York 1953)

Stevens, C. E., *The Building of Hadrian's Wall* (Kendal 1966)

Toynbee, J. M. C., *Art in Roman Britain* (London 1962): 159–60, no. 86, pl. 88

Vermeule, C., 'Graeco-Roman Statues: Purpose and Setting', *Burlington Magazine* CX (1968): 545–58, 607–13; 'Some Erotica in Boston', *Antike Kunst* XIII (1969): 9–15 and plates 4–8

Wainwright, G. J., 'The Excavation of a Fortified Settlement at Walesland Rath', *Britannia* II (1971): 48–108

On Ai Khanoum inscription:

Robert, L., 'Inscriptions Grecques Nouvelles de la Bactriane', *Comptes Rendus, Académie des Inscriptions et Belles-Lettres* (1968): 416–57, esp. 424–6

In addition, recent discoveries are reported in the *Journal of Hellenic Studies* (*JHS*) or the Archaeological Reports that accompany it; in the *Journal of Roman Studies* (*JRS*); and, for Britain, in *Britannia*

PART IV. MEDIEVAL EUROPE

For general reading

Bloch, M., *Feudal Society* (London 1960)

Brooke, E. C., *Europe in the Central Middle Ages, 962–1154* (London 1964)

Chadwick, N. K. (ed.), *Studies in Early British History* (Cambridge 1952)

Davis, H. W. C., *Medieval Europe* (London 1960)

Douglas, D., *The Norman Achievement* (London 1969)

Foot, P. G. and Wilson, D. M., *The Viking Achievement* (London 1970)

Hussey, J. M., *The Byzantine World* (London 1957)

Lopez, R. S., *The Birth of Europe* (London 1967)

Loyn, H. R., *Anglo-Saxon England and the Norman Conquest* (London 1962)

Southern, R. W., *The Making of the Middle Ages* (London 1953)

Thomas, C., *Britain and Ireland in Early Christian Times, AD 400–800* (London 1971)

Wallace-Hadrill, J. M., *The Barbarian West, 400–1000* (London 1952) *Medieval Archaeology*, an annual journal, first published in 1957, devoted to the archaeology of medieval Britain and its European context (London)

More specialised reading

Alcock, L., *By South Cadbury is that Camelot . . . The Excavation of Cadbury Castle 1966–1970* (London 1972)

Beckwith, J., *Early Medieval Art* (London 1964)

Biddle, M., 'Archaeology and the Beginnings of English Society' in Clemoes, P., and Hughes, K. (eds), *England before the Conquest: Primary Sources Presented to Dorothy Whitelock* (Cambridge 1971); (ed.), 'Urban Archaeology', *World Archaeology*, 2, no. 2 (1971)

Brown, P., *The World of Late Antiquity* (London 1971)

Hawkes, S. C. and Dunning, G., 'Soldiers and Settlers in Britain, Fourth to Fifth Century', *Medieval Archaeology* XI: (10) 87–104.

Hensel, W., 'The Origins of Western and Eastern Slav Towns', *World Archaeology* 1, no. 1 (1970): 51–60

Hitti, P. K., *A History of the Arabs* (London 1953)

Jones, G., *A History of the Vikings* (Oxford 1968)

Latouche, R., *Les Origines de l'économie Occidentale* (Paris 1956)

Lopez, R. S., 'Mahommed and Charlemagne: A Revision', *Speculum* XVIII (1943): 14–38

Lopez, R. S. and Raymond, I. W., *Medieval Trade in the Mediterranean World* (New York 1955)

Luzzatto, G., *An Economic History of Italy* (London 1961)

Pirenne, H., *Mahommed and Charlemagne* (London 1939)

Thompson, M. W., *Novgorod the Great* (London 1967)

White, L., *Medieval Technology and Social Change* (Oxford 1962)

Wilson, D., *The Vikings and their Origins* (London 1970)

Index